# Monetary and Fiscal Actions in India

**By the Same Author**

- Ecology and Quality of Life in Urban Slums : *An Empirical Study*
- Women Empowerment and Family Management in Tribal Region
- Economics of Social Sector and Environment

---

**The Authors**

**Udai Prakash Sinha** (*b.* 1956) is Professor of Economics, T.M. Bhagalpur University, Bhagalpur. He has authored many books including Planned Development of Resources in a Developing Region (1985), Socio-Economic Dimensions of Integrated Development in India (1991) and IRDP for Weaker Sections (1996). He is editing 'Journal of Economic Issues' since 2000 published by Planning Forum, and Anga Economic Society, University, Bhagalpur. He has also completed two UGC Major Research Projects and contributed more than 50 research papers to reputed national and international journals of Economics and other social-sciences. Micro-level planning and the regional economics are the areas of his interest and research.

**K.D. Prasad** (*b.* 1965) is presently Regional Director of IGNOU, Regional Centre, Connaught Place, New Delhi. He has contributed more than 15 research papers to the reputed National and International Journals of Statistics, Economics and other Social Sciences. Prior to that, he taught at NEHU, Shillong as lecturer for five years. He also participated and-presented paper in National/International Symposium.

# Monetary and Fiscal Actions in India

## An Empirical Evidence

U.P. Sinha

K.D. Prasad

CONCEPT PUBLISHING COMPANY PVT. LTD.

NEW DELHI-110059

ISBN-13-978-81-8069-664-0 ISBN-10-81-8069-664-2

First Published 2010

*Published and Printed by*

Concept Since 1974

**Concept Publishing Company Pvt. Ltd.**
**Regd. Office:**
A/15-16, Commercial Block, Mohan Garden
New Delhi-110059 (India)
*Phones* : 25351460, 25351794, *Fax* : 091-11-25357109
*Email* : publishing@conceptpub.com,
*Website:* www.conceptpub.com

**Editorial Office:**
H-13, Bali Nagar, New Delhi-110 015, India.

Cataloging in Publication Data-- *Courtesy:* D.K. Agencies (P) Ltd. <docinfo@dkagencies.com>

**Sinha, U. P. (Udai Prakash),** 1956-
Monetary and fiscal actions in India : an empirical evidence / U.P. Sinha, K.D. Prasad.
p. cm.
Includes bibliographical references (p. ).
Includes index.
ISBN 13: 9788180696640 ISBN 10: 8180696642

1. Monetary policy--India. 2. Fiscal policy--India. 3. Economic development--India. 4. India--Economic policy--1991- I. Prasad, K. D., 1965-, joint author. II. Title.

DDC 332.40954 22

# Preface

The Monetarist-Fiscalist controversy has been on for long, dating back to the 1940s. At a time when the Keynesian theory was gaining ground, a few economists began to take interest in examining the relative importance of the real and the monetary forces in the economy, a direction which later lead to an endless tug of war between some of the most distinguished economists.

The early systematic work on the Monetarist-Fiscalist controversy was made by Clark Warburton (1945), Milton Friedman and Garry Bocker (1957) and Karl Burner and Anatole Balbach (1960). This debate sparked more by the work of Friedman and Muscleman (1963) and extended by the work of Andersen and Jorden (1968), Moroney and Mason (1971). Aristics, Frowen and Karakitses (1978), Stephens (1980), Bladen *et. al*, (1982), Batten and Hafer (1983) and Darrat (1984).

Present study concentrates on one of the most important hypothesis of the monetarists: the crowding out hypothesis. In its earliest form, the crowding out hypothesis was used by monetarists to show that a pure expansionary fiscal policy action is unable to increase the real GNP of an economy on a permanent level. Monetarists argued that a pure fiscal policy—a fiscal action unaided by an increase in the money supply—could lead to an increase in interest rates and/or general price level, and/or domestic exchange rate. An increase in general price level would, of course, lead to inflation. Finally, an increase in domestic exchange rate would reduce the value of domestic currency in international markets. So, even if a pure fiscal policy temporarily stimulated real GNP, the secondary effects of it may eventually eliminate nay long-term gain in real GNP.

A reduction in gross domestic investment caused by higher interest rates that results from an increase in government expenditure in traditionally called 'crowding out'. In recent years, however, other dimensions to the crowding out effect have been recognized. These are the price level and exchange rate effects mentioned above. Therefore, one can now argue that an initial increase in government expenditure that can cause a deficit in the governmental budget can also be responsible for raising the general price level, as well as the interest rates. Further, a government budget deficit, if not supported by the simultaneous increase in excess saving over investment, can also be responsible for a deficit in the nation's trade balance. A budget deficit is, therefore, also responsible for increasing the domestic exchange rate, defined as the number of domestic currency units available for one unit of foreign currency. Hence, it is possible to argue that an expansionary fiscal policy leads to a simultaneous existence of 'twin deficit' inflation and a devaluated domestic currency.

The present book is a modest attempt to highlight on the impact of monetary and fiscal action on economic development in India. There are eight chapters in the study, which are crucial for economic development. In fact, the Indian economy presents a classic example of an overly active government sector that has been running a deficit in its budget for the last twenty-five years. It has been claimed that the Indian private sector is prosperous, but hampered by an extensive network of licensing, regulation, other policy controls and corruption. Its economic growth has been impressive in some years, disastrous in some others, but has been much less than potential in almost all the years. Prices have been increasing rapidly, interest rates have been traditionally high, the rupee value in international market has been deteriorating, and India's balance of payments has been consistently showing deficits in its current. Therefore, India serves as a good nation for an empirical test of the crowding out hypothesis.

**Udai Prakash Sinha**
**Kumar Dharmendra Prasad**

# Acknowledgements

The present book attempts to give one of the many possible explanations as to how in a global economy that was characterised by rapid change and high uncertainty, India calibrated a less unstable but significant changes in the economic policy, in general, and in money, finance and export sectors in particular.

Acknowledgements are due to Several Institutions where these lectures were delivered. These are Bank for International Settlements (BIS), Basel; Confederation of Indian Industry, Mumbai; Indian Banks' Association and Punjab National Bank, New Delhi; Indian Econometric Society; Institute for Social and Economic Change, Bangalore and Reuters Group, Mumbai.

Several Professional of RBI have provided valuable assistance through Bulletins/Journals and many reading materials in this regards and we are grateful to them. In particular, we would like to make a mention of Y.V. Reddy, V. Leeladhar, Rakesh Mohan, Raj Kumar Sen, P.K. Bhargava, Sajal Mukherjee and many others who have always provided an excellent window not only to communicate with the rest of the world but also to insist on prompt and faithful feedback.

Our sincere thanks are also due to Prof. N. Jha, Prof. A.K. Sinha, Prof. A.K. Tiwary and all the colleagues of the Department who have gone through the proofs of the most complicated chapter of the work.

We are thankful to Mr. Raj Madhvan for Cartographic and technical work and Mr. Saquib for computation work.

At the end, our sincere thanks to Prof. Rekha Sinha who has forgone her holidays and comforts during the work.

**U.P. Sinha**
**K.D. Prasad**

# Contents

# LIST OF TABLES

# LIST OF FIGURES

# 1 INTRODUCTION

In macro economic policies, high employment, rising output of goods and services and relatively stable prices are three widely accepted goals. Responsibility has been assigned to monetary and fiscal authorities to achieve these goals through economic stabilization measures. But there has been growing controversy among them in examining the relative importance of monetary and fiscal actions in influencing macro economic variables. Opinions on this issue have varied greatly from decade to decade, and still vary from economist to economist. The above proposition has been extensively tested abroad (especially in developed countries) but has received little empirical attention in India. In the present study we wish to subject the proposition to econometric test using Indian data. This will enable us to determine the extent of the relative effectiveness of monetary and fiscal policy adopted in the past years and as a guide to future policy formulation and implementation.

The Monetarist-Fiscalist controversy has been on for long, dating back to the 1940s. At a time when the Keynesian theory was gaining ground, a few economists began to taken interest in examining the relative importance of the real and the monetary forces in the economy, a direction which later lead to an endless tug of war between some of the most distinguished.

The early systematic work on the Monetarist-Fiscalist controversy was made Clark Warburton (1945), Miltan Friedman and Garry Bercher (1957) and Kark Brunner and Anatole Balbach (1960). This debate sparked more by the work of Friedman and Meiselman (1963) and extended by the work of Andersen and Jordan (1968), Moroney and Mason (1971). Aristice, Frowen and Karakitsos (1978), Stephens (1980), Bladen *et al.* (1982), Batten and Hafer (1983) and Darrat (1984). While making a contribution to the staff studies for the Commission of Money and Credit, came to a conclusion that money was more closely related to the consumption level than the autonomous expenditures, implying that the monetary forces were more important in influencing the economic activities than the real factors. The conclusion followed from the study of the stability of the income velocity as compared with the investment multiplier, both related to the consumption levels, where the consumption level was a proxy for the economic activity.

Several attempts have been made to evaluate the relative impact of monetary and fiscal variables using either St. Louis equation estimate by Andersen and Jordan (1968) or modified St. Louis equation proposed by Darrat (1984). The empirical results based on these equations show different results across the countries and the effectiveness of monetary and fiscal policy differs from country, depending upon the nature of the economy of the country.

The reduced form equation that Andersen and Jordan (1968) estimated was of the form:

$$\Delta Y_t = \alpha + \sum_{i=0}^{3} \beta_i \Delta M_t + \sum_{i=0}^{3} r_i \Delta E_{t-i} + u_t$$

Where,

$Y_t$ = Total spending (GNP) in current prices.
$E_t$ = Government expenditures and $M_t$ = Money Stock ($M_1$)

They found that the monetary policy is more effective, more reliable, more stable and quicker than fiscal policy in influencing national income.

The research of Andersen and Jordan (1968) was criticized for four main reasons:

(i) that there was a simultaneity Bias,
(ii) that, the indictors for the policy chosen were not appropriate,

(iii) that the model was misspecified,
(iv) that there was inappropriate restriction incorporated in the model.

**The Modified Single Reduced from St. Louis Equation**

It is of interest that despite so much of debate and tests on the St. Louis Model, its basic structure has more or less remained unaltered.

Some minor modifications have, however, occurred as a consequence of more research and discussion on the model.

The basis equation of Andersen and Jordan (1968) still contains the monetary and fiscal measures lagged over past quarters, with the monetarist characteristics that the estimated sum of coefficients of the lagged monetary measures being close to unity while that of the fiscal measures being close to zero, also that monetary actions have no effect on the real magnitudes. Changes have occurred in the respecification of the model. The variables of monetary and fiscal action are now not the first differences of money stock and high employment government expenditures but are now in the growth rates form.

The estimation procedure for these measures has remained unchanged Almon's lag Estimation technique for the lagged variables and OLS for the other variables.

The modified St. Louis Equation may now be put as:

$$Y_t = \alpha o + \alpha l\, Z_t + \sum_{i=0}^{3} \beta_i M_{t-i} + \sum_{i=0}^{3} r_i E_{t-i} + \sum_{i=0}^{3} \delta E X_{t-i} + \Sigma_t$$

Where,

$Y_t$ = Total spending (GNP) in current prices.
$E_t$ = Government expenditures & $M_t$ = Money Stock ($M_1$)
$Z_t$ = Dummy variable

It is a reduced form equation in which the rate of growth in the nominal GNP of the current quarter is regressed on the contemporaneous and the past values of the rate of growth of money stock (M) and current and past values of the rate of growth of government expenditure as well as on those of the exports.

(1) *The Rate of Change Form*: The advantage in putting the values in terms of Rates of growth rather than first differences was realized in the 1970's when the first differenced form began to exhibit heteroskedasticity (Carison, 1978). The rate of change form would work in the direction of eliminating this problem and would, therefore, improve the quality of the estimates.

(2) *Addition of two more Exogenous variables*: In the 1970's (1973-74 in particular) new developments became quite pronounced in most economies, largely originating from the sharp oil price increases by the OPEC countries. There became a need to modify the original St. Louis specification to incorporate such complex factors. (Rasche and Tatom, 1977). Also, it was felt necessary to capture the velocity shifts, which became clear after 1981. Rate of growth of exports (Ext.) lagged over three quarters and a Dummy variable ($Z_t$) were added to the total spending equation. This was to provide a crude way of capturing the shifts in the velocity after 1981.

(3) *The Shortened lag on money*: A further change in the St. Louis equation is the shortening of the lag on money. It became necessary to take the measure of money stock growth rates only over three quarters rather than four. The rate of growth of export was also lagged over three quarters.

## The Indian Evidence on the Relative Effectiveness of Monetary and Fiscal Policy on Economic Activity

In spite of the fact that India has been going through a period of stagflation, little work has been done on the study of the relative efficacy of fiscal and monetary policies.

The work done by Mehta and Bishnoi, published in 1977, was based on annual data running over the post-independence period, 1950-51 to 1970-71. The main concern was to examine which of the two policies was stronger, more predictable and faster on the level of economic activity. They opted for a single equation approach of the St. Louis reduced form type. The variables included a measures of economic activity taken as current national income regressed on the total government spending and money stock ($M_1$). They were entered in the first difference form. A measure for other unknown factors was also represented by an intercept term. Since, the fiscal data do change frequently, they made several adjustment to make the data of different period comparable.

Regression analysis was then carried and the result showed conclusions consistent with those of Andersen-Jordan with a few exceptions:

(i) Whereas they find both policies to important, Andersen and Jordan (1968) ruled out the importance of fiscal policy and attributed all importance to the monetary policy. However, like Andersen and Jordan, they also found the Beta coefficients of the money stock to be stronger than those of the fiscal changes.

(ii) Mehta and Bishnoi found the fiscal actions to be more reliable than the monetary measures. But Andersen and Jordan observed the opposite.

(iii) Because of the constraint of the data being confined to annual data, Mehta and Bishnoi failed to allow longer lags than one to get a more clear view of the dynamic path of response by seeing which of the two policies reach its peak first. They only resorted to the analysis of the speed of response of the two policies by comparing the size of the regression coefficients of the current changes in the money supply with those of the Government expenditures. Their conclusion on this issue was, however, the same as that of Andersen and Jordan.

The problem of lack of erogeneity for the policy measures incorporated in the St. Louis equation, which became a centre of debt in the later years was also noted by Mehta and Bishnoi. They did not adjust the fiscal measures for the cyclical changes. Their model gave little attention to the dynamic aspects of adjustments in the money, income and expenditure relationship.

A second study on the Indian economy on this topic is much more recent. This was carried on by Chowdury, A.R. (1986). This study was also based on the annual data over the period extending form 1955 to 1981. He investigated similar propositions as the earlier researches had done although he went further to investigate the stability of the relationships for policy purposes. The model applied was the modified St. Louis form, containing export measures and variables entering as growth rates rather than first differences.

As different from the study of Mehta and Bishnoi, this investigation included loner lags running up to fine years. The method used in the estimation of the lagged value coefficients was different from that of Andersen and Jordan (1968).

The test of structural stability of the model was done by the application of both Chow and Farley and Hinich tests. Both tests showed that the money, income and expenditure relationship is a stable function, which strengthens the use of the St. Louis equation for policy in the determination of the economic activity magnitudes. Darrat (1984) also reached a similar conclusion although that was on the Latin American Economy. The result in interesting since most studies done in the developed and the underdeveloped economies show money measures to be important in influencing economic activity in the short run, although some of these give importance to fiscal actions as well. But since it is true that most studies done so far have concentrated on the developed economies, the study of the underdeveloped economies may show much differences.

By using dynamic multipliers to study the dynamic response of the economic activity to the policy changes, he observed that fiscal measures, taken as Government expenditure, had a larges and stronger effect distributed over five years, while the monetary measures, taken as the monetary baser had negligible effect, on the economic activity after the first year. Both expenditure and the monetary base would reach their peak in the first year but the effect of Government expenditure would be stronger than that of the monetary base.

Although study of Chowdhury on the Indian economy had made some advance in that here the modified model of the St. Louis had been applied, some comments are worth noting:

(i) Government expenditure has not adjusted to remove the effects of the other factors on it so that its erogeneity is questionable. In the modified model, such a measure ought to be adjusted for the cyclical fluctuations. Chowdhury has not reported of any such precautions.

(ii) It is also true, as Mehta and Bishnoi had earlier noted, that fiscal measures in India are not easily comparable due to frequent changes in their classification. Chowdhury has not made any adjustment to remove this weakness of the Indian Data.

(iii) He gave no explanation as to why monetary base is considered to reflect the monetary actions better than $M_1$.

Overall, none of the Indian studies has used quarterly data. A better result would be expected with the quarterly data since this would us to take a closer view of the dynamic path of response of the economic activity to the policy actions. As such, there is still a gap to be filled.

**The Equations**

Eight different specifications were put in terms of equations and estimated with quarterly data on the Indian economy.

(1) The unmodified model with no lags.

(2) The unmodified model with lags.
(3) The unmodified model with the variable (E/Y) substituted in place of E.
(4) The modified with no lags.
(5) The modified model with lags.
(6) The modified model with variable (E/Y) substituted in place of $\hat{E}$.
(7) The modified model with Unadjusted Reserve Money ($RM^u$) taken in place of $M_1$.

## The Hypotheses to be Tested

The propositions that fiscal policy is (i) Stronger, (ii) more predictable, and (iii) faster than monetary policy in influencing economic activity, also, (iv) that the model is stable for policy uses. Additional hypotheses tested are; (v) the Fiscal Policy has more longer effects on the total spending, (vi) other factors not included in the model have significant influence on economic activity, (vii) fiscal action is more effective when taken alone, and (viii) there is no significant difference in the performance of the original model and the modified form in the case of India.

## The Data: National Income (V)

Quarterly series of National income prepared by S.L. Lodha (1988) is used in this study. The original data came from various issues of National Accounts Statistics.

Income form the various sectors of the economy was classified by Lodha as:

(i) Income from agricultural sector,
(ii) Industrial Sector, and
(iii) From the 'Rest of the Sectors'.

The 'Rest of the Sectors' included much of the service sector e.g. transport, communication, storage, banking and insurance, real estate, trade, hotels and Restaurants, Public Administration, Defence and other Services. These were added to obtain the Net Domestic Product (NDP) Index which was converted to constant prices with 1970-71 as the base year.

**Government Expenditure**

This was obtained from the Reserve Bank of India Bulletins. The aggregate was computed as the net expenditures of the Central Government after the Defence drawings had been deducted.

**Money Supply**

This data been obtained from the Reserve Bank of India occasional paper Vol. 3, No. 1, June 1982. It was originally taken from the RBI Bulletins.

The $M_1$ concept is used, $M_1$ includes the total demand deposits with commercial bank and all the Co-operative Banks in India as in line with the redefinition effected since March 1970. Adjustment has been made to account for the reclassification of Money which became in effect since March 1978 whereby 85 per cent of savings deposits have been treated as time deposits and only 15 per cent entered in as demand deposits.

**Exports**

This has been obtained from the Reserve Bank of India Bulletins. The foreign trade data as a whole as defined in the Bulletin relate to total sea, air and land trade on private and government accounts. It excludes the direct transit trade, transshipment trade, ships, stores and passengers baggage. But it includes silver (other than current coins), notes and coins withdrawn from circulation or those not yet issued, indirect transit trade and trade by parcel post.

In this study, only exports that included re-exports taken. The valuation was based on the general system of recording where exports are valued on f.o.b. basis inclusive of export duties. The export figures for the period November 1970 to March 1973 are based on the original copy of the shipping bills but the figures for the rest of the period are based on the finally passed shipping bills. All the data references are quarterly data.

# 2 GENESIS OF THE STUDY

Against the background of a contra-seasonal expansion in bank credit, higher credit-deposit ratio and continued pressure on bank's resources resulting in smaller investment in government securities by the commercial banks and smaller repayments by them against borrowings from the Reserve Bank during the 1970 slack season (Table 2.1), the Reserve Bank stepped up the Statutory Liquidity Ratio (SLR) from 27 per cent to 28 per cent (Table 2.3) and the Net Liquidity Ratio (NLR) from 32 per cent to 33 per cent in August 1970 (Table 2.4). Measures were also announced to regulate advances against shares with a view to preventing the use of bank finance for speculative purposes.

**Table 2.1** : Seasonal Variations in Scheduled Commercial Bank's Data

*(Amount in Rs. Crores)*

| | *Slack 1970* | *Busy 1970-71* | *Slack 1971* | *Busy 1971-72* | *Slack 1972* | *Busy 1972-73* |
|---|---|---|---|---|---|---|
| 1. Bank Credit: | -226 | +394 | +163 | +351 | +67 | +897 |
| (a) Food procurement advances | +35 | +70 | +156 | -76 | -1 | +5 |
| (b) Other advances | +191+324 | | +7 | +427 | +68 | +892 |
| 2. Investment govt. and other approved securities: | +187+115 | | +249 | +244 | +619 | +4 |
| (a) In govt. securities | +155 | +39 | +208 | +144 | +519 | -89 |
| (b) In other approved securities. | +32 | +76 | +41 | +100 | +100 | +93 |
| 3. Cash and balances with the R.B.I. | +31 | +12 | +59 | +2 | +57 | +60 |
| 4. Money at call and short notice | -6 | -11 | +70 | -5 | +13 | +72 |
| 5. Aggregate deposits: | +449+439 | | +624 | +590 | +705 | +811 |
| (a) Demand deposits | +175+190 | | +190 | +296 | +262 | +335 |
| (b) Time deposits | +274+245 | | +422 | +294 | +443 | +476 |
| 6. Borrowings from Reserve Bank of India | -86 | +40 | -172 | +4 | -16 | +17 |
| 7. Inland bills purchased and discounted by R.B.I | – | – | – | – | -10 | +19 |

(Contd.)

(Contd.)

| | *Slack 1973* | *Busy 1973-74* | *Slack 1974* | *Busy 1974-75* | *Slack 1975* | *Busy 1975-76* | *Slack 1976* | *Busy 1976-77* |
|---|---|---|---|---|---|---|---|---|
| 1. | +346+10 | 05 | -129 | -893 | +665 | +1758 | +1070 | +1064 |
| (a) | -57 | +189 | +170 | +317 | +173 | +874+489 | | +175 |
| (b) | +402 | +816 | +299 | +576 | +492 | +884+581 | | +889 |
| 2. | +282 | +156 | +472 | +269 | +302 | +393+663 | | +641 |
| (a) | +187 | +71 | +349 | +223 | +120 | +345+398 | | +599 |
| (b) | +95 | +85 | +123 | +46 | +182+48 | | +265 | +42 |
| 3. | +444 | -218 | +118 | -102 | -86 | +125+178 | | +234 |
| 4. | -41 | -103 | +61 | +29 | -13 | -114 | +54 | +38 |
| 5. | +899 | +683 | +912 | +716 | +1210 | +1218 | +1861 | +1803 |
| (a) | +252 | +452 | +298 | +294 | +956 | +395+579 | | +1174 |
| (b) | +647 | +231 | +614 | +422 | +754 | +823 | +1282 | 1174 |
| 6. | +56 | +253 | -27 | +183 | -38 | +627 | -83 | -304 |
| 7. | +15 | +244 | -171 | +59 | -80 | +44 | +22 | +21 |

(Contd.)

| | *Slack 1977* | *Busy 1977-78* | *Slack 1978* | *Busy 1978-79* | *Slack 1979* | *Busy 1979-80* | *Slack 1980* | *Busy 1980-81* |
|---|---|---|---|---|---|---|---|---|
| 1. | +507 | +938 | +1418 | +1674 | +1615 | +1631 | +1133 | +2971 |
| (a) | -10 | -28 | +219 | +14 | +457 | -691 | -150 | -146 |
| (b) | +517+12 | 18 | +1199 | +1660 | +1158 | +2322 | +1283 | +3117 |
| 2. | -563 | +1539 | +725 | +1074 | +503 | +1085 | +1505 | +1427 |
| (a) | +328+14 | 11 | +479 | +802 | +139 | +767+985 | | +1167 |
| (b) | +235 | +128 | +246 | +272 | +364 | +318+520 | | +269 |
| 3. | +577 | +443 | +88 | +834 | +901 | -102 | 669 | -116 |
| 4. | +147 | -155 | -7 | -34 | +5 | -30 | +48 | +71 |
| 5. | +1870 | +2276 | +1900 | +2673 | +2820 | +2422 | +2630 | +3447 |
| (a) | +689+11 | 50 | +237 | +1250 | +966 | -132 | -2147 | -1133 |
| (b) | +1181 | +1126 | +1753 | +1423 | +1854 | +2554 | +4777 | +4580 |
| 6. | -256 | -203 | +90 | +142 | +293 | -260 | +50 | +76 |
| 7. | -41 | 64 | -17 | +35 | +5 | -24 | -63 | -1 |

(Contd.)

| | *Slack 1981* | *Busy 1981-82* | *Slack 1982* | *Busy 1982-83* | *Slack 1983* | *Busy 1983-84* |
|---|---|---|---|---|---|---|
| 1. Bank Credit: | +1090 | +1584 | +1649 | +3789 | +1246 | +4009 |
| (a) Food procurement advances | +328+189 | | +265 | +445 | +893 | +773 |
| (b) Other advances | +762 | +1395 | +1384 | +3344 | +353 | +3236 |
| 2. Investment govt. and other approved securities: | +765 | +1415 | +1994 | +1884 | +1453 | +1407 |

(Contd.)

(Contd.)

| | | | | | | |
|---|---|---|---|---|---|---|
| (a) In govt. securities | +349 | +1010 | +1193 | +1462 | +1041 | +726 |
| (b) In other approved securities. | +416 | +405 | +800 | +423 | +4181 | +680 |
| 3. Cash and balances with the R.B.I. | +653 | +1115 | +529 | -968 | +598 | +127 |
| 4. Money at call and short notice | +108 | -247 | +142 | -104 | -9 | +199 |
| 5. Aggregate deposits: | +1667 | +2256 | +3783 | +3639 | +3422 | +3701 |
| (a) Demand deposits | +339 | +237 | +54 | +695 | +880 | +755 |
| (b) Time deposits | 2328 | +2019 | +7242 | +2944 | +2543 | 2947 |
| 6. Borrowings from Reserve Bank of India | +16 | +13 | -270 | +127 | -37 | +463 |
| 7. Inland bills purchased and discounted by R.B.I. | -2 | - | - | - | - | - |

(Contd.)

| | *Slack 1984* | *Busy 1984-85* | *Slack 1985* | *Busy 1985-86* | *Slack 1986* | *Busy 1986-87* | *Slack 1987* | *Busy 1987-88* |
|---|---|---|---|---|---|---|---|---|
| 1. | +3228 | +3949 | +2623 | +4755 | +2333 | 4327 | +3158 | +4874 |
| (a) | +921 | +633 | +125 | +186 | -375 | -1244 | -791 | 1595 |
| (b) | +2307 | +3316 | +2498 | +4569 | +2708 | +5511 | +3949 | -16469 |
| 2. | +2638 | +4188 | +2013 | +2524 | +855 | +4153 | +5232 | +2823 |
| (a) | +1723 | +3674 | +729 | +1474 | -290 | +3074 | +3764 | +1973 |
| (b) | +915 | +514 | +1284 | +1050 | +1145 | +1079 | +1468 | +580 |
| 3. | +784 | -1376 | +2755 | +289 | +4886 | +1427 | 2390 | +1818 |
| 4. | -7 | -49 | +501 | +178 | +1591 | -811 | -635 | +1789 |
| 5. | +5795 | +5862 | +6600 | +6668 | +7734 | +8549 | +8506 | +8703 |
| (a) | +867 | +1733 | +515 | -1106 | +835 | +2290 | +191 | +7027 |
| (b) | +4929 | +4129 | +6085 | +15562 | +6899 | +6259 | +8315 | +7027 |
| 6. | +4929 | -331 | -64 | -164 | +132 | -245 | +1855 | -592 |
| 7. | - | - | - | - | - | - | - | - |

(Contd.)

| | *Slack 1988* | *Busy 1988-89* | *Slack 1989* | *Busy 1989-90* | *Slack 1990* | *Busy 1990-91* |
|---|---|---|---|---|---|---|
| 1. Bank Credit: | +5096 | +11050 | 6321 | 10631 | 2970 | 1339 |
| (a) Food procurement advances | -898 | -126 | -59 | 987 | 1756 | 1125 |
| (b) Other advances | +5994 | +11174 | 6380 | 9644 | 1214 | 12265 |
| 2. Investment govt. and other approved securities: | +4668 | 41107 | 5250 | 5413 | 6304 | 5017 |
| (a) In govt. securities | +3150 | 2831 | 3354 | 4075 | 4401 | 3816 |

(Contd.)

(Contd...)

| | | | | | | |
|---|---|---|---|---|---|---|
| (b) In other approved securities. | 1528 | +1276 | 1896 | 1338 | 1903 | 1201 |
| 3. Cash and balances with the R.B.I. | +2786 | +2077 | 450 | 2166 | 2868 | 1045 |
| 4. Money at call and short notice | +737 | +329 | 5250 | 2433 | -1179 | 250 |
| 5. Aggregate deposits: | +11536 | +11927 | 13946 | 13234 | 11310 | 1558 |
| (a) Demand deposits | +1556 | +1878 | 3626 | 2653 | 928 | 2860 |
| (b) Time deposits | +9980 | +10049 | 10320 | 10581 | 10382 | 12648 |
| 6. Borrowings from Reserve Bank of India | -370 | +2797 | -94 | 152 | -46 | 4551 |
| 7. Inland bills purchased and discounted by R.B.I | - | - | - | - | - | - |

**Table 2. 2 :** Cash Reserve Ratio in India

| *Effective From* | *CRR (% age)* | *Extent of Increase* | *Extent of Decrease* | *Additional Cash Reserves on Incremental Net DTL over a base data* |
|---|---|---|---|---|
| June 29, 1973 | 5.0 | 2 | - | 50% of the increase in net DTL over May 5, 1960 |
| Sept. 8, 1973 | 6.0 | 1 | - | " |
| Sept. 22, 1973 | 7.0 | 1 | - | " |
| June 29, 1974 | 5.0 | - | 2 | " |
| Dec. 14, 1974 | 4.5 | - | 0.5 | " |
| Dec. 28, 1974 | 4.0 | - | 0.5 | " |
| Sept. 4, 1976 | 5.0 | 1 | - | " |
| Nov. 13, 1976 | 6.0 | 1 | - | " |
| Jan. 14, 1977 | - | - | - | 10 % of Net DTL occurring since Jan. 14, 1977 |
| Oct. 31, 1980 | - | - | - | 10 % incremental as withdrawn |
| July 31, 1981 | 6.5 | 05 | - | The balance not released |
| Aug. 31, 1981 | 7.0 | 0.5 | - | - |
| Nov. 27, 1981 | 7.25 | 0.25 | - | - |
| Dec. 25, 1981 | 7.50 | 0.25 | - | - |
| Jan. 29, 1982 | 7.75 | 0.25 | - | - |
| April 9, 1982 | 7.25 | - | 0.5 | - |
| June 11,1982 | 7.00 | - | 0.25 | - |
| May 27, 1983 | 7.50 | 0.5 | - | - |
| July 29, 1983 | 8.00 | 0.5 | - | - |
| Aug. 27, 1983 | 8.50 | 0.5 | - | - |
| Nov. 12, 1983 | - | - | - | One-fifth addition cash balance as on 31.10.1980 released two installments on these dates. |

(Contd...)

**Table 2.2 :** *(Contd...)*

| | | | | |
|---|---|---|---|---|
| Feb. 28, 1987 | 9.50 | 0.5 | - | - |
| oct. 24, 1987 | 10.00 | 0.5 | - | - |
| july 21, 1988 | 10.50 | 0.5 | - | - |
| july 30, 1988 | 11.00 | 0.5 | - | - |
| dec. 30, 1988 | 15.00 | 4.5 | - | - |

**Table 2.3 :** Net Liquidity Ratio in India

| *Effective from* | *NLR (on age of DTL)* | *Extent of* | |
|---|---|---|---|
| | | *Increase* | *Decrease* |
| April 1970 | 32 | - | - |
| August 1970 | 33 | 1 | - |
| January 1971 | 34 | 1 | - |
| November 1972 | 36 | 2 | - |
| March 1973 | 37 | 1 | - |
| June 1973 | 39 | 2 | - |
| September 1973 | 40 | 2 | - |
| November 1975 | Discontinued | | |

*Source:* R.B.I. Report on Currency and Finance, Vo.1, Various issues.

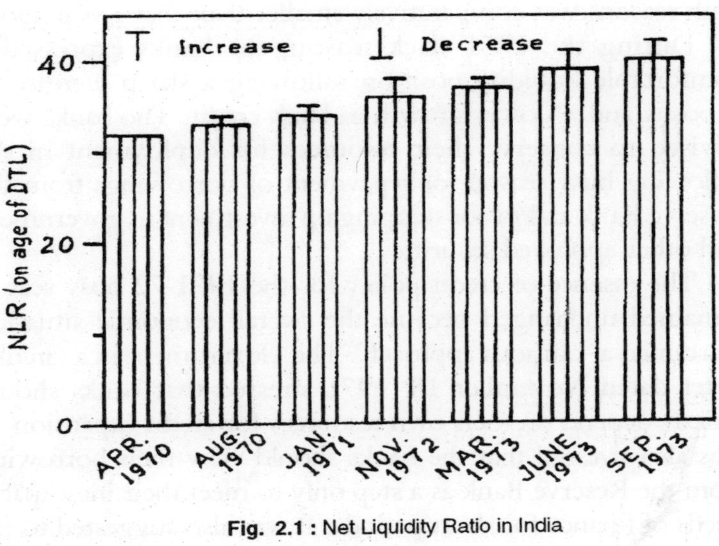


**Fig. 2.1 :** Net Liquidity Ratio in India

While fully appreciating the need for credit restraint, the Reserve Bank considered a higher level of credit expansion in 1970-71 busy season unavoidable so as to maintain the tempo of economic expansion and to ensure and uninterrupted supply of credit for priority sector and backward areas.

At the time of mid-term review of monetary and credit situation on February 4, 1971, the Governor expressed satisfaction at the slowing down of the rate of expansion in bank credit and reduction in borrowing from the Reserve Bank. He attributed these developments to the tightening of the credit control measures. At the same time he stressed the need for continued restraint in credit and for greater efforts towards deposit mobilization. The governor also advised banks to initiate measures for a gradual replacement of the exiting cash credit system will bills and loans.

During 1971-72, the Reserve Bank continued its policy of credit restraint and of ensuring adequate credit facilities for all legitimate productive activities and directing the flow of credit to desired channels. In this year, the expansion in bank credit in both reasons was comparatively smaller than that a year ago.

During the 1971 slack season, the banks expressed a comfortable liquidity position following a sharp increase in deposits and a slower growth in bank credit. The banks were advised to conserve their resources for deployment in the following busy season for repayment of borrowings from the Reserve Bank and/or for stepping up investment in government and other approved securities.

The essence of credit policy for the 1971-72 busy season remained unchanged because the overall economic situation warranted a 'cautious approach'. The Government in a circular letter dated November 18, 1971 stressed that banks should strictly depend on their own resources for credit expansion. It was also stressed that the banks should view their borrowing from the Reserve Bank as a step only to meet their inescapable needs of finance for short periods. It was also suggested to the banks that their borrowing at the end of busy season should not exceed those as at the end of the 1970-71 busy season. But, following the out break of Indo-Pak war in November 1971, the Reserve Bank made certain modification in its credit policy to enable banks to meet on a priority basis additional credit needs for defence purposes. At a meeting with bankers on February 7, 1972, the Governor pointed out that while the banking system has operated in a flexible manner to meet overall credit expansion during the busy season, the overall monetary situation, however, called for a cautions approach. Accordingly, it was decided to continue the credit policy along with the limited relaxations that were made following the out break of the Indo-Pak conflict.

The first and second half of the year 1972-73 witnessed contrasting monetary trends. The conventional 1972 slack season (May to October) witnessed a pronounced increase in the liquidity position of the banking system due partly to continued growth in deposits (though at a somewhat lower pace) and partly to smaller expansion in bank credit. But, during 1972-73 busy season, there took place a spurt in bank credit for purposes other than food procurement particularly after January 1973.

As a result, the Reserve Bank took credit restraining measures on March 17, 1973. These included: (i) restraining bank's access to Reserve Bank's refinance window, and (ii) raising the cost of funds-both from the Reserve Bank and the public.

Despite these measures, the credit expansion continued apace which called for more stringent measures. Accordingly, the Reserve Bank, on June 29, 1973 raised bank rate from 6 to 7 per cent (Table 2.5), Cash Reserve Ratio (CRR) from 3 to 5 per cent (Table 2.2) and Net Liquidity Ratio (NLR) from 37 to 39 per cent (Table 2.4). In the context of continuing excess liquidity in the banking system and as a follow up on the measures already adopted, the Bank introduced a few other measures in July 1973. These included the withdrawal of virtually all refinance facilities at the bank rate or below; a further increase in reserve requirements (Table 2.2) to 7 per cent (in two stages) and an increase in the NLR from 39 to 40 per cent effective from September 8, 1973 (Table 2.4).

**Table 2.4:** Statutory Liquidity Ratio in India

| *Effective from* | *SLR (as age of DTL)* | *Extent of* | |
|---|---|---|---|
| | | *Increase* | *Decrease* |
| September 16, 1964 | 25 | - | - |
| March 5, 1970 | 26 | 1 | - |
| April 24, 1970 | 27 | 1 | - |
| August 28, 1970 | 28 | 1 | - |
| August 4, 1972 | 29 | 1 | - |
| November 17, 1972 | 30 | 1 | - |
| December 8, 1973 | 32 | 2 | - |
| June 29, 1974 | 33 | 1 | - |
| December 8, 1978 | 34 | 1 | - |
| September 25, 1981 | 34.5 | 0.5 | - |
| October 30, 1981 | 35.0 | 0.5 | - |
| July 28, 1984 | 36.0 | 0.5 | - |
| June 8, 1985 | 36.5 | 0.5 | - |
| July 6, 1985 | 37.0 | 0.5 | - |
| April 25, 1987 | 37.5 | 0.5 | - |
| January 2, 1988 | 38.5 | 1.0 | - |
| September 22, 1990 | 38.0 | - | 0.5 |
| Budget (1992-93) | 36.75 | - | 1.25 |
| January 6, 1993 | 37.25 | 1 | - |
| October 16, 1993 | 34.75 | - | 2.5 |

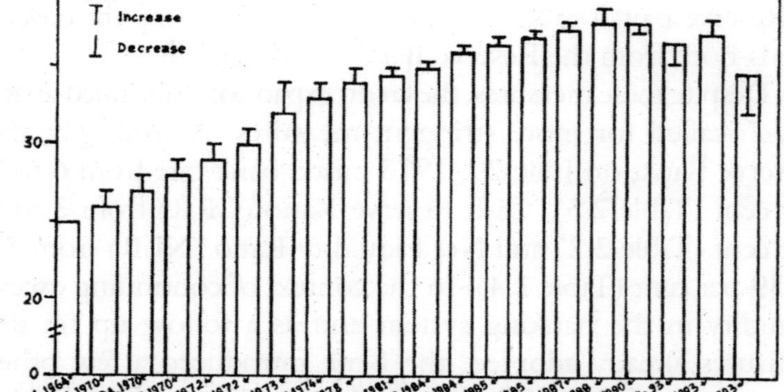


**Fig. 2.2 :** Statutory Liquidity Ratio in India.

**Table 2.5** : Bank Rate in India

| *Effective from* | *Level of Bank Rate (per cent)* | *Absolute change (percentage)* |
|---|---|---|
| November 16, 1951 | 3.5 | 0.5 |
| May 16, 1957 | 0.4 | 0.5 |
| January 2, 1963 | 4.5 | 0.5 |
| September 25, 1964 | 5.0 | 0.5 |
| February 17, 1965 | 6.0 | 1.0 |
| March 2, 1968 | 5.0 | -1.0 |
| January 9, 1971 | 6.0 | 1.0 |
| May 31, 1973 | 7.0 | 1.0 |
| July 23, 1974 | 9.0 | 2.0 |
| July 11, 1981 | 10.0 | 1.0 |
| July 4, 1991 | 11.0 | 1.0 |
| October 16, 1991 | 12.0 | 1.0 |

*Source:* RBI, Report.

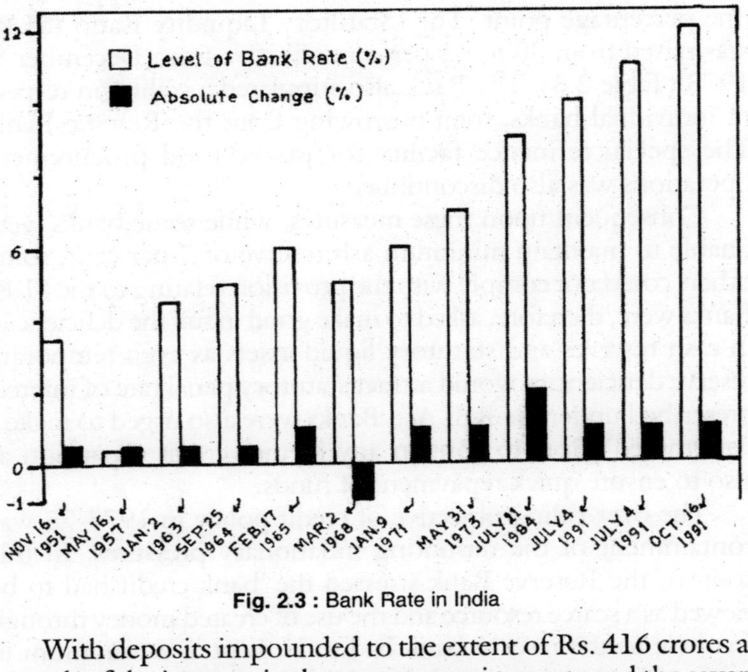


**Fig. 2.3** : Bank Rate in India

With deposits impounded to the extent of Rs. 416 crores as a result of the increase in the reserve requirements and the severe curtailment of refinance facilities, the increase in the reserve requirements and the severe curtailments of refinance facilities, the resource position of the banks at the beginning of 1973-74 busy season was far from comfortable. At the same time, the overall outlook on the monetary and price fronts made it imperative that credit expansion during the busy season be kept to the minimum level. Hence, the reserve Bank further tightened the already prevailing restrictive measures. The banks were advised to minimize their lending. This was followed up with the indication of a 'quantitative ceiling on credit expansion in 1974'. It was also indicated that recourse to refinance facilities from the Reserve Bank would not be automatic even within the NLR system bunt would be on a discretionary basis. The minimum rate of borrowing from the Reserve Bank was stepped up from 12 to 15 per cent with effect from November 16, 1973 applicable to an NLR level of below 33 per cent. The maximum rate on export credit and that on bill finance was stepped up by one percentage point. The (Statutory Liquidity Ratio (SLR) was raised from 30 to 32 per cent effective from December 8, 1973 (Table 2.3). The Bank also stipulated a ceiling in respect of individual banks' total borrowing from the Reserve Bank. The special refinance facility for public food procurement operations was also discontinued.

Consequent upon these measures, while some banks were unable to maintain minimum ash reserve of 7 per cent, some others could not comply with the provision relating to the SLR. Banks were, therefore, asked to make good in full the deficiencies in cash reserves and statutory liquid assets as even temporary reserve deficiencies would attract statutory penal rate of interest prescribed under the RBI Act. Banks were also urged to make a determined effort to contain any further credit expansion as also to ensure quick repayment of funds.

The over-riding objective of credit policy in 1974-75 was containment of the mounting inflationary pressures. In this context, the Reserve Bank stressed the 'bank credit had to be viewed as a scarce resource and the use of created money through recourse to the reserve bank had to be kept at a minimum in terms of both amount and duration of use'.

In pursuance of these objectives, banks were asked even at the onset of the 1974 slack season to give prime attention to the liquidation of their obligations to Reserve Bank which had increased substantially by Rs. 253 crores in addition to an increase of Rs. 244 crores under bills rediscounting scheme in the preceding busy season. In addition, the SLR was raised from 32 to 33 per cent in June 1974 (Table 2.3). These requirements of borrowings, liquidation and additional investment did not permit much further scope for credit expansion and it was felt that over the 1974 slack season period as a whole not more than 33 to 35 per cent of the additional deposits could be used increasing credit. Banks were also asked to reduce the limits of bills rediscounted with the Reserve Bank to about 40 per cent of the outstanding level at the end of the previous busy season. During 1974-75 busy season, the main elements of credit policy were: (i) an indication of the priorities to be observed in credit deployment; and (ii) a further extension of the principle of discretionary lending by the Reserve Bank.

As a part of the overall objective of limiting the use of created money for credit expansion, the minimum statutory reserve ratio was reduced from 5 to 4 per cent of demand and time liabilities in two installments of 0.5 per cent each (Table 2.2). This provided banks with lendable resource of Rs. 120 crores. At the same time automatic access to Reserve Bank funds was further restricted with the extension of the policy of discretionary accommodation to the rediscounting of bills. The minimum net liquidity ratio, relevant to borrowing at the bank rate was reduced from 40 to 39 per cent effective from December 28, 1974, but the maximum rate charged on such borrowings continued at 18 per cent. The corresponding basic quota for bills was fixed at 10 per cent of the total in land bills purchased and discounted as on the last Friday of September 1974. Rediscount limits in excess of this were to be allowed at the Reserve Bank's discretion, not only in regard to amount but in respect of rates of interest also, within the range of 10 to 15 per cent. In addition, the Reserve Bank followed the policy of moral suasion which provided an opportunity to "note only to maintain a close touch with the major banks throughout the year but also enabled it to have a 'feel' of the situation".

In 1975- 76 too, the prevention of inflationary conditions continued to be the main objective of credit policy. To this end, the general accent of credit policy in the 1975 slack season continued to be restrictive "consistent with the need for sustaining investment and assisting production in the core sectors and other essential lines as well as mass consumption goods and exports". Bank were told that the credit expansion would have to be limited to their own resources and that all special discretionary limits granted (other than for food procurement) would be gradually withdrawn by the end of October 1975. With a view to providing additional incentives to the export sector, some relaxations in terms of export credit were however, made. Further, in view of the need for stimulating investment, commercial banks were asked to step up their term-lending for projects of high priority in specified areas. In its credit policy for the 1975-76 busy season announced on November 1, 1975 the Reserve Bank retreated the need to continue the policy of credit restraint despite an improvement in the overall supply and price situation. The Reserve Bank announced that every assistance would be provided to boost production, investment and export but at the same time stressed that care would have to be taken to ensure that addition to inventory did not take place on the basis of bank credit and bank's resource to the Reserve Bank was kept at the minimum.

With a view to regulating both the cost and availability of refinance more effectively, the system of relating refinance to the NLR of the banks in operation since September 1964 was discontinued (Table 2.4). The discretionary refinance of one per cent of DTL was, however, continued but this accommodation was available at the Reserve Bank's discretion of policy objectives, sectoral deployment of funds, credit, deposit ratio, credit, etc. special discretionary assistance provide for financing petroleum companies and public sector undertaking was also discontinued. The Reserve Bank also imposed, effective from March 15, 1976, a ceiling on lending rates charged by commercial banks at 16.5 per cent with a view to bringing about an appropriate relationship between the bank rate and the lending rate of the commercial banks.

In 1976, the credit policy of the Reserve Bank did not undergo any significant change except that it stressed the need to relate additional availability of bank credit to the increase in real output and sales. But with a view to mopping up the inflationary tendencies, the credit policy was made more restrictive towards the second half of the year 1976-77 when the CRR was increased three times between September 1976 and January 1977 (see, Table 2.2). The changes in the CRR were intended to immobilize about Rs. 390 crores. The SLR was also raised by one percentage point in September 1976.

In 1977-78, the Reserve Bank continued using its credit policy in a flexible manner, while in this year the Reserve Bank kept its statutory and liquidity requirements unchanged, these measures were further buttressed by making the refinances and rediscount accommodation from the Reserve Bank more selective and discretionary. It was announced on May 27, 1977 that the limit of one per cent of banks' demand and time liabilities was not to be regarded as an automatic entitlement for augmenting resource but to be used only for meeting the day-to-day operational requirements. Any refinance in excess of the entitlement, however, continued to be available at the discretion of the Reserve Bank in regard to quantum, duration as well as rate on interest. The bill rediscounting facilities equal to 10 per cent of inland bill purchased and discounted was made entirely discretionary.

In the context of the relative price stability achieved as the year progressed and in tune with 1978-79 fiscal policy, measures, were taken by the Bank for a downward revision in the structure of lending rates while keeping the bank rate unchanged. The lower lending rates were expected to "improve the investment climate and stimulate production and growth in the economy".

Simultaneously some realignment in deposit rates of bank was also effected with a view to reducing the cost of deposit rates of without unduly affecting the flow of saving to banks'.

In the context of a sizable monetary expansion in two successive years 1976-77 and 1977-78 the Reserve Bank credit policy during 1978-79 aimed at restraining credit expansion and relating it to the increase in production, economic activity and employment creation. While this objective, the Reserve Bank on November 30, 1978 introduce incremental credit-deposit ratio as the norm for prescribing the ceilings on expansion of non-food credit. It raised the SLR from 33 to 34 per cent with effect from December 1, 1978. The Reserve Bank also impressed on the bank that:

(i) they should monitor the utilization of bank credit by borrowers more closely than before and implement the norms set by the Tandon Committee;
(ii) they should ensure that there was no leakage of credit from large or small borrowers to socially undesirable sector; and
(iii) they should not extend concessions in interest charges to relatively large borrowers.

In mid-March 1979, the Reserve Bank again impressed on bank the necessity to ensure that any further increase in credit was related strictly to the needs of increase in production. Banks were further advised (i) to strengthen their internal machinery of data collection and monitoring to enable them to keep a close watch over credit expansion from week to week; (ii) to review credit limits of Rs. 50 lakhs and above in respect of accounts where 60 to 65 per cent of the existing credit limit was already utilized; grant of further credit was to be strictly scrutinized and to be related to increase in production or existing commitments; and (iii) to keep to minimum their reliance on borrowings from call money market and issue of participation certificates.

Despite the raising of the RLR, banks had not increased their investment in government securities, rather continued to expand credit by recourse to money market and issue of participation certificates. Accordingly, a graduated system of penal rates on the non-observance of SLR and CRR was introduced with effect from March 30, 1979, in respect of bank which did not maintain the SLR of 34 per cent of DTL and/or defaulted in respect of stipulated reserve ratios, access to refinance/rediscount facilities was not to be available until such deficiencies were fully made good. In addition to default as above, on March 3, 1979, banks which had refinance/rediscount facilities, and additional interest of 3 per cent was to be charged on the portion of refinance re-discount accommodation equivalent to the shortfall in SLR and CRR.

The monetary policy was made more stringent as the year 1979-80 progressed. The increased stringency found expression in both the cost and availability of Reserve Bank lending to commercial bank. In this year, the following measures were implemented;

(i) In May 1979, banks were asked to institute procedures to reduce dependence of large borrowers on the banking system for working capital finance;
(ii) In June 1979, the impounding of deposits relating to the two non-resident deposit schemes was discontinued;
(iii) Effective from July 1979, participation certificates were treated as deposits and made subject of CRR and SLR obligations. In addition, banks were instructed to kept with the RBI and additional daily balance of at least to 10 per cent to the increase in partition certificates (PC's) over the level outstanding of July 28;
(iv) Refinance policies were made more restrictive in particular for food and small farmers' refinance;
(v) The maximum lending rate on short-term advances was increased from 15 to 18 per cent for large bank and from 16 to 19 per cent for smaller banks; and

(vi) The continuing restriction on the effective drawing power of credit limits was further extended until end June 1980. Thus in 1979-80 as a whole commercial banks' access to non-deposit resources was reduced.

The Reserve Bank's credit policy, which had been one of restraint and caution since November 1978 remained basically, unchanged during 1980-81. As a step towards maximum restraint on credit expansion, the Reserve Bank issued in May 1981 broad guidelines to bank regarding non-food credit expansion during the first half of 1981-82, the 1981 slack season as well as the financial year as a whole. With a view to reducing the growth of primary liquidity in the banking system and slowing down the pace of monetary expansion, the Reserve Bank in May 1981 raised CRR from 6 to 7 per cent (in two stages (Table 2.3) and interest rate on discretionary refinance and on rediscounting of bills from 11 to 14 per cent. In order to further contain inflationary pressures, the Reserve Bank, on July 11, 1981, raised to bank rate from 9 per cent to 10 per cent (Table 2.5). Following the raising of the bank rate, upward adjustments were made in interest rates on certain refinance facilities provided by the Reserve Bank. The SLR was also raised from 34 to 35 per cent in two stages 34.5 per cent from September 25, 1981 and 35 per cent from October 30, 1981 (Table 2.3). In addition, the effective data of the second phase of the increase in CRR from 6.5 to 7 per cent which was earlier stipulated as September 11, 1981 was advanced to August 21, 1981 (Table 2.2).

The growth in $M_3$ in the first half of 1981-82 was higher that in the first half of 1980-81 whereas the anticipated growth in real national income in 1981-82 was substantially lower (4.5 per cent) than in 1980-81 (7.7 per cent). According, a lower growth rate in national income called for a slower pace of monetary expansion. With this end in view, the Reserve Bank raised in mid-October 1980-81, the CRR from 7 per cent to 8 per cent in four stages (Table 2.2). Banks were however, asked to meet the increase in reserve requirement (CRR) from their own resources and also to correct the excessive expansion in non-food credit.

Beginning from the early November 1980-81 till the last week at February 1952, there took place a perceptive slow down in the pace of deposit accretions. As a result, a large number of banks defaulted in the maintenance of CRR and SLR. In addition, the flow of credit to number of seasonable industries and other vital sectors like sugar, tractors, trucks and export was adversely affected.

In view of these developments, the last phase of the increase in CRR which was to be effective from February 26, 1982 was initially deferred to April 30 and later rescinded on March 22, 1982. The Reserve Bank also provided substantial refinance accommodation to banks on a selective case by case basis taking into account the overall resources of the banks concerned and the credit needs of seasonal industries and the vital sectors.

To ease the liquidity position of banks and also to enable them to meet the credit requirement of the 1982 rabi food procurement and the legitimate requirements of other vital sectors, the Reserve Bank modified on April 8, 1982 some of the credit policy measures which included the reduction in the CRR from 7.75 per cent to 7.25 (and further to 7 per cent with effect from June 11, 1982) and the application of only the minimum CRR of 3 per cent from April 9, 1982 in respect of deposits under the Non-Resident External Rupee Accounts Scheme. These measures were intended to ensure that, among other, the sanctity of the CRR and SLR was made inviolate and the banks were required to rectify CRR defaults by the April 1982 and SLR default by end-June 1982 and also to restore normalcy in banking operations. Excepting a couple of banks, the banking system was able to rectify the defaults within the stipulated time.

During April-June 1982, while deposit growth and the rise in food credit were broadly in alignment with Reserve Bank, expectations, outstanding non-food credit on July 2, 1982 did not show much variation over end March 1982 level. It, therefore, appeared that normalcy in credit operations had not been fully restored by some banks. With a view to enabling banks to normalize their credit operations so that they could fully meet legitimate credit requirements of vital sector, the credit policy was liberalized in July 1982. The various measures adopted included; (i) introduction of scheme graduated penalties in cases of small involuntary defaults by bank in maintaining the CRR; (ii) liberalization of Reserve Bank's stand by refinance facility; and (iii) raising of the cut-off point for working capital limit under Credit Authorization Scheme (CAS) for private sector borrowers from Rs. 2 crores to Rs. 3 crores. With the uncertainties evident in October 1982 regarding the kharif crop and the relatively slow down of industrial output, there seemed to be a continuing need for slowing down of the creation of primary money. At the same time there was also a need to provide stimulus to certain vital sectors of the economy characterized by sluggishness of demand. With a view to facilitating the attainment of these twin objectives, a number of measures were devised in October 1982 which included realignment of interest rates on deposits of various maturities. Measures were also undertaken to enhance the banks ability to increase export credit without any constraint and to stimulate investment in capital and intermediate goods.

A review in April 1983 of monetary and credit trends indicated that the real rate of growth of the economy in 1982-83 was perceptibly lower than in 1981-82 while primary money creation was comparatively considerably large. It was, therefore, considered necessary to contain the inflationary potential implicit in excess liquidity without hurting processes in production. Accordingly, the CRR was enhance from 7 to 8 per cent in two stages (Table 2.2).

Against the backdrop of a large increase in primary money and its impact on growth of overall liquidity, the focus of credit policy during 1983-84 was on moderating growth of primary money base and on immobilizing primary money already created on the economy. The basic emphasis, however, continued to be on fully supporting all productive activities. During the 1983 slack season, the CRR was raised (Table 2.2) with a view to smoothening liquidity over the year. As expansion in primary money and deposit growth continued to be large and the price situation was causing concern, the CRR was raised in May, July, August and November 1983 and again in February 1984 (Table 2.2). Besides raising the cut-off point for food refinance, the Reserve Bank altered the export credit refinance formula to provide a strong incentive to bank to expand credit to that sector.

The growth of primary money and overall liquidity in the economy on the one hand and the disconcerting price situation despite record food grains production on the other, emphasized the need for moderating growth of liquidity and curbing inflationary expectations with a view to providing resource for vital public sector investment, it was decided to raise the SLR of bank from 35 to 36 per cent in two stages from July 28 and September 1, 1984 (Table 2.3). It was also decided to release to be banks into equal instalments on September 29 and October 27, 1984 one-fifth of additional cash balances maintained under the stipulation of the 10 per cent incremental CRR as on October 31, 1980. This was intended to enable banks to plan their resource allocation in smooth manner before the onset of the 1984-85 busy season. They Reserve Bank understood to provide on merits discretionary refinance for short periods to banks which might experience difficulty in meeting the enhance reserve requirements to enable them to smoothly adjust to the higher cash reserve requirement.

The underling objective of credit policy during 1984-85 continued to be one of lowing down the growth of reserve money. At the same time, the credit policy had to be geared to meet the needs of vital public sector investments and the consequent on a swelling of public distribution system on account of successively high procurement during 1984-85. During the period under review, the main instruments of credit policy used were reserve ratio, refinance facilities, interest rates and selective credit controls. Whereas in 1983-84, the main emphasis was on the use of CRR as an instrument for controlling the growth of reserve money, in 1984-85 reliance was placed on the SLR which was raised in a phased manner from 35 to 36 per cent by September 1, 1984 and again in phased manner to 37 per cent by July 6, 1985 (Table 2.3). Thus, the policy of containing the growth of reserve money which was a feature of the 1983-84 measures was pursued vigorously in 1984-85.

In the context of a large increase on volume of reserve money, the containment of overall liquidity continued to the major objective of credit policy during 1985-86. While reserve ratios, refinance facilities, interest rates and selective credit regulations continued to be the main instruments of credit policy in this year, greater emphasis was laid on effective maintenance of a graduated scheme of penalties for defaults in daily maintenance of SLR from March 28, 1985. Further, the banks were asked to conserve resources and rectify shortfalls, if any, in the maintenance of reserve requirements. Banks were also asked to ensure an effective and smooth transition to proper maintenance of SLR on a daily basis.

In a review of the credit policy in April 1986, it was noted that as a result of the various policy measures adopted, there was a slowdown in the rate of expansion of overall liquidity and a perceptible deceleration in the rate of inflation in 1985-86. However, the growth of reserve money in 1985-86 was substantially higher than that in the previous year. In the interest of containing inflationary pressures, it was considered necessary to restrict the rate of growth of $M_3$ in 1986-87 to a level below the average for the previous three years. Accordingly, reserve requirements with special emphasis on an effective maintenance of SLR on a daily basis continued to remain the major instrument of credit policy. The CRR was also raised on February 1987 and the release of impounded cash balances announced earlier was partly rescind in March 1987 (Table 2.2).

But the growth overall liquidity during 1986-87 was in

excess of what was necessary to support productive activity. Various measures were, therefore, taken to moderate the pace of monetary expansion. These inter alia included: (i) the extinguishing of the 4 per cent band of waiver for maintaining SLR with effect from October 11, 1976 (ii) introduction of a scheme for 1982-Days treasury bills; (iii) Effective from April 1987, banks were to be provided refinance equivalent to 50 per cent to their holding of 1982-Days treasury bills at the interest rate of 10 per cent per annum; (iv) Discontinuation of the practice of bringing forward the base year for calculating the export refinance limits of banks; (v) Increase in the CRR from 9.0 to 9.5 per cent effective from February 28, 1987; and (vi) Effective from October 30, 1986, banks were permitted to draw discretionary refinance without prior sanction by the Reserve Bank upto an amount equivalent to 0.5 per cent to their average per annum for a period not exceeding 14 days followed by a cooling off period of 14 days.

In order to check the emergence of inflationary pressures, it was considered desirable to work towards containing the growth of overall liquidity ($M_3$) in 1987-88 to a rate well below that in 1986-87. In 1987-88 too, the stance of credit policy continued to be one of restraining the growth of overall liquidity ($M_3$). During the first half of the year, the commercial banks faced implementation of daily maintenance of SLR. To ease the situation effective from August 17, 1987 banks' access to discretionary refinance was raised at rate of interest ranging between 14 to 15 per cent depending upon the period and amount of refinance. Further the limit of refinance against 182-Days treasury bill was raised from 50 to 75 per cent.

In view of the decoration in the rate of growth of the economy and the need to control inflationary pressures, the main thrust of credit policy during 1987-88 busy reason was to meet fully the credit requirements of agriculture, industry and export while preventing excess monetary growth. With a view to achieving these twin objectives, the Reserve Bank raised CRR by 0.5 percentage point with effect from October 24, 1987

(Table 2.2). The banks were also directed to give a positive and effective response to the serious problems caused by severe drought and floods and to accord high priority to the provision of agricultural credit. Further, effective from December 5, 1987, banks access to the existing discretionary refinance facility without prior sanction from the Reserve Bank was lowered to one per cent to their average aggregate deposit in 1986-87. In addition, the SLR was raised from 37.5 per cent to 38.0 per cent in January 2, 1988.

During 1988-89, supporting the production activities and at the same time containing inflationary pressures continued to be the major objective of monetary policy in 1988-89, the Reserve Bank also took efficiency in the operations of the financial system. Towards this end, several changes in financial policies were initiated which included the easing of operational constraint in the credit delivery system, the introduction of new money market instruments and strengthening of the existing instruments.

The changes introduced during 1989-90 in the traditional instrument of monetary control such as the CRR, deposit rates, lending rates and the money market regulations are of special significance. The prescription of uniform CRR of 15 per cent, while it did not mean additional burden for most banks, simplified to whole CRR operation. The raising of the short-term deposit rates during the year was a logical extension of the process of rationalizing of the whole structure of deposit rates which began in April 1985. Likewise the prescription of a minimum lending rate on the general category of borrowers effective from May 1, 1989, thus replacing the long-term ceiling rate made a significant qualitative difference to the system of administered interest rates.

The introduction of two kinds of inter-bank participation certificates, namely, with risk and without risk, enabled banks over to overcome their temporary liquidity problems. The withdrawal of the requirement of prior authorization under the Credit Authorisation Scheme and its replacement by post sanction scrutiny and the freedom of borrowers to transfer accounts as between banks. Provided considerable flexibility both to borrowers and the banks.

Against the backdrop of large fiscal deficit, a large expansion of non-food credit, slowing down of industrial growth and increased resource to the capital market and the stance of credit in policy had to be clearly one of restraint. Accordingly, a number of measures were adopted in 1980-90 which included a reduction in access to the export refinance facility, increase in SLR and the stipulation of an incremental non-food credit deposit ratio. A number of other policy measures were undertaken during the year which could be broadly categorized under three heads: First, those measures which aimed at imparting greater discipline and prudence in the bank's operations, Seconds, those which sought to carry forward several measures already put in place with a view to introducing greater flexibility and reducing rigidities in general promoting a more competitive environment in the money and financial market; and Third, measures in response to price and output developments relating to sensitive commodities wherein more frequent modifications of minimum margins and credit ceilings on bank advances against sensitive commodities be were effected.

## A Critical Appraisal

Thus the containment of inflation has been the primary objective of monetary policy since 1970 in India. For this purpose, the Reserve Bank continued adopting a restrictive monetary policy with some relaxations for ensuring an uninterrupted supply of credit to the desired channels. During this period, it continued increasing the CRR and the SLR till January 1988 so as to restrict the lendable capacity of commercial banks. It also continued restricting its refinance facilities and made these more and more discretionary so as to contain the expansion of money supply in the economy. As a extreme step to control the expansion of bank credit, the Reserve Bank started prescribing quantitative ceiling on the expansion in bank credit (non-food or total) from 1974-75 busy season and in terms of the expansion in $M_3$ from 1985-86, the year when it adopted the policy of monetary targeting.

**Table 2.6:** Annual Percentage Change in Wholesale Prices in India (WPI)

| *Year* | *WPI (in seventies)* | *Year* | *WPI (in eighties)* |
|---|---|---|---|
| 1970-71 | 3.02 | 1980-81 | 15.78 |
| 1971-72 | 7.19 | 1981-82 | 2.62 |
| 1972.73 | 12.94 | 1982-83 | 6.13 |
| 1973.74 | 29.70 | 1983-84 | 9.69 |
| 1974.75 | 15.67 | 1984-85 | 6.16 |
| 1975-76 | -9.20 | 1985-86 | 5.05 |
| 1976-77 | 12.34 | 1986-87 | 5.08 |
| 1977-78 | 0.54 | 1987-88 | 10.44 |
| 1978-79 | 2.82 | 1988-89 | 6.63 |
| 1979-80 | 23.32 | 1989-90 | 8.60 |

*Source:* R.B.I., Report on Currency and Finance.

Despite these restrictive measures, prices continued rising (Table 2.6). Prices rose at a double digit rate in the economy from 1972-73 upto 1980-81 except in the year 1975-76 when prices fell and 1977-78 and 1978-79 when the prices depicted more or less stability. During the eighties too, prices continued increasing but at a smaller pace. Indeed, during this period, excepting the years 1983-84, 1987-88 and 1989-90 when the price rise was comparatively higher, beginning from 1982-83, the rate of inflation ranged between 5 to 6 per cent.

It may be mentioned here that there seems to be a definite relationship between the rate of growth of wholesale prices and the excess of the rate of growth of money supply over national product at constant prices. Table 2.7 presents a comparison of the annual compound rates of growth of $M_3$, national product at constant prices and wholesale prices for the decade 1971-80 and 1981-90 and taking the period as a whole. This table clearly shows that higher the excess of the rate of growth of money supply over the rate of growth national product, higher is the rate of growth wholesale prices and vice versa.

**Table 2.7 :** Annual Compound Rate of Growth of $M_3$ National Product at constant Prices and Wholesale in India

| *Year* | *Per Annum Rate Growth (per cent)* | | |
|---|---|---|---|
| | $M_3$ | *National Product at constant price* | *Wholesale Prices* |
| 1970-71 to 1979-80 | 17.39*** (39.986) | 3.41*** (8.476) | 9.09*** (7.961) |
| 1980-81 to 1989-90 | 17-29*** (92.907) | 5.10*** (18.932) | 6.79*** (32.021) |
| 1970-71 to 1989-90 | 17.45*** (155.828) | 4.11*** (27.366) | 8.37*** (27.291) |

*Note:* 1. Figure in parentheses are t-values.
2. Significant at one per cent level.

Thus, inflation in India can be attributed partly to the excessive expansion in money supply. It implies that the policy of quantitative ceiling adopted since 1974-75 busy season has failed in restricting the expansion in money supply in India.

This becomes evident from Table 2.8, which depicts the performance of banks in complying with credit/money expansion guidelines since 1973-74 busy season. The Table shows that until 1976-77, the quantitative ceilings were prescribed in terms of the expansion in non-food credit (as in 1973-74 busy season) or in terms of the incremental credit-deposit ratio (as in 1974-75 and 1975-76) or in terms of the expansion in total credit (1976-77). However, in 1978-79, the quantitative ceiling was prescribed in terms of incremental non-food credit-deposit ratio and during 1979-80 to 1982-83 it was prescribed in terms of the expansion in non-food credit. However, following the adoption of monetary targeting in 1985-86, the quantitative ceiling was prescribed in terms of the expansion in $M_3$.

Thus, it can be seen from the table that excepting the years 1974-75 and 1981-82, the actual expansion in bank credit (non-food or total) $M_3$ has been far in excess of the prescribed ceilings.

**Table 2.8 :** Performance of Banks in Complying with Credit/Money Supply ($M_3$) Expansion Guidelines

| *Period* | *Ceiling Prescribed in terms of* | *Prescribed ceiling* | *Actual* |
|---|---|---|---|
| 1973-74 | Non-food credit expansion | +600-650 | +1111 |
| 1974 (Slack Season) | Incremental credit-deposit | 33-35% | 32.80% |
| 1974-75 | " | 63-35% | 62.80% |
| 1975-76 | " | 63-64% | 90.85% |
| 1976-77 | Expansion in bank credit | +1207 | +1627 |
| Dec. 78 to March 79 | Incremental gross non-food credit-deposit ratio | 40% | 72% |
| 1979-80 | Non-food credit | +2816 | +2967 |
| 1980 (Slack season) | " | +1052 | +1283 |
| April-Sept. 1981 | " | +775 | +1677 |
| 1981 (Slack season) | " | +1282 | +2078 |
| 1982-83 (April-March) | " | 21.5% | 16.5% |
| 1982-83 | " | 16.8% | 18.2% |
| 1985-86 | $M_3$ | Less than the level of 1984-85 (Rs. 101957) | 118.338 |
| 1986-87 | $M_3$ | Less than the average of three previous year (102065) | 140633 |
| 1987-88 | $M_3$ | Less than 1986-87 (140633) | 162060 |
| 1988-89 | $M_3$ | Less than the average of the previous three years (1403440) | 192085 |

Table 2.9 present the component-wise seasonal expansion in bank credit in India during the period of the operation of the policy of quantitative ceiling on bank credit expansion. The table indicates that the non-food procurement advances constituted the major contributor to the expansion in bank credit in India. It may be mentioned here that most of the increase in non-food advances was due to the increase in bank credit to public sector under taking/enterprises. Likewise Table 2.10 showing sources of money supply indicates that net bank credit to government sector alone constituted around 50 per cent of money supply in

India. The extent of bank credit to government sector is usually determined by the fiscal operations of the government and is used mostly for non-productive purposes. Hence, if the government is to restrict the expansion in money supply in India then it must observe a fiscal discipline. In this regard a close co-ordination between the fiscal and the monetary authorities is require. The success of this technique would hinge very much on the political will of government to restrict the non-productive expenditure and its readiness to play the game according to the rules. The observance of this requirement implies greater maneuverability for the Reserve Bank to conduct the monetary policy.

**Table 2.9 :** Component with Seasonal Expansion in Bank Credit

| *Year* | *Bank Credit* | | *Total* |
|---|---|---|---|
| | *Procurement advances (1)* | *Non-food procurement advances (2)* | *(1+2)* |
| Busy 1973-74 | +189 | +816 | +1005 |
| Slack 1974 | +170 | +299 | +469 |
| Busy 1974-75 | +317 | +576 | +893 |
| Slack 1975 | 173 | +492 | +665 |
| Busy 1975-76 | +874 | +884 | +1758 |
| Slack 1976 | +489 | +581 | +1070 |
| Busy 1976-77 | +175 | -889 | +1064 |
| Slack 1977 | -10 | +517 | +507 |
| Busy 1977-78 | -28 | +1218 | +938 |
| Slack 1978 | +219 | -1199 | +1418 |
| Busy 1978-79 | +14 | -1660 | +1674 |
| Slack 1979 | +457 | -1158 | +1615 |
| Busy 1979-80 | -691 | +2322 | +1631 |
| Slack 1980 | -150 | +1283 | +1133 |
| Busy 1980-81 | -146 | +2118 | +2971 |
| Slack 1981 | +328 | +762 | +1090 |
| Busy 1981-82 | +189 | +1395 | +1584 |
| Slack 1982 | +208 | +1284 | +1649 |
| Busy 1982-83 | +445 | +3344 | +3789 |
| Slack 1983 | +893 | +353 | +1246 |

*Source* : R.B.I. Report

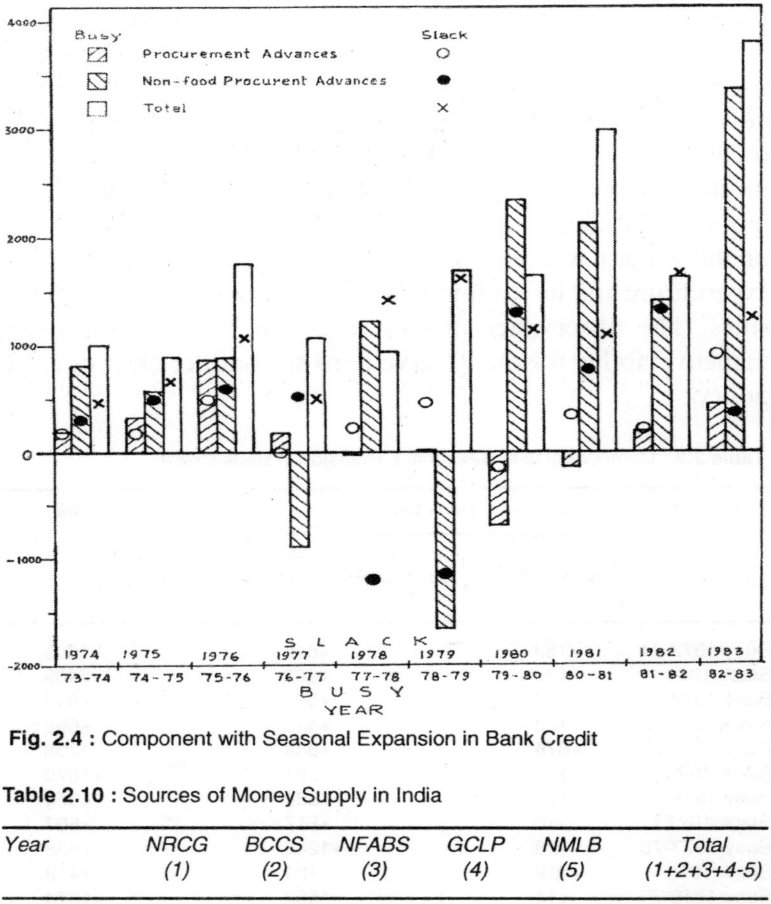


**Fig. 2.4** : Component with Seasonal Expansion in Bank Credit

**Table 2.10** : Sources of Money Supply in India

| *Year* | *NRCG (1)* | *BCCS (2)* | *NFABS (3)* | *GCLP (4)* | *NMLB (5)* | *Total (1+2+3+4-5)* |
|---|---|---|---|---|---|---|
| 1986-87 | 72020 | 94741 | 4815 | 1192 | 31236 | 141632 |
| | (50.85) | (66.89) | (3.39) | (0.84) | (21.28) | (100.00) |
| 1987-88 | 84370 | 107487 | 5672 | 1380 | 34634 | 164275 |
| | (51.35) | (65.44) | (3.45) | (0.84) | (21.08) | (100.00) |
| 1988-89 | 97373 | 132663 | 6800 | 1475 | 38066 | 200245 |
| | (48.62) | (66.25) | (3.39) | (0.73) | (19.01) | (100.00) |
| 1989-90 | 118093 | 156765 | 6818 | 1555 | 44047 | 239184 |
| | (49.37) | (65.55) | (2.85) | (0.65) | (18.41) | (100.00) |

# 3 ECONOMIC OUTLOOK OF ASIA AND INDIA

## Place of Asian Economies in the Global Economy

It is reasonable to hold that the economies of the Asian region are emerging as the new engines of growth in the global economy. Asia is a host to three of the ten largest economies (China, Japan and India) and accounting for more than 35 per cent of world GDP. Today Asia's share in world GDP exceeds that of European Union and the US (IMF, 2006). Being the fastest growing economies of the world, over the past two years, China and India contributed 73 per cent to the Asian growth and 38 per cent to the world GDP growth (IMF, 2005). With the setting of recovery in Japan, it is expected to be another engine of growth for the Asian as well as the global economy. Thus, for poles of growth—Japan, East Asia, China and India—forming a sort of quadrangle—have been emerging in Asia, and these could henceforth be the new sources of sustaining the global growth engine. It is interesting to note that among the top four economies in terms of GDP based on purchasing power parity, three Asian economies of this quadrangle, viz., China, Japan and India are ranked second, third and fourth, respectively.

It is also important to recognize the growing significance of the Asian economies in financial stability and global trade. For example, there has been a continued substantial accumulation of foreign exchange reserves by several countries of Asia reflecting increasing trade and financial integration of the region with rest of the world. Today, Asia holds foreign exchange reserves of US$ 3 trillion, which is 62 per cent of total foreign exchange reserves of the world. Further, the Asian region has increasingly become a major center of world trade, global capital flows and other macro-economic parameters. Today, the contribution of Asia to global trade has increased substantially to about 27 per cent.

**Dynamics of Asian Economic Integration**

There is increasing integration within Asia, as reflected in the pace of change in intra-regional trade flows. Intra-regional trade is growing as countries have positioned themselves at different stages of a regional supply chain. The rise of China and India is helping Asia to not only grow but to become more integrated. Asian countries are working to create a cohesive Asian community that allows for both complementary growth and positive competition. This phenomenon has been facilitated by an array of Free Trade Agreements (FTAs) in Asia. Intra-Asian trade as a share of the region's total trade has risen to more than 50 per cent in 2004 from about 30 per cent in 1980 (IMF, 2006). In less than 10 years, trade between China and the rest of Asian increased fourfold; trade between China and Japan/Korea tripled over the same period: intra-ASEAN trade doubled, and trade between ASEAN and India has tripled (Mandelson, 2005). In recent years, there is an impressive ongoing transformation in the composition of production and trade within Asia as the comparative advantage of many Asian economies continues to change. In particular, economies with relatively high wage costs are shifting toward higher value-added products, including services. The shift of labour-intensive manufacturing our of Hong Kong into mainland China and the associated boost to Hongs Kong's economy from the growth of trade in financial services in perhaps the most appropriate example of this on-going process.

Financial flows within the region have also become more significant. Although the developing countries of Asia still rely on London and New York to intermediate foreign savings of the region, Japan continues to remain the world's largest exporter of capital. Moreover, Hong King and Singapore, with their well-capitalised banks, efficient clearing and settlement system, and expanding range of financial products, have also emerged as major financial centers. Increasingly, these centers are intermediating savings within Asia, as well as channeling savings to Asia from other parts of the world. In particular, Hong Kong in the main conduit for investment in China and arranges a significant proportion of Asia's syndicated borrowing. Singapore, for its parts, has evolved into the main baking center for Southeast Asia.

## Asian Emerging Market Economies (AEMEs) : Some Generalisations in the Current Context

The growing importance of the Asian economies in the global economy and the dynamics of the Asian economic integration are also reflected in the added significance of the Asian EMEs (AEMEs) as the sub-set of the EMEs in the global economy. While the AEMEs are not homogenous in their economic system, structure and size, it may be useful to consider some generalisations in the current context recognising the severe limitations of such generalisations whenever a country-context becomes the focus. Development in the Japanese economy are very critical to the AEMEs and there is scope for considerable applied research in this area, recognising the signs of resurgence in the Japan's economy. The narration that follows essentially relates to the AEMEs, commencing with favourable factors.

(1) They currently enjoy strong global demand for their exports, favourable terms of trade and easy access to external financing.
(2) Comfortable foreign currency reserves along with reduced external debt as percentage of GDP serve as cushion against any sudden external shocks.
(3) Though public debt in some Asian economies still remains at elevated levels, most of the debt is of longer maturity, with higher proportions in local currency.

(4) The banking system has been strengthened through restructuring and supervisory systems have improved. Financial markets have evolved considerably in most of these economies.
(5) The resilience to external shocks in reinforced by a combination of lower balance sheet exposure to exchange rate risks, lower refinancing risks in debt structures, strong financial systems and above all, an observed tendency for greater policy flexibility.
(6) Most of the economies display strong growth-performance and reasonably well-anchored inflation expectations.

There are, however, several challenges being faced by the fast-growing AEMEs, particularly in sustaining the hard-won stability while maintaining growth momentum.

First, while growth impulses are strong in Asia and easing of oil-prices should moderate inflationary pressures, there are concerns about inflationary pressures being reinforced by ample liquidity driven by excess capital flows and rapidly rising credit. Strong capital inflows into Asia pose a challenge to monetary management. While some appreciation of currencies of countries enjoying current account surplus is evident, the macro policy may need to be predominantly governed by the compulsions of domestic supply and demand considerations. The currency appreciation or depreciation could, at times, be steep and sudden, resulting in possible disruption in the real sector and therefore there is a need for containing excess volatility in foreign exchange markets. Further, sterilisation costs may have to be often shared between the disc, the banking sector and the central bank balance sheets. While, to meet the surge in capital inflow, liberal capital outflows are recommended, they do not, in fact, take place at the time when they are liberalized. Further deepening of financial markets may help in absorption of large capital inflows in the medium term, but it may not give immediate succour at the current stage of financial sector development in many

AEMEs, particularly when speed and magnitude of flows are very high.

Second, significant improvements have taken place in developing local currency markets, especially bond markets. However, the operations of large players in financial markets in some Asian global needs than that of host country. Further, some multinational non-financial corporates operating in these economies may have large treasury operations, and their operations, could often make the assessment of risks in financial markets somewhat difficult. While supervisory skills in many AEMEs have been strengthened, new instruments, especially derivatives, new players such as hedge funds, and large OTC operations tend to diffuse and relocate risk making their assessment for policy purposes sometime difficult.

Third, the banking sector has been strengthened and non-banking intermediation expanded providing both stability and efficiency to the financial sector in many AEMEs. Yet, sometimes aligning the operations of large financial conglomerates and foreign institutions with local public policy priorities remains a challenge for domestic financial regulators in many AEMEs. Further, competition in financial sector in somewhat limited in many Asian economies. Large players in developed economies compete with each other intensely, while it is possible that a few of them dominate in each of Asian financial markets. A few of the financial intermediaries could thus wield dominant position in the financial markets of these countries, increasing the concentration risk.

## Performance of the Indian Economy

There is widespread and intense interest in the Indian economy, but merely by way of recollecting. It is useful to mention some features of the economic performance.

First, the average growth rate of the Indian economy over a period of 25 years since 1980-81 (financial year beginning April) has been about 6.0 per cent, with the growth rate averaging 9.1 per cent during the last two years.

Second, the economy has shown considerable resilience during the recent years, as evidenced by the avoidance of adverse contagion impact of several shocks in the EMEs and the ability to cope with oil price increases. The strengthening of economic activity in the recent years has been supported by persistent increase in domestic investment rate from 22.9 per cent of GDP in 2001-02 to 33.8 per cent in 2005-06 coupled with more efficient use of capital domestic saving rate has also improved from 23.5 to 32.4 per cent during the same period. While the services sector continues to the driver of growth with a share of around 60 per cent in the overall GDP and contributing almost three-fourth to overall growth, a noteworthy development during the recent years has been the continued recovery in industrial sector, particularly the manufacturing sector, supported by domestic as well export demand.

Third, the inflation rates since the second half of the 1990s have been by and large benign despite sustained external capital flows and continued surge in fuel prices. In the recent period, the headline inflation as measured by the Wholesale Price Index (WPI) has been higher crossing 6.0 per cent level in January to March 2007— a matter of concern at this juncture.

Fourth, the common intention of the Government and the Reserve Bank of India is to maintain annual inflation below 5 per cent in the medium term. A welcome development in this regard is that the fiscal position of the Government, both Central and States, is undergoing consolidation in terms of targeted reduction in fiscal deficit Indicators. The improvement in the fiscal position of several States in particularly impressive.

Fifth, the financial sector has acquired greater strength, efficiency and stability by the combined effect of competition, regulatory measures, policy environment and motivation among the market players including banks. Keeping in view the diverse investor needs in tune with the Reserve Bank's liquidity management, thereby facilitating the conduct of monetary policy, the money market has been progressively developed. The government securities market is quite deep, liquid and vibrant and well developed in terms of instruments/processes/ participants. The exchange rate of the rupee has been flexible, particularly, in the last few years and the turnover in the foreign exchange market has increased considerably. The stock market has been opened to foreign institutional investors and is comparable with major international equity markets in terms of market capitalisation, turnover and systems and processes. The corporate debt market in India is relatively underdeveloped but has a large potential to raise resources particularly for infrastructure projects, housing and for corporate and municipal needs.

Sixth, India's external sector has become resilient with the current account deficit being maintained at very modest levels after a couple of year's marginal surplus. Exports have been growing at an average rate of around 25 per cent during the last three years. Sustained growth in export of services and remittances continued to provide buoyancy to the surplus in the invisible account which enabled financing a large part of trade deficit. There was a significant strengthening in the capital account with the foreign exchange reserves close to US $ 200 billion and the reserves currently exceed the country's external debt of about US $ 140 billion as at end September 2006, thereby reflecting improved solvency of the economy. However, the imparting of human skills needed to cope with global competition is perhaps the most daunting task to ensure employment and thus, social tranquility.

## Challenges for the Indian Economy

There are, undoubtedly, many challenges the Indian economy, but is useful to focus on a few of these: the "usual suspects", I may say, in the eyes of analysis that track the developments in the Indian economy.

First, the poor state of the physical infrastructure, both in terms of quantity and quality is considered to be most critical hindrance for India's progress by many. The most important issue here is regulatory framework and overall investment climate, which are being addressed by the Government. Technological developments and rapid enhancement of domestic construction capabilities should aid the process of speedy and efficient implementation. Given the strengths of the domestic financial sector and the enhanced interest of foreign investors. Funding should not pose any serious problem. One other concern has been the cost recovery in infrastructure, which is expected to improve with more public-private partnerships. Again, with rapid growth in manufacturing and services. A sudden and intense pressure has developed in regard to availability and quality of urban infrastructure and urban services.

Second, fiscal consolidation still remains a matter of concern, especially in the eyes of the rating agencies. The recent Budget of the Central Government brings the consolidation on track. Our studies on State finances in Reserve Bank of India give grounds for optimism in regard to their fiscal health. We recognise two important areas the, if addressed would result in fiscal empowerment. One is elimination of subsidies, which are not directly targeted to the poor or inappropriate, and elimination of most of the tax exemptions, which are patently distortionary. While in any polity, fiscal consolidation in hard, it is particularly so in our setting of democratic compulsions, but there are grounds for optimism.

Third, and perhaps the most challenging issue relates to development of agriculture. While over 60 per cent of the workforce is dependent on agriculture, the GDP growth generated from agriculture is only marginally above the rate of growth of the population, which is not adequate to ensure rapid poverty reduction. The results of recent surveys on poverty in India, however, provide grounds for optimism in regard to accelerated reduction in absolute poverty since the reform period. To facilitate a more rapid growth in agriculture, legislative, institutional and attitudinal changes to supplement enhanced public and private investment are needed. There is an increasing recognition of this issue among policy makers.

Fourth, delivery of essential public services such as education and health to large parts of our population is a major institutional challenge. It is strongly felt that education will empower the poor to participate in the growth process and the large gaps in availability of health in terms of minimum access to the poor needs to be filled. Similarly, the judicial processes need to be aligned with the compulsions of a fast-growing globalizing economy, especially in terms of timeliness. All these are being intensely debated, and one should hope for significant improvements.

## Strengths of the Indian Economy

There are certain 'not easily quantifiable strengths', which our economy possesses and I would like to highlight them here.

First, a vast pool of science and technology graduates and the million who are familiar with English language are sources of strength for the emerging India so far. India is a country of great diversities but with incredibly harmonious co-existence of various religions, languages and a unified culture. The familiarity with multiple languages in India prepares the people to adapt better to multi-lingual environment, making it easier for them to fit into international systems very smoothly.

Second, India also enjoys the distinction of being the largest democracy of the world. The existence of a free press provides some insurance against excesses and makes Governments at all levels more alert and accountable.

Third, the political climate is characterised by what may be termed as political system stability, despite the coalition cabinets and periodic elections both at the Centre and in several States.

Fourth, India will remain one of the youngest countries in the would in the next few decades. This 'demographic divided' is seen as an inevitable advantage provided prerequisites such as skill-upgradation and sound governance to realise it are put in place. More important, the demographic transition is likely to be stretched over a longer period since States in India are at different stages of such transition from Kerala to Uttar Pradesh.

Fifth advantage is India's business culture. In terms of

business environment, the impressive growth coupled with market orientation of the economy has been a bottom-up exercise, with a very broad-based growing entrepreneurial class. These tendencies are perhaps reflective of a penchant for innovation among growing entrepreneurial class in India, imbued with professionalism and seeking to be globally competitive.

Sixth, the workers enjoy considerable freedom of movement, expression and right, especially through unionisation which, while making some changes difficult, ensures a vibrancy and timely improvisation to deal with competition. The migration of labour in India is sometimes seasonal and also related to a particular nature of work such as large construction activity.

**Current Priorities for India**

In the current context, the real challenge for India is to manage several transitions occurring simultaneously.

First, the structural shift in the domestic economy to higher growth.

Second, the lagged supply response.

Third, supply shock of oil followed by another of primary commodities, influencing inflation expectations.

Fourth, manage the consequences of the global excess liquidity, global imbalances, and sudden re-pricing of risks in international financial markets.

Fifth, the potential for excess volatility in the cross-border capital flows.

These challenges are managed involving several trade-offs. While pre-commitment to a set of reforms is useful, some flexibility in policies may be needed to respond to ongoing developments. Such a flexibility to review, rationalise and constantly rebalance the pace and sequencing of various measures impacting financial markets in considered desirable and the financial markets are generally kept informed of these developments. In fact, there are grounds for the financial markets to be comfortable with such flexibilities in policy measures that add to the overall financial stability.

To conclude, there are reasons to believe that these transitions in India will be managed smoothly by public policy, in general, and monetary policy, in particular. Of special interest of this gathering may be the fact the India does not contribute to global imbalances either positively or negatively. The corporate, banking and government balance sheets are not unduly exposed to currency risks, financial sector including financial markets, are generally considered to be robust and fairly efficient. There seem to be reasonably good prospects for continuing the current growth momentum in an enabling policy environment of contextual re-emphasis or price stability.

# 4 MONETARY POLICY TRANSMISSION IN INDIA

Key to the efficient conduct of monetary policy is the condition that it must exert a systematic influence on the economy in a forward-looking sense. A priori economic theory backed by some empirical evidence has identified the main channels through which monetary policy impacts its final targets, viz., output, employment and inflation. Broadly, the vehicles of monetary transmission can be classified into financial market prices (e.g., interest rates, exchange rates, yields, asset prices, equity prices) and financial market quantities (money supply, credit aggregates, supply of government bonds and foreign currency denominated assets). It is recognised that, whereas these channels are not mutually exclusive, the relative importance of each channel may differ from one economy to another depending on a number of factors including the underlying structural characteristics, state of development of financial markets, the instruments available to monetary policy, the fiscal stance and the degree of openness.

Traditionally, four key channels of monetary policy transmission are identified, viz., interest rate, credit aggregates, asset prices and exchange rate channels. The interest rate channel emerges as the dominant transmission mechanism of monetary policy. An expected to lead to a lowering of the cost of loanable funds, which, in turn, raises investment and consumption demand and should eventually get reflected in aggregate output and prices. Monetary policy also operates on aggregate demand through changes in the availability of loanable funds, *i.e.*, the credit channel. It is, however, relevant to note that the 'credit channel' is not a distinct, free-standing alternative to the traditional transmission mechanism but should rather be seen as a channel that can amplify and propagate conventional interest rate effects (Bernanke and Gertler, 1995). Nevertheless, it is fair to regard the credit channel as running to produce monetary effects on real activity (RBI, 2002). Changes in interest rates by the monetary authorities also induce movements in asset prices to generate wealth effects in terms of market valuations of financial assets and liabilities. Higher interest rates can induce an appreciation of the domestic currency, which in turn, leads to a reduction in net exports and, hence, in aggregate demand and output.

In the recent period, a fifth channel-expectations—has assumed prominence in the conduct of forward-looking monetary policy in view of its influence on the traditional four channels. For example, the link between short- and long-term real rates is widely believed to follow from the expectation hypothesis of the term structure of interest rates. In a generalised context, the expectations channel of monetary policy postulates that the beliefs of economic agents about future shocks to the economy as also the central bank's reactions can affect the variables that are determined in a forward-looking manner. Thus, "open-mouth operation" by the Central Bank, *i.e.*, an announcement of future central bank policy influences expectations in financial markets and leads to changes in output and inflation. Clearly, the credibility of the monetary authority drives the expectations channels.

The rest of the paper focuses on the Indian experience with monetary policy transmission. Section I delineates the objectives of monetary policy in India. Section II present the framework and instruments of monetary policy alongside the evolution of institutional developments which were to have a fundamental bearing on the monetary policy transmission. Section III discusses the monetary policy transmission channels: operating procedures, channel of bank lending and rates, debt market channel, exchange rate channel, and communication and expectation channel. Section IV makes an assessment of monetary transmission in terms of the ultimate objectives of monetary policy: price stability and growth. Section V discusses what is needed to improve monetary transmission. Section VI sums up the challenges and dilemmas of monetary policy.

## Objectives of Monetary Policy

The short title to the Reserve Bank of India Act, 1934 sets out the objectives of the Bank: "to regulate the issue of Bank notes and the keeping to reserves with a view to generally to operate the currency and credit system of the country to its advantage". Although, there has not been any explicit objectives of monetary policy in India are widely regarded as (i) price stability and (ii) sectors of the economy so as to support aggregate demand and ensure high and sustained growth. With the increasing openness of the Indian economy, greater emphasis has been laid in recent years on strengthening the institutional capacity in the country to support growth consistent with stability in the medium term. Given the overarching consideration for sustained growth in the context of high levels of poverty and inequality, price stability has evolved as the dominant objective of monetary policy. The underlying philosophy is that it is only in a low and stable inflation environment that economic growth can be sustained.

In recent years, financial stability has assumed priority in the conduct of monetary policy in view of the increasing openness of the Indian economy, financial integration and possibility of cross border contagion. Strong synergies and complementarities are observed between price stability and financial stability in India. Accordingly, regulation, supervision and development of the financial system remain in India within the legitimate ambit of monetary policy, broadly interpreted.

## Framework and Instruments

Prior to the mid-1980s, there was no formal enunciation of monetary policy objectives, instruments and transmission channels in India other than that of administering the supply/allocation of and demand for credit in alignment with the needs of a planned economy. Over the period from 1985 to 1997, India followed a monetary policy framework that could broadly be characterised as one of loose and flexible monetary targeting with feedback. Under this approach, growth in broad money supply ($M_3$) was projected in a manner consistent with expected GDP growth and a tolerable level of inflation. The $M_3$ growth thus worked out was considered a nominal anchor for policy. Reserve Money (RM) was used as the operating target and bank reserves and the operating instrument. As deregulation increased the role of market forces in the determination of interest rates and the exchange rate, monetary targeting, even in its flexible mode, came under stress. Capital flows increased liquidity exogenously, put upward pressure on the money supply, prices and the exchange rates, the latter having gained importance *vis à vis* quantity variables. While most studies in India showed that money demand functions had been fairly stable, it was increasingly felt that financial innovations and technology had systematically eroded the predictive potential of money demand estimations relative to the past. Interest rates gained relative influence on the decision to hold money. Accordingly, the monetary policy framework was reviewed toward the late 1990s, and the Reserve Bank switched over to a more broad-based multiple indicator approach from 1998-99.

In this approach, policy perspectives are obtained by return in different markets (money, capital and government securities markets), which are available at high frequency with medium and low frequency variables such as currency, credit extended by banks and financial institutions, the fiscal position, trade and capital flows, inflation rate, exchange rate, refinancing and transactions in foreign exchange and output. For simplicity and to facilitate greater understanding, the quarterly policy statements of the Reserve Bank continue to be set in a framework in terms of money, output and prices.

Since the late 1980s, there has been an enhanced emphasis by many central banks on securing operational freedom for monetary policy and investing it with a single goal, best embodied in the growing independence of central banks and inflation targeting as an operational framework for monetary policy, which has important implications for transmission channels. In this context, the specific features of the Indian economy have led to the emergence of a somewhat contrarian view: "In India, we have not favoured the adoption of inflation targeting, while deeping the attainment of low inflation as a central objective of monetary policy, along with that of high and sustained growth that is so important for a developing economy. Apart from the legitimate concern regarding growth as a key objective, there are other factors that suggest that inflation targeting may not be appropriate for India.

First, unlike many other developing countries we have had a record of moderate inflation, with double digit inflation being the exception, and largely socially unacceptable.

Second, adoption of inflation targeting requires the existence of an efficient monetary transmission mechanism through the operation of efficient financial markets and absence of interest rate distortions. In India, although the money market, government debt and forex markets have indeed developed in recent years, they still have some way to go, whereas the corporate debt market is still to develop. Though interest rate deregulation has largely been accomplished, some administered interest rates still persist.

Third, inflationary pressures still often emanate from significant supply shocks related to the effect of the monsoon on agriculture, where monetary policy action may have little role.

Finally, in an economy as large as that of India, with various regional differences, and continued existence of market imperfections in factor and production markets between regions, the choice of a universally acceptable measure of inflation is also difficult" (Mohan, 2006b).

The success of a framework that relies on indirect instruments of monetary management such as interest rates is contingent upon the extent and speed with which changes in the central bank's policy rate are transmitted to the spectrum of market interest rates and exchange rate in the economy and onward to the real sector. Clearly, monetary transmission cannot take place without efficient price discovery, particularly, with respect to interest rates and exchange rates. Therefore, in the efficient functioning of financial markets, the corresponding development of the full financial market spectrum becomes necessary. In addition, the growing integration of the Indian economy with the rest of the world has to be recognized and provided for. Accordingly, reforms focused on improving operational effectiveness of monetary policy have been put in process, while simultaneously strengthening the regulatory role of the Reserve Bank, tightening the prudential and supervisory norms, improving the credit delivery system and developing the technological and institutional framework of the financial sector.

### Market Development

Given the pivotal role of the money market in transmission, efforts initiated in the late 1980s were intensified over the full spectrum. Following the withdrawal of the ceiling on inter-bank money market rates in 1989, several financial innovations in term of money market instruments such as certificate of, commercial paper and money market mutual funds were introduced in phases. Barriers to entry were gradually eased by increasing the number of players and relaxing the issuance and subscription norms in respect of money market instruments, thus fostering better price discovery. Participation in the call money market was widened to cover primary and satellite dealers and corporates (through primary dealers), besides other participants. In order to improve monetary transmission as also on prudential considerations, steps were initiated in 1999 to turn the call money market into a pure inter-bank market and, simultaneously, to develop a repo market outside the official window for providing a stable collateralized funding alternative, particularly to non-banks who were phased out of the call segment, and banks. The Collateralised Borrowing and Lending Obligation (CBLO), a repo instrument developed by the Clearing Corporation of India Limited (CCIL) for its members, with the CCIL acting as a central counter-party for borrowers ad lenders, was permitted as a money market instrument in 2002. With the development of market repo and CBLO segments, the call money market has been transformed into a pure inter-bank market, including primary dealers, from August 2005. A recent noteworthy development is the substantial migration of money market activity from the uncollateralised call money segment to the collateralised market repo and CBLO markets. Thus, uncollateralised overnight transaction are now limited to banks and primary dealers in the interest of financial stability (Table 4.1).

**Table 4.1 :** Activity in Money Market Segments

| *Year/Month* | *Average Daily Turnover (One leg)* | | | | *Commercial Paper (Outstanding)* | *Certificates of Deposit (Outstanding* |
|---|---|---|---|---|---|---|
| | *Call Money Market* | *Market Repo* | *CBLO* | *Term Money Market* | | |
| **1** | **2** | **3** | **4** | **5** | **6** | **7** |
| 2003-04* | 86 | 26 | 3 | 3 | 78 | 32 |
| 2004-05* | 71 | 43 | 34 | 3 | 117 | 61 |
| 2005-06* | 90 | 53 | 100 | 4 | 173 | 273 |
| 2006-07 | | | | | | |
| April | 85 | 55 | 163 | 5 | 165 | 441 |
| May | 90 | 90 | 172 | 5 | 169 | 502 |
| June | 87 | 106 | 138 | 6 | 197 | 564 |
| July | 91 | 97 | 157 | 4 | 211 | 592 |
| August | 107 | 78 | 156 | 5 | 229 | 656 |
| September | 118 | 92 | 148 | 6 | 244 | 653 |
| October | 132 | 97 | 170 | 5 | 232 | 658 |
| November | 128 | 94 | 161 | 4 | 242 | 689 |
| December | 121 | 72 | 155 | 5 | 233 | 686 |

**CBLO** : Collateralised Borrowing and Lending Obligation.

: The average daily turnover (one leg) for a year is arrived at by adding daily turnover (one leg) and then dividing the sum by the number of days in the year.

*Source* : Macroeconomic and Monetary Development, various issues, Reserve Bank of India.

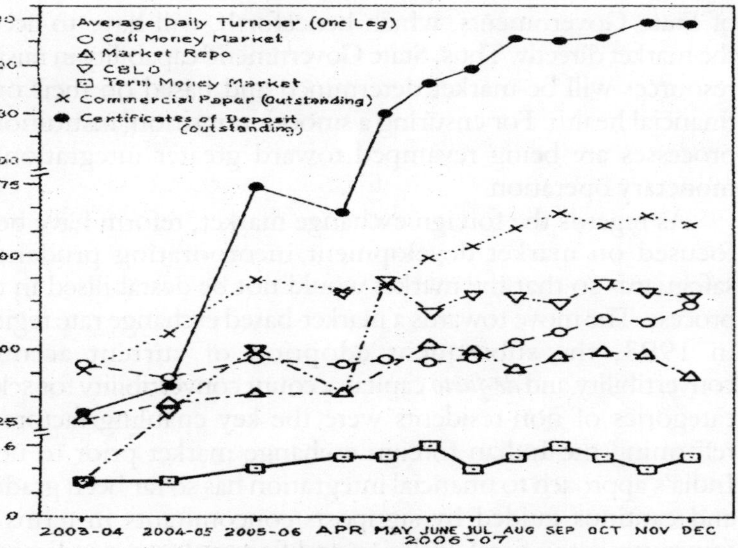


**Fig. 4.1 : Activity in Money Market Segments**

The government securities markets is important for the entire debt market as it serves as a benchmark for pricing other debt market instruments, thereby aiding the monetary transmission across the yield curve. The key policy development that has enabled a more independent monetary policy environment as well as the development of government securities market was the discontinuation of automatic monetization of the government's fiscal deficit since April 1997 through an agreement between the Government and the Reserve Bank of India in September 1994. Subsequently, enactment of the Fiscal responsibility and Budget Management Act, 2003 has strengthened the institutional mechanism further: from April 2006 onwards, the Reserve Bank is no longer permitted to subscribe to government securities in the primary market. This step completes the transition to a fully market based system for government securities. Looking ahead, consequent to the recommendations of the Twelfth Finance Commission, the

Central Government would cease to raise resources on behalf of State Governments, which henceforth, will have to access the market directly. Thus, State Government' capability in raising resources will be market determined and based on their own financial health. For ensuring a smooth transition, institutional processes are being revamped toward greater integration in monetary operation.

As regards the foreign exchange market, reform have been focused on market development incorporating prudential safeguards so that the market would not be destabilised in the process. The move towards a market-based exchange rate regime in 1993, the subsequent adoption of current account convertibility and *de-facto* capital account convertibility for select categories of non-residents were the key enabling factors in reforming the Indian foreign exchange market prior to now. India's approach to financial integration has so far been gradual and cautious guided by signposts/concomitants in terms of improvement in fiscal, inflation and financial sector indicators, *inter alia,* efforts are currently underway to move towards fuller capital account convertibility even for residents. In the period 2000-06, a number of measures were initiated to integrate the Indian forex market with the global financial system, with increasing freedom given to banks to borrow abroad and fix their own position and gap limits.

The development of the monetary policy framework has also involved a great deal of institutional initiatives in the area of trading, payments and settlement systems along with the provision of technological infrastructure. The interaction of technology with deregulation has also contributed to the emergence of a more open, competitive and globalised financial market. While the policy measures in the pre-1990s period were essentially devoted to financial deepening, the focus of reforms in the last decade and a half has been engendering greater efficiency and productivity in the banking system. Legislative amendments have also been carried out to strengthen Reserve Bank's regulatory jurisdiction over financial markets, providing greater instrument independence and hence, ensuring monetary transmission.

The relative weights assigned to various channels of transmission of monetary policy also reflect a conscious effort to move from direct instruments of monetary control to indirect instruments. Illustratively, the Cash Reserve Ratio (CRR) which had been brought down from a peak of 15 per cent in 1994-95 to 4.5 per cent by June 2003, before the onset of withdrawal of monetary accommodation since October 2004 is now 6.0 per cent. The recent amendment to the RBI Act in 2006 will further strengthen monetary maneuverability since it allows for the removal of the floor of 3 per cent and ceiling of 20 per cent on CRR. Monetary control is also exercised through the prescription of a Statutory Liquidity Ratio (SLR), which is a variant of the secondary reserve requirement is several countries. It is maintained in the form of specified assets such as cash, gold and 'approved' and unencumbered securities – the latter being explicitly prescribed – as a proportion to Net Demand and Time Liabilities (NDTL) of banks. Accordingly, the SLR is also important for prudential purposes, *i.e.*, to assure the soundness of the banking system. The pre-emption under the SLR, which had increased to about 38.5 per cent of NDTL in the beginning of the 1990s, was brought to its statutory minimum of 25 per cent by October 1997. Banks, however, continue to hold more government securities than the statutory minimum SLR, reflecting risk perception and portfolio choice. The statutory minimum SLR of 25 per cent has been removed now (January 2007) to provide for greater flexibility in the Reserve Bank's monetary policy operation. The reform of the monetary and financial sectors has, thus, enabled the Reserve Bank to expand the array of instruments at its command and enhanced its ability to respond to evolving circumstances.

## Operating Procedure for Monetary Policy

Short-term interest rates have emerged as the key indicators of the monetary policy stance all over the world. It is also recognised that stability in financial markets is critical for efficient price discovery and meaningful signaling. Since the interest rate and exchange rate are key price reflecting the cost of money, it is particularly important for efficient functioning of the economy that they be market determined and easily observed.

Central banks follow a variety of operating framework and procedures for signaling and implementing the monetary policy stance on a day-today basis, with a view to achieving the ultimate objectives-price stability and growth. The choice of policy framework in any economy is always a difficult one and depend on the stage of macroeconomic and financial sector development and is somewhat of an evolutionary process (Mohan, 2006a). In a market-oriented financial system, central banks typically use instruments that are directly under their control: required reserve ratios, interest charged on borrowed reserved (discount window) provided directly or through rediscounting of financial assets held by depository institutions, Open Market Operations (OMOs) and selective credit controls. These instruments are usually directed at attaining a prescribed value of the operating target. Typically bank reserves and/or a very short-term interest rate (usually the overnight interbank rate). The optimal choice between price and quantity targets would depend on the sources of disturbances in the goods and money markets (Poole, 1970). If money demand is viewed as highly unstable, greater output stability can be attained by stabilizing interest rates. If, however, the main source of short-run instability arises from aggregate spending or unsterilised capital inflows, a policy that stabilizes monetary aggregates could be desirable. In reality, it often becomes difficult to trace out the source of instability. Instead, monetary policy is implemented by fixing, at least over the short time horizon, the value of an operating target or policy instrument. As additional information about the economy is obtained, the appropriate level at which to fix the policy instrument/target changes.

The operating procedures of monetary policy of most central banks have largely converged to one to the following three variants: (i) a number of central banks, including the US Federal Reserve, estimate the demand for bank reserves and then carry out open market operations to target short-term interest rates: (ii) another set of central banks, of which the Bank of Japan used to be a part until recently, estimate market liquidity and carry out open market operations to target bank reserves, while allowing interest rates to adjust; and (iii) a growing number of central banks, including the European Central Bank and the Bank of England, modulate monetary conditions in terms of both quantum and price of liquidity, through a mix of OMOs, standing facilities and minimum reserve requirement and changes in the policy rate. The operating procedure, followed in India, however, presents a fourth variant.

## Money Markets and the Liquidity Adjustment Facility

In the Indian context, reforms in the monetary policy operating framework, which were initiated in the late 1980s crystallised into the Liquidity Adjustment Facility (LAF) in 2000 . Under the LAF, the Reserve Bank sets its policy rates, *i.e.*, repo and reverse repo rates and carries out repo/reverse repo operations, thereby providing a corridor for overnight money market rates. The LAF avoids targeting a particular level of overnight money market rate in view of exogenous influences impacting liquidity at the shorter end, *viz.*, volatile government cash balances and unpredictable foreign exchange flows.

Although repo auctions can be conducted at variable or fixed rates on overnight or longer-term given market preference and the need to transmit interest rate signals quickly, the LAF has settled into a fixed rate overnight auction mode since April 2004. With the introduction of Second LAF (SLAF) from November 28, 2005 market participants now have a second window during the day to fine-tune their liquidity management. LAF operations continue to be supplemented by access to the reserve Bank's standing facilities linked to repo rate: export credit refinance to banks and standing liquidity facility to the primary dealers.

The introduction of LAF has had several advantages. First and foremost, it made possible the transition from direct instruments of monetary control to indirect instruments. Since LAF operations enabled reduction in CRR without loss of monetary control, certain dead weight loss for the system was saved. *Second*, LAF has provided monetary authorities with greater flexibility in determining both the quantum of adjustment as well as the rates by responding to the needs of the system on a daily basis. *Third* and most importantly, though there is no formal targeting of a point overnight interest rate. LAF helped to stabilise overnight call rates within a specified corridor, the difference between the fixed repo and reverse repo rates currently being 150 basis points. It has thus enabled the central bank to affect demand for funds through policy rate changes. In this sense, LAF rates perform the role of nominal anchor effectively. Although call money rates edged above the repo rate during January-February 2006, the rates in the collteralised segment of the money market-market repos and CBLO, which account for nearly 80 per cent of the market turnover-remained below the repo rate.

### Market Stabilisation Scheme

In the context of increasing openness of the economy, a market-determined exchange rate and large capital inflows, monetary management may warrant sterilizing foreign exchange market intervention, partly or wholly, so as to retain the intent of monetary policy. Initially, the Reserve Bank sterilised capital inflows by way of OMOs. Such sterilisation, however, involves cost in terms of low returns on international assets *vis à vis* domestic assets. The finite stock of government securities with the Reserve Bank also limited its ability to sterilise. The LAF operations, which are essentially designed to take care of frictional daily liquidity began to bear the burden of stabilisation disproportionately.

The Reserve Bank, therefore, signed in March 2004 a Memorandum of Understanding (MoU) with the Government of India for issuance of Treasury Bills and dated Government Securities under the Market Stabilisation Scheme (MSS), in addition to normal Government borrowings. The new instrument empowered the Reserve Bank to absorb liquidity on a more enduring but still temporary basis while leaving LAF for daily liquidity management and using conventional OMO on more enduring basis. The MSS has provided the Reserve Bank flexibility not only to absorb but also inject liquidity in times of need by way of unwinding. Therefore, short-term instruments are generally preferred for MSS operations.

The various tools of liquidity management have thus enabled the Reserve Bank to maintain liquidity conditions, orderly movement in both exchange rates and interest rates and conduct monetary policy n accordance with its stated objectives Table 4.2.

**Table 4.2 :** Phases of Bank's Liquidity Management Operations

*(Rupees billion)*

| *Item* | *Variation during* | | | | |
|---|---|---|---|---|---|
| | *2003-04* | *2004-05* | *2005-06* | *2006-07Q1* | *2006-07Q2* |
| 1 | 2 | 3 | 4 | 5 | 6 |
| A. Drivers of Liquidity **(1+2+3+4)** | **721** | **581** | **-317** | **355** | **-158** |
| 1. RBI's Foreign Currency Assets (adjusted for revaluation) | 1414 | 1150 | 688 | 285 | 105 |
| 2. Currency with the Public | -434 | -409 | -573 | -215 | -1 |
| 3. Surplus Cash Balances of the Centre with Reserve Bank | -177 | 5 | -227 | 402 | -262 |
| 4. Others (residual) | -83 | -165 | -205 | -118 | -1 |
| **B. Management of Liquidity (5+6+7+8)** | **-464** | **-567** | **580** | **-390** | **320** |
| 5. Liquidity impact of LAF Repos | -332 | 153 | 121 | -353 | 407 |
| 6. Liquidity impact of OMO (Net)* | -176 | 12 | 107 | 5 | 1 |
| 7. Liquidity impact of MSS | 0 | -642 | 351 | -42 | -88 |
| 8. First round liquidity impact due to CRR change | 35 | -90 | 0 | 0 | 0 |
| **C. Bank Reserves (A+B)#** | **357** | **14** | **263** | **-35** | **162** |

(+) —Indicates injection of liquidity into the banking system.
(-) —Indicates absorption of liquidity from the banking system.
(#) —Includes vault cash with banks and adjusted for first round liquidity impact due to CRR change.
(*) —Adjusted for Consolidated Sinking Funds (CSF) and other Investments and including private placement.
*Note* —Data pertain to March 31 and last Friday for all other months.
*Source*—Annual report and Macroeconomic and Monetary Development, various issues, Reserve Bank of India.

Government cash balances with the Reserve Bank often display sizeable volatility. *First*, due to operational requirements which are difficult to predict (except for salary payments, coupon/interest payments, redemption of loans and the like) Government needs to maintain a substantial cash position with the Reserve Bank. *Second*, there is the need for maintaining or building up cash balances gradually over many weeks ahead of large, known disbursements such as lumpy redemption of bonds contracted for financing high fiscal deficit and, particularly, benchmark bonds, if markets are not to be disrupted. *Third*, while a major part of outflows from government cash balances is regular, inflows by way of direct tax revenues and other sources are lumpy and irregular in nature.

Accumulating Government cash balances with the central banks, in effect, act as withdrawal of liquidity from the system and have the same effect as that of monetary tightening, *albeit* without any intention to do so by the monetary authority. Similarly, there would be injection of liquidity into the system if Government cash balances maintained with the central bank decline, despite a situation in which, for instance, monetary policy is biased towards tightening liquidity. Thus, volatile Government cash balances could cause unanticipated expansion or contraction of the monetary base, and consequently, money supply and liquidity, which may not necessarily be consistent with the prevailing stance of the monetary policy cash balance, the task of monetary management becomes complicated, often warranting offsetting measures, partly or wholly, so as to retain the intent of monetary policy.

## Bank Credit and Lending Rate Channels

There is some evidence of the bank lending channel working in addition to the conventional interest rate channel. In view of the asymmetry in the resource base, access to non-deposit sources, asset allocation and liquidity, big and small banks are found to respond in significantly different ways. In particular, small banks are more acutely affected by concretionary monetary policy shocks as compared to big banks, *i.e.*, smaller banks curtail their lending more sharply *vis* à *vis* large banks (Pandit *et al*, 2006). Available empirical evidence also indicates that prudential norms, as proxied by banks' capital adequacy ratios, exert a significant influence on bank lending (Nag and Das, 2002: Pandit *et al*, 2006).

The monetary policy stance of the Bank is often articulated as a commitment to ensure that all genuine requirements for bank credit are adequately met in order to support investment and export demand consistent with price stability. Liquidity operations are conducted with a view to ensuring that the demand for reserves in satisfied and credit projections consistent with macroeconomic objectives are achieved. Simultaneously, improvements in the delivery of bank credit are pursued failure in efficiently auctioning credit. An integral element of the conduct of monetary policy has, therefore, been the direction of bank credit to certain sectors of priority such as agriculture, exports, small scale industry, infrastructure, housing, micro-credit institutions and self help groups. An on going policy endeavour is enhancing and simplifying the access to credit with a view to securing the widest inclusion of society in the credit market (Table 4.3).

Available empirical evidence covering the period September 1998 to March 2004 suggests that the interest rate pass-through from changes in the policy rate was 0.61 and 0.42 for lending and deposit rates, respectively, *i.e.*, a reduction/increase of 100 basis points (bps) in the Bank Rate led to a reduction/increase of almost 40 bps in the banks' deposit rates and 60 bps in their

**Table 4.3:** Sectoral Shares in Non-food Bank Credit

*(Per cent)*

| *Sector/Industry* | *Outstanding on October 12, 2006* | *March 2006* | *March 2005* | *March 2004* |
|---|---|---|---|---|
| **Non-food Gross Bank Credit** | **100** | **100** | **100** | **100** |
| 1. Agriculture and Allied Activities | 12 | 12 | 13 | 12 |
| 2. Industry (Small, Medium and Large) | 39 | 39 | 43 | 43 |
| 2.1 Small Scale Industries | 6 | 6 | 8 | 9 |
| 3. Services | 2 | 3 | 3 | ... |
| 3.1 transport Operators | 1 | 1 | 1 | ... |
| 3.2 Professional and Others | 1 | 1 | 1 | ... |
| 4. Personal Loans | 26 | 25 | 25 | ... |
| 4.1 Housing | 14 | 13 | 13 | ... |
| 4.2 Advances against Fixed Deposits | 2 | 3 | 3 | 4 |
| 4.3 Credit Cards | 1 | 1 | 1 | ... |
| 4.4 Education | 1 | 1 | 1 | ... |
| 4.5 Consumer Durables | 1 | 1 | 1 | 1 |
| 5. Trade | 6 | 6 | 6 | 3 |
| 6. Others | 9 | 14 | 11 | 41 |
| 6.1 Real Estate Loans | 2 | 2 | 1 | 1 |
| 6.2 Non-Banking Financial | 2 | 2 | 2 | 2 |
| Memo Item: | | | | |
| Bank Credit-GDP ratio | 40.3* | 42.2 | 35.2 | 30.4 |

* Approximately.

*Note:* Sectoral shares may not add up to 100 due to rounding off.

*Source: Annual Report 2005-06,* Reserve Bank of India.

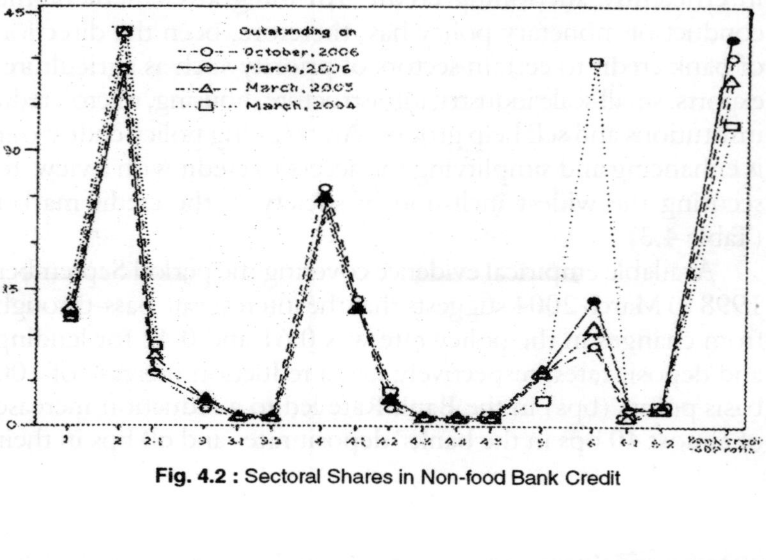


**Fig. 4.2 :** Sectoral Shares in Non-food Bank Credit

prime lending rate (Table 4.4 and 4.5). Rolling regressions suggest some improvement in pass-through to lending rates and deposits. Thus, though pass-through is less than complete, there are-signs of an increase in pass-through over time (RBI, 2004b).

The improvement in the pass-through can be attributed to policy efforts to impart greater flexibility to the interest rate structure in the economy through various measures such as advising banks: to introduce flexible interest rate option for new deposits: to review their maximum spreads over Prime Lending Rate (PLR) and reduce them wherever they are unreasonably high: to announce the maximum spread over PLR to the public along with the announcement of their PLR: and, to switch over to "all cost" concept for borrowers by explicitly declaring the various charges such as processing and service charges (Table 4.6). Besides, interest rates have emerged as a more potent instrument than before with the move towards floating as against fixed rate products under which the transmission is limited at the margin.

From October 18, 1994, banks have been free to fix the lending rates for loans above Rupees 2,00000. Bank were required to obtain the approval of their respective boards for the PLR which would be the minimum rate changed for loans above Rs. 2,00,000, in the interest of small borrowers as also to remove the disincentive for credit flow to such borrowers. PLR was converted into a celling rate for loans up to Rs. 2,00,000 in 1998-99. Sub-PLR lending was allowed in 2001-02 a keeping with international practice. For customers' protection and meaningful competition, bank-wise quarterly data on PLR, and maximum and minimum lending rates have been placed at the Reserve Bank's website, starting from June 2002. Towards greater transparency in loan pricing in the context of sticky behaviour of lending rates, the system of BPLR (i.e., benchmark PLR) was introduced in 2003-04. Banks were advised to specify their BPLR taking into account (a) actual cost of funds, (b) operating expense, and (c) a minimum margin to cover regulatory requirement of provisioning and capital charge, and profit margin. Whereas, conceptually the BPLR should turn out to be a median lending rate in practice, the specification of BPLR by banks has turned out to be sticky. Movements in the actual interest rate charged take place less transparently through changes in the proportion of loans above or below the announced BPLR. The share of sub-BPLR lending has, in recent times, increased to over 75 per cent reflecting the overall decline in interest rates, until recently. This has undermined the role of BPLR as a reference rate, complicating the judgment on monetary transmission in regard to lending rates.

**Table 4.4:** Outstanding Term Deposits of Scheduled Commercial Banks by Interest Rate (At the end of March)

*(Per cent to total deposits)*

| *Interest Rate Slab* | *1996* | *1997* | *1998* | *1999* | *2000* | *2001* | *2002* | *2003* | *2004* | *2005* |
|---|---|---|---|---|---|---|---|---|---|---|
| 1 | 2 | 3 | 4 | 5 | 6 | 7 | 8 | 9 | 10 | 11 |
| < 8% | 10.8 | 11.2 | 11.5 | 13.3 | 16.8 | 16.9 | 25.0 | 53.7 | 74.0 | 86.4 |
| 8-9% | 2.4 | 5.2 | 4.8 | 6.1 | 6.5 | 10.5 | 22.6 | 16.4 | 9.9 | 5.8 |
| 9-10% | 4.5 | 7.1 | 6.4 | 9.0 | 14.3 | 16.1 | 19.8 | 12.0 | 7.3 | 3.1 |
| 10-11% | 15.2 | 14.1 | 13.7 | 17.7 | 20.9 | 23.9 | 17.3 | 10.5 | 5.1 | 2.5 |
| 11-12% | 13.9 | 14.3 | 16.3 | 20.2 | 19.2 | 17.9 | 9.1 | 4.5 | 2.3 | 1.1 |
| 12-13% | 23.4 | 20.9 | 22.3 | 19.2 | 13.9 | 9.1 | 4.3 | 2.3 | 1.1 | 0.5 |
| > 13% | 29.8 | 27.2 | 25.0 | 14.5 | 8.4 | 5.6 | 1.9 | 0.8 | 0.5 | 0.7 |

*Source: Basic Statistical Returns of Scheduled Commercial Banks in India*, various issues, Reserve Bank of India.

**Table 4.5:** Outstanding Loans of Scheduled Commercial Banks by Interest Rate (At the end of March)

| *Interest Rate Slab* | *1990* | *1995* | *1997* | *1998* | *1999* | *2000* | *2001* | *2002* | *2003* | *2004* | *2005* |
|---|---|---|---|---|---|---|---|---|---|---|---|
| 1 | 2 | 3 | 4 | 5 | 6 | 7 | 8 | 9 | 10 | 11 | 12 |
| < 6% | 2.7 | 2.3 | 1.1 | 1.0 | 0.3 | 0.2 | 0.2 | 0.1 | 0.1 | 0.4 | 0.4 |
| 6-10% | 6.8 | 2.1 | 0.5 | 0.4 | 3.7 | 1.0 | 0.6 | 3.2 | 5.3 | 13.6 | 19.5 |
| 10-12% | 4.8 | 2.3 | 1.4 | 2.3 | 3.3 | 7.9 | 17.0 | 24.5 | 22.9 | 16.1 | 17.5 |
| 12-14% | 21.4 | 10.6 | 10.7 | 13.2 | 20.3 | 26.8 | 28.6 | 22.5 | 25.1 | 25.7 | 22.4 |
| 14-15% | 4.4 | 6.7 | 10.9 | 14.9 | 9.7 | 11.5 | 12.6 | 14.1 | 19.4 | 16.2 | 16.6 |
| > 15% | 59.8 | 76.0 | 75.4 | 68.2 | 62.7 | 52.6 | 41.0 | 35.6 | 27.1 | 28.0 | 23.6 |

*Source: Basic Statistical Return of Scheduled Commercial Banks in India*, various issues, Reserve Bank of India.

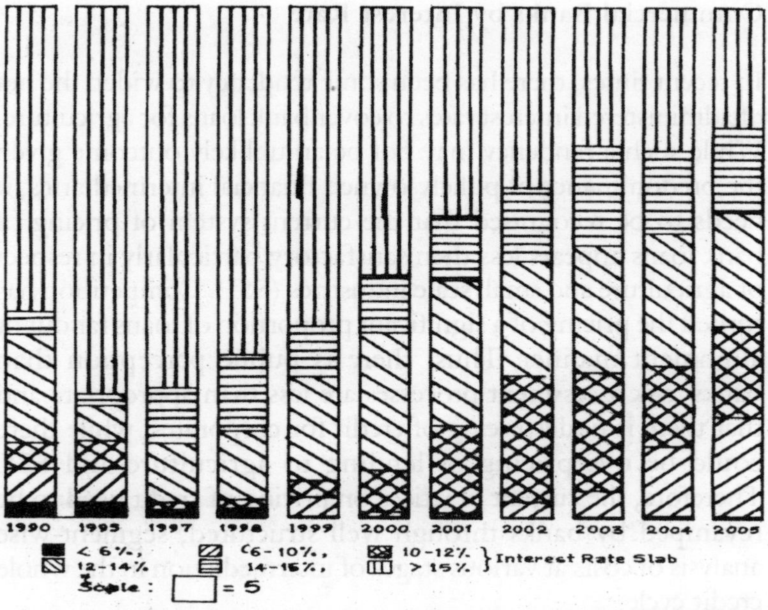


**Fig. 4.3 :** Outstanding Term Deposits of Scheduled Commercial Banks by Interest Rate

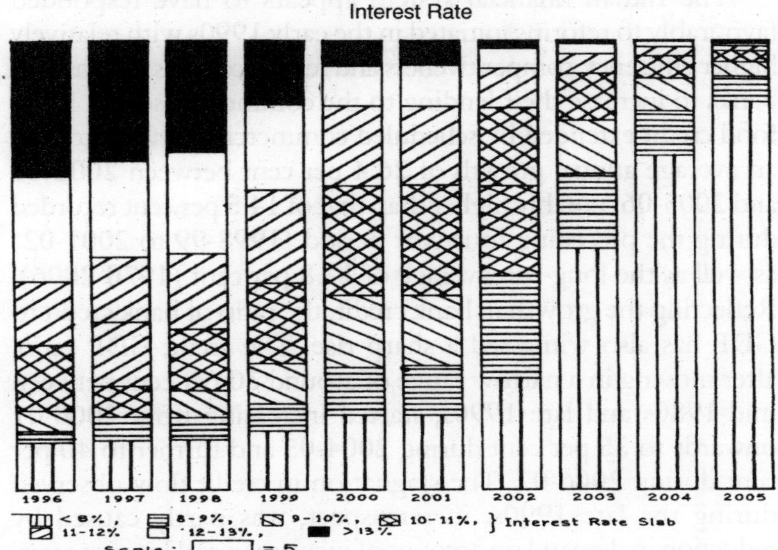


**Fig. 4.4 :** Outstanding Loans of Scheduled Commercial Banks by Interest Rate

## Commercial Banks by Interest Rate

In recent times, there has been some tendency to widen the net of administered interest rates to cover bank loans for agriculture. While such a tendency may not be an unlikely outcome given the predominance of pulicly-owned financial intermediaries, it needs to be recognised that the current system of pricing of bank loans appears less then satisfactory particularly in respect of agriculture and small scale industries (SSI). Competition has turned the pricing of a significant proportion of loans far out of alignment manner. Thus, there is public perception than banks' risk assessment processes are less than appropriate and that there is underpricing of credit for corporates, while there could be overpricing of lending to agriculture and SSI. Therefore, the current practices on pricing of credit need to be revamped by banks through well structured, segment-wise analysis of costs at various stages of intermediation in the whole credit cycle.

The Indian financial system appears to have responded favourably to reforms initiated in the early 1990s with relatively higher efficiency, competitiveness and resilience. This has enabled banks to increase their lending to the commercial sector. Non-food credit extended by scheduled commercial banks recorded an average annual growth of 26.4 per cent between 2002-03 and 2005-06, notably higher than that of 14.5 per cent recorded during the preceding four-year period (1998-99 to 2001-02) as well as the long-run average of 17.8 per cent (1970-2006). Reflecting the growth in bank credit, the ratio of bank credit to GDP has also witnessed a sharp rise. The credit-GDP ratio, after moving in a narrow range of around 30 per cent between mid-1980s and late 1990s, started increasing from 2000-01 onwards to 35 per cent during 2004-05 and further to 40 per cent during 2006-07. The stagnation in credit flow observed during the late 1990s, in retrospect, was partly caused by reduction in demand on account of increase in real interest rates, the cyclical down turn and the significant business restructuring

**Table 4.6** : Lending Rates of Scheduled Commercial Banks in India

(Percentage)

| | *Public Sector Banks* | | *Foreign Banks* | | *Private Sector Banks* | |
|---|---|---|---|---|---|---|
| | *Demand Loans* | *Term Loans* | *Demand Loans* | *Term Loans* | *Demand Loans* | *Term Loans* |
| *1* | *2* | *3* | *4* | *5* | *6* | *7* |
| Jun-02 | 12.75-14.00 | 12.75-14.00 | 13.00-14.50 | 13.00-15.50 | 13.75-16.00 | 14.00-16.00 |
| Sep-02 | 12.00-14.00 | 12.25-14.00 | 13.00-14.75 | 12.75-14.50 | 14.00-16.00 | 13.50-15.00 |
| Dec-02 | 11.58-14.00 | 12.25-14.00 | 12.00-14.75 | 11.70-13.63 | 13.50-15.75 | 13.50-15.00 |
| Mar-03 | 11.50-14.00 | 12.00-14.00 | 10.50-12.75 | 10.25-13.50 | 13.50-15.50 | 13.00-15.00 |
| Jun-03 | 11.50-14.00 | 11.50-14.00 | 10.00-14.00 | 9.73-13.00 | 13.00-15.00 | 12.50-14.75 |
| Sep-03 | 11.50-13.50 | 11.00-13.50 | 9.50-12.75 | 9.25-13.50 | 13.00-14.50 | 12.00-14.50 |
| Dec-03 | 11.50-13.00 | 11.00-13.25 | 7.75-13.65 | 9.00-13.00 | 12.50-14.50 | 11.50-14.50 |
| Mar-04 | 11.00-12.75 | 11.00-12.75 | 7.50-11.00 | 8.00-11.60 | 12.00-14.00 | 11.25-14.00 |
| Jun-04 | 10.50-12.50 | 10.75-12.75 | 6.50-11.50 | 7.25-11.00 | 11.25-13.25 | 9.50-13.00 |
| Sep-04 | 10.50-12.50 | 9.50-12.25 | 6.75-9.00 | 7.25-11.00 | 11.25-13.25 | 9.50-13.00 |
| Dec-04 | 9.00-12.50 | 8.38-12.13 | 7.25-9.00 | 7.38-10.95 | 10.00-13.00 | 9.25-13.00 |
| Mar-05 | 9.00-12.50 | 8.38-12.00 | 7.13-9.00 | 7.63-9.50 | 10.00-12.50 | 9.00-13.00 |
| Jun-05 | 8.00-12.13 | 8.00-11.88 | 7.75-9.00 | 7.50-9.50 | 10.00-12.75 | 9.00-13.00 |
| Sep-05 | 8.00-11.63 | 8.00-11.88 | 7.00-10.25 | 7.35-9.50 | 10.00-12.50 | 9.00-13.00 |
| Dec-05 | 8.00-11.63 | 8.00-11.63 | 7.00-9.50 | 7.20-9.50 | 10.00-13.00 | 9.25-13.00 |
| Mar-06 | 8.00-11.63 | 8.00-11.63 | 8.00-9.75 | 7.53-9.75 | 9.50-13.00 | 9.00-13.18 |
| Jun-06 | 8.00-11.25 | 8.00-12.00 | 7.63-9.75 | 7.53-9.75 | 9.75-13.50 | 9.23-13.75 |
| Sep-06 | 8.25-11.50 | 8.50-12.13 | 8.08-9.57 | 7.85-9.75 | 10.00-13.50 | 9.45-13.50 |
| Dec-06 | 8.00-11.88 | 8.50-12.00 | 8.05-10.00 | 8.00-9.50 | 10.00-13.13 | 9.23-12.63 |

*Note* : Median lending rates in this table are the range within which at least 60 per cent business is contracted.

*Source* : Reserve Bank of India, available at http://rbidocs.rbi.org.in/lendingrate/home.html.

that occurred during that period. The sharp expansion in bank credit in the past 4-5 year also reflects, in part, policy initiatives to improve flow of credit to sectors like agriculture. While demand for agricultural and industrial credit has remained strong in the current cycle, increasingly, retail credit has emerged as the river of growth. The strengthening of the banking system has thus worked towards financial widening monetization and financial inclusion are extending the net of the formal financial system and hence, enhancing the scope of monetary transmission.

The increasing reach of formal finance has gradually expanded to cove larger segments of the population. The 'demographic divided' of a larger and younger labour force has meant that banks have been able to expand their loan portfolio rapidly, enabling consumers to satisfy their lifestyle aspirations at a relatively young age with an optimal combination of equity and debt to finance consumption and asset creation. In the process, interest has become a much more potent tool of monetary policy, affecting consumption and investment decisions of the population in a fashion much more rapidly than was the case earlier. This is evident in the share of retail credit in total bank credit, increasing from around 6 per cent in March 1990 to over 22 per cent in March 2005. A large part of this increase has taken place in the past 5-6 years. In view of likely that household consumption decision, in the coming years, may be more strongly influenced by monetary policy decisions with implications for the monetary transmission mechanism. Consequently, the monetary authority may need to contend increasingly with public opinion on monetary management, much more than hitherto in the context of the rising share of personal/household loans. In the context of large scale public ownership of banks, such pressures of public opinion would also manifest themselves into political pressures.

In brief, there is increasing evidence that the bank credit and lending rates channels of monetary transmission are gaining in strength with the widening and deepening of the financial system and the progress towards greater price discovery. A number of constraints continue, however, to interfere with monetary transmission. *First*, the stipulation of priority sector lending of 40 per cent of net bank credit affects flexibility in sectoral credit allocation even though there is no interest rate stipulation for the priority sector. *Second*, allocational flexibility is further constrained under the extant prescription of a SLR of 25 per cent of net demand and time liabilities (NDTL), though now the relevant Act has been amended to give the Reserve Bank flexibility to reduce this statutory liquidity ratio. *Third*, the system of BPLR for credit pricing has proved to be relatively sticky downward and more so for specific sectors like agriculture and SSI. As the BPLR has ceased to be a reference rate, assessment of the efficacy of monetary transmission has become difficult. *Fourth*, the Government of India continues to own around 70 per cent of Banks' assets. While the Government, as a legitimate owner, is entitled to issue direction to public sector banks, such exercise by the Government infuses elements of uncertainty and market imperfection, impacting monetary transmission.

**Debt Market Channel**

While government debt management was one of the motivating factors for the setting up of central banks in many countries, currently the function with is focus on lowering the cost of public debt in often looked upon as constraining monetary management, particularly when compulsions of monetary policy amidst inflation expectations may necessitate a tighter monetary policy stance. Therefore, it is now widely believed that the two functions-monetary policy and public debt management-need to be conducted in a manner that ensures transparency and independence in monetary operation. The fuller development of financial market, reasonable control over the fiscal deficit and necessary legislative changes are regarded as pre-conditions for separation of debt management from monetary management. The Reserve Bank currently performs the twin function of public debt and monetary management.

"The logical question that follows is whether the experience of fiscal dominance over monetary policy would have been different if there had been separation of debt management from monetary management in India? Or, were we served better with both the functions residing in the Reserve Bank? What has really happened is that there was a significant change in thinking regarding overall economic policy during the early 1990s, arguing for a reduced direct role of the Government in the economy. A conscious view emerged in favour of fiscal stabilisation and reduction of fiscal deficits aimed at eliminating the dominance of fiscal policy over monetary policy through the prior practice of fiscal deficits being financed by automatic monetisation. It is this overall economic policy transformation that has provided greater autonomy to monetary policy making in the 1990s.

The Indian economy has made considerable progress in developing its financial markets, especially the government securities market since 1991. Furthermore, fiscal dominance in monetary policy formulation has significantly reduced in recent years. With the onset of a fiscal consolidation process, withdrawal of the Reserve Bank from the primary market of Government securities and expected legislative changes permitting a reduction in the statutory minimum Statutory Liquidity Ratio (SLR), fiscal dominance would be further diluted.

All of these changes took place despite the continuation of debt management by the Reserve Bank. Thus, one can argue that effective separation of monetary policy from debt management is more a consequence of overall economic policy thinking rather than adherence to a particular view on institutional arrangements (Mohan, 2006b).

The Fiscal Responsibility and Budget Management (FRBM) Act, 2003 has set the stage for a front-loaded fiscal correction path for the Central Government. Similar enactments have also taken place in a number of States. As already mentioned, the FRBM Act, 2003 has prohibited the Reserve Bank from participating in primary issuances of government securities with effect from April 1, 2006, except under exceptional circumstances. In preparation, the institutional structures within the Reserve Bank have been modified to strengthen monetary operations with a view to moving towards functional separation between debt management and monetary operations. Accordingly, a new Financial Markets Department (FMD) has been constituted to undertake (i) monetary operations, (ii) regulation and development of money market instruments, and (iii) monitoring of money, government securities and foreign exchange markets. The enactment of the FRBM Act has arguably strengthened monetary transmission through the debt market. It has also mitigated the possibility of conflict in monetary policy in order to contain the cost of Government borrowing.

The auction-based issue of government debt according to a pre-announced calendar has enabled price discovery and liquidity in the market. A Negotiated Dealing System (NDS) was introduced in February 2002 to facilitate electronic bidding, secondary market trading and settlement and to disseminate information on trades on a real-time basis. In the context of the Reserve Bank's absence from primary auctions, 'when, as and if issued' market in government securities as been allowed recently.

Vibrant secondary market trading has helped to develop a yield curve and the tem structure of interest rate. This has facilitated pricing of debt instruments in various market segments and, thereby, monetary transmission across maturity and financial instrument. While market yield, at times, turn out to be puzzling, particularly in the wake of global policy signaling as also in times of re-pricing of risks, the reserve repo rate set out by the Reserve Bank remains the overnight floor for the market. The falling interest rate scenario witnessed up to 2003-04 and the comfortable liquidity position in the system had helped to bring down the yields and the yield curve turned relatively flat. The long-term yields, however, continue to be impervious across the globe to subsequent reversal of the interest rate cycle, giving rise to a 'conundrum' *a la* Greenspan (2005). In the Indian context, the transmission from shorter to longer end of the yield curve has been vacillating linked, *inter alia*, to change in monetary policy rates, inflation rates, international interest rates and, on other occasion, the SLR stipulation. With increasing openness of the domestic economy, it appears that international economic developments are set to exert a greater influence on the domestic yield curve than before. Thus, even in the absence of fuller capital account convertibility, monetary transmission may need to contend with impulses that arise from international development. Furthermore, the process of fiscal consolidation currently underway could potentially lead to a situation of excess demand for government securities in relation to their supply, which would, in turn, impact the shape of the yield curve and, thereby, impede monetary transmission. The stipulation for SLR could also undergo a change guided by prudential consideration, affecting, in the process, the demand for government securities and thereby, the yield curve as banks reamin invested with government securities for the purpose of SLR. Such developments, however, may not be in consonance with the monetary policy stance and hence, could come in the way of intended monetary transmission.

While the government securities market is fairly well

developed now, the corporate debt market remains to be developed for facilitating monetary signaling across various market, the demand for debt instruments has largely concentrated on government securities with the attendant implications for the yield curve and, in turn, for monetary transmission. The secondary market for corporate debt has suffered from lack of market making resulting in poor liquidity. Corporates continue to prefer private placements to public issues for raising resources in view of ease of procedures and lower costs. There is a need for development of mortgage-backed securities, credit default swaps, bond insurance institutions for credit enhancement, abridgment of disclosure requirements for listed companies, rating requirement for unlisted companies, real time reporting of primary and secondary trading, retail access to bond market by non-profit institutions and small corporates and access to RTGS. A concerted effort is now being made to set up the institutional and technological structure that would enable the corporate debt market to operate. Furthermore, the on-going reforms in the area of social security coupled with the emergence of pension of provident funds are expected to increase the demand for long-term debt instrument. In the process, the investor base for government securities would be broadened, extending the monetary transmission across new players and participant.

**Exchange Rate Channel**

The foreign exchange market in India has acquired increasing depth with the transition to a market determined exchange rate system in March 1993 and the subsequent gradual but significant liberalisation of restrictions on various external transaction. Payments restrictions on all current account transactions have been removed with the acceptance of the obligations of Article VIII of the IMF's Articles of Agreement in August 1994. While the rupee remains virtually convertible on the capital account for foreign nationals and non-resident Indian (NRIs), similar moves are on course for the domestic resident. Significant relaxations have been allowed for capital outflows in the form of direct and portfolio investment, non-resident deposits, repatriation of assets and funds held abroad. Indian residents can now open foreign currency accounts with banks in India.

The major initiative taken to widen and deepen the Indian forex market and to link it with the global financial system have been: (i) freedom to banks to fix net overnight position limits and gap limits, initiate trading positions in the overseas markets, and use derivative products for asset-liability management; (ii) permission to autorised dealers (Ads) in foreign exchange to borrow abroad up to limits related to their capital based as a prudential measure; and (iii) freedom to corporates to hedge anticipated exposures, cancel and rebook forward contact. The CCIL has commenced settlement of forex operations for inter-bank US Dollar/Indian rupee spot and forward trades from November 2002 and inter-bank US Dollar/Indian rupee cash ad tom trades from February 2004.

The annual turnover in the foreign exchange market has increased more than threefold from US $ 1434 billion in 2000-01 to US $ 4413 billion in 2005-06 (Table 4.7). The inter-bank transactions continue to account for bulk of the transactions in the forex market, *albeit* with a declining share over the years. The forward market segment (swaps plus forward) is also growing at a faster pace. Reflecting the build-up of forex reserves, the strong capital flows and the confidence in the Indian economy, the forward premia has come down sharply from the peak reached in 1995-96. Under the market determined exchange rate regime, the Indian rupee has exhibited two way movements and the foreign exchange market has displayed stable conditions as reflected in the annual coefficient of variation of 0.9-2.3 per cent during 2000-01 to 2005-06. The exchange rate policy of the Reserve Bank in recent years has been guided by the broad principles of careful monitoring and management of exchange rates with flexibility, without a fixed target or a pre-announced target or a band, coupled with the ability to intervene, if and when necessary.

Exchange rate flexibility, coupled with the gradual removal of capital controls, has widened the scope for monetary maneuverability, enabling transmission through exchange rates.

In the event of interest rate arbitrage triggered by monetary policy action, foreign exchange inflows can tend to pick up until the interest rate parity is restored by exchange rate adjustment. An appreciating exchange rate, in turn, would have a dampening effect on aggregate demand, containing inflationary pressures. However, if large segments of economic agents lack adequate resilience to withstand volatility in currency and money markets, the option of exchange rate adjustments may not be available, partially of fully. Therefore, the central bank may need to carry out foreign exchange operations for stabilizing the market. In the process, the injection of liquidity into the system by the central bank would go against it policy stance and weaken monetary transmission. Thus, monetary management becomes complicated, and the monetary authority may need to undertake offsetting sterilisation transactions in defence of monetary stability intended transmission. In the Indian context, faced with similar circumstances, sterilisation operations are being carried out from 2004 by issuances of government securities under the MSS.

**Table 4.7 :** Foreign Exchange Market-Activity Indicators

| *Year* | *Foreign Exchange Market-Annual Turnover (US $ billion)* | *Gross Volume of BoP Transactions (US $ billion)* | *RBI's Foreign Currency Assets* (US $ billion)* | *C.V. of Exchange Rate of Rupee (per cent)* | *Col. 2 over Col. 3* | *Col. 2 over Col. 4* |
|---|---|---|---|---|---|---|
| *1* | *2* | *3* | *4* | *5* | *6* | *7* |
| 2000-01 | 1434 | 258 | 40 | 2.3 | 5.6 | 36 |
| 2001-02 | 1487 | 237 | 51 | 1.4 | 6.3 | 29 |
| 2002-03 | 1585 | 267 | 72 | 0.9 | 5.9 | 22 |
| 2003-04 | 2141 | 362 | 107 | 1.6 | 5.9 | 20 |
| 2004-05 | 2892 | 481 | 136 | 2.3 | 6.0 | 21 |
| 2005-06 | 4413 | 657 | 145 | 1.5 | 6.7 | 30 |

* At end-March. BoP: Balance of Payments, C.V.: Coefficient of Variation.
*Source:* Reserve Bank of India.

•

Available evidence suggests that exchange rate depreciation has the expected effect of raising domestic prices and the coefficient of exchange rate pass-through to domestic inflation ranges between 8-17 basis point (depending upon the measure of inflation) *i.e.*, a 10 per cent depreciation of the Indian rupee (*vis-à-vis* the US Dollar) would, other things remaining unchanged, increase consumer inflation by less than one percentage point and the GDP deflator by 1.7 percentage points. Rolling regressions suggest some decline in exchange rate pass-through coefficient in the recent years (RBI, 2004b). The coefficient of the exchange rate exhibits a declining trend although the estimates turn out to be somewhat imprecise. This suggests a possible decline in exchange rate pass-through to domestic inflation. The decline in pass-through during the 1990s is consistent with the cross-country evidence. In India, inflation rates have declined significantly since the second half of the 1990s and this could be one explanation for the lower pass-through. Another key factor that could have lowered the pass-through is the phased decline in tariffs as well as non-tariff barriers such as quotas. Average import duties are now less than one-third of what they were a decade ago. This steep reduction in tariffs could have easily allowed domestic producers to absorb some part of the exchange rate depreciation without any effect on their profitability.

Another factor that could reduce the pass-through is related to globalisation and "Walmartisation". The increased intensity of globalisation and the commodification of many goods have perhaps reduced the pricing power of producers, particularly of low technology goods in developing countries, whereas the pricing power of large retailers like Walmart has rise. The decline in pass—through across a number of countries, as suggested by various studies, has implication for the efficacy of exchange rate as an adjustment tool. The lower pass-through suggests that, in the new globalised economy, exchange rate adjustments as a means of correction of imbalances may have become less potent: if so, then the swing in exchange rates to correct emerging imbalances will have to be much larger than before, bringing in their wake greater instability eventually (Mohan, 2004).

## Communication and Expectations Channel

In a market-oriented economy, well-informed market participants are expected to enable and improved functioning of the markets, and it is held that a central bank is in the best position to provide such useful information to the market participants. Whether providing information would result in shaping and managing expectations, and if so, whether it is desirable, remain unsettled issues. There are several dilemmas faced by central banks while designing an appropriate communication policy. What should be communicated and to what degree of disaggregation? The second set relates to: at what stage of evolution of internal thinking and debate should there be dissemination? The third set relates to the timing of communication with reference to its market impact. The fourth relates to the quality of information and the possible ways in which it could be perceived. Thus, alleged incoherence or and element of ambiguity at times on the part of central bankers in explaining policies is as much a reflection of the complexity of the issues as it is of the differing perceptions of a variety of audiences to which the communication is addressed. It is essential to appreciate that communication policy is not merely about explaining or getting a feedback on policy, but may include elements of influencing the policy direction itself. A central bank does this through several channels, including research publication and speeches (Reddy; 2001; 2006). It is recognised that credible communication and creative engagement with the market and economic agents have emerged as the critical channel of monetary transmission as against the traditional channels. For example, the US Federal Reserve, since 1994, appears to have been providing forward guidance, while the European Central Bank appears to be in the mould of keeping the markets informed rather than guiding it.

With the widening and deepening of inter-linkages between various segments of financial markets, the Reserve Bank has adopted a consultative process for policy making in order to ensure timely and effective implementation of the measures. The Bank has taken a middle path of sharing its analysis in addition to providing information, but in now way guiding the market participants. However, in doing so, the Reserve Bank has the benefit of the process of two-way communication, of information as well as perceptions, between the market participants and the Reserve Bank. In the process, the Bank's signaling/announcements are increasingly seen to have an influence on the expectations formation in the market.

The more complex is the mandate for the central bank, the more is the necessity of communication (Mohan, 2005). The Reserve Bank of India clearly has complex objective. Apart from pursuing monetary policy, financial stability is one of the overriding concerns of the Reserve Bank. Within the objective of monetary policy, both control of inflation and providing adequate credit to the productive sectors of the economy so as to foster growth are equally important. This apart, the Reserve Bank acts as a banking regulator, public debt manager, government debt market regulator and currency issuer. Faced with such multiple tasks and complex mandate, there is an utmost necessity clearer communication on the part of the Reserve Bank.

In general, for a central bank, there is necessity of three kinds of communication, *viz*., (a) policy measures, (b) reasons behind such policy measures, and (c) analysis of the economy. The Reserve Bank is engaged with all these three kinds of communication. In fact, by international standards the Reserve Bank has a fairly extensive and transparent communication system. Policy statements (quarterly since April 2005 onwards and bi-annual prior to this period) have traditionally communicated the Reserve Bank's stance on monetary policy in the immediate future of six months to one year. The proactive of attaching a review of macroeconomic developments to the quarterly reviews gives an expansive view of how the centrai bank sees the economy. In the bi-annual policy meetings with leading bankers, the Governor explains the rationale behind the measures at length. These policy meetings are not one-way traffic. Each banker present in the meeting interacts with the Governor to express his or her reaction to the policy announcement is over, the Governor addresses a press conference in the afternoon. The Deputy Governor in charge of monetary policy normally gives live interviews to all the major television channels on the same day. The Governor also gives interviews to print and electronic media over the next few days' after the monetary policy announcement.

Communication of policy also takes place through speeches of the Governor and Deputy Governor, and various periodic reports. A significant step towards transparency of monetary policy implementation is formation of various Technical Advisory Committees (TACs) in the Reserve Bank with representatives from market participants, other regulators and experts. In line with the international best practices and with a view to further strengthening the consultative process in monetary policy, the Reserve Bank, in July 2005, set up a Technical Advisory Committee on Monetary Policy (TACMP) with external experts in the areas of monetary economics, central banking, financial markets and public finance. The Committee meets at least once in a quarter, review macroeconomic and monetary developments and advises the Reserve Bank on the stance of monetary policy. The Committee has contributed to enriching the inputs and processes of monetary policy setting in India. Recognising the importance of expectations in the conduct and formulation of monetary policy, the Reserve Bank has recently initiated survey of business and inflation expectations.

Finally, in the context of growing openness of the Indian economy and increasing integration with the rest of the world, global economic and financial developments-much as monetary policy decisions of the US Federal and other major economies and trends in international crude oil prices-are also shaping expectations. The Reserve Bank takes such factors and expectations also into account.

The process of monetary policy formulation in India is now relatively transparent, consultative and participative with external orientation and this has contributed to stabilising expectations of market participants. Illustratively, an important element in coping with liquidity management has been smoothening behavour of the Reserve Bank and its communication strategy. In August 2004, the headline inflation rate shot up to 8.7 per cent, partly on account of rising global oil prices and partly due to resurgence in manufacturing inflation. The turning of the interest rate cycle looked imminent. The issue was addressed through burden sharing by appropriate monetary and fiscal coordination and by preparing markets for a possible interest rate reversal. In measured and calibrated steps the monetary policy stance was changed and measures such as those on CRR and reverse repo were taken in a phased manner. Also, banks were allowed to transfer HFT (Held for Trading) and AFS (Available for Sale) securities to HTM (Held to Maturity) category, thereby affording them some cushion against the possible interest rate shock. Markets were prepared with a careful communication on the stance of the monetary policy that the central bank would strobe for provision of appropriate liquidity while placing equal emphasis on price stability. Monetary management thus succeeded in building credibility and keeping inflation expectation low.

Illustratively, the Reserve Bank in its Annual Policy Statement for 2006-07 (April 2006) stressed that: "Domestic Macroeconomic and financial conditions support prospects of sustained growth momentum with stability in India. It is important to recognise, however, that there are risks to both growth and stability from domestic as well as global factors. At the current Juncture the balance of risks is tilted towards the global factors. The adverse consequences of further escalation of international crude prices and/or of disruptive unwinding of global imbalances are likely to be pervasive across economies, including India. Moreover, in a situation of generalised tightening of monetary policy, India cannot afford to stay out of step. It is necessary, therefore, to kept in view the dominance of domestic factors as in the past but to assign more weight to global factors than before while formulating the policy stance" (RBI, 2006).

In brief, there has been noteworthy improvement in the operational efficiency of monetary policy from the early 1990s. Financial sector reforms and the contemporaneous development of the money market, government securities market and the foreign exchange market have strengthened monetary transmission by enabling more efficient price discovery, and improving allocative efficiency even as the Reserve Bank has undertaken developmental efforts to ensure the stability and smooth functioning of financial markets. The approach has been one of simultaneous movement on several, fronts, graduated and calibrated, with an emphasis on institutional and infrastructural development and improvements in market microstructure. The pace of the reform was contingent upon putting in place appropriate systems, and procedures, technologies and market practices. There has been close co-ordination between the Government and the Reserve Bank, as also between different regulators, which helped in orderly and smooth development of the financial markets in India. Markets have now grown in size, depth and activity, paving the way for flexible use of indirect instruments. The Reserve Bank has also engaged in refining the operating procedures and instruments as also risk management systems, income recognition and provisioning norms, disclosure norms, accounting standards and insolvency in line with international best practices with a view to fostering the seamless integration of Indian financial markets with global markets.

## How Well do Monetary Transmission Channels Works?

Turning to an assessment of monetary policy transmission, it would be reasonable to assert that monetary policy has been largely successful in meeting its key objectives in the post-reforms period. There has been a fall in inflation worldwide since the early 1990s, and in India since the late 1990s. Inflation has averaged close to five per cent per annum in the decade gone by, notably lower than that of eight per cent in the previous four decade. Structural reforms since the early 1990s coupled with improved monetary-fiscal interface and reforms in the government securities market enabled better monetary management from the second half of the 1990s onwards. More importantly, the regime of low and stable inflation has, in turn, stabilised inflation expectations and inflation tolerance in the economy has come down. It is encouraging to note that despite record high international crude oil prices, inflation remain low and inflation expectation also remain stable (Table 4.8). Since inflation expectations are a key determinant of the actual inflation outcome, and given the lags in monetary transmission, the Reserve Bank has been taking pre-emptive measures to keep inflation expectations stable. As discussed earlier, a number of instruments, both existing as well as new, were employed to modulate liquidity conditions to achieve the desired objectives. A number of other factors such as increased competition. Productivity gains and strong corporate balance sheets have also contributed to this low and stable inflation environment, but it appears that calibrated monetary measures had a substantial role to play as well.

In the context of the recent firming up of core as against headline inflation particularly in industrial countries, primarily on account of higher non-oil commodity prices, issues of proper measurement of inflation and inflationary pressures have attracted renewed debate. In particular, the debate involves the relevance of core inflation as a guide for the conduct of monetary policy *vis-à-vis* the use of headline inflation. In India, core inflation is not considered as relevant for several reasons, but specially because the two major sources of supply shock, food and fuel, account for a large share of the index. Further, in the absence of a harmonised consumer price index for India, use of core inflation based on wholesale prices may not be much meaningful. While the permanent component is judgmental, broad magnitudes could be perceived and articulated. Such an explanatory approach to headline and underlying inflation pressure in monetary policy has added credibility to the policy and influenced and guided the inflation expectations in India.

**Table 4.8 :** Wholesale Price Inflation (WPI) and Consumer Price Inflation (CPI)

*(Year-on-Year)*

| *Inflation Measure* | *March 2000* | *March 2001* | *March 2002* | *March 2003* | *March 2004* | *March 2005* | *March 2006* | *March 2007* |
|---|---|---|---|---|---|---|---|---|
| 1 | 2 | 3 | 4 | 5 | 6 | 7 | 8 | 9 |
| WPI Inflation (end-Month) | 6.5 | 5.5 | 1.6 | 6.5 | 4.6 | 5.1 | 4.1 | 6.6+ |
| CPI-IW | 4.8 | 2.5 | 5.2 | 4.1 | 3.5 | 4.2 | 4.9 | 6.9* |
| CPI-UNME | 5.0 | 5.6 | 4.8 | 3.8 | 3.4 | 4.0 | 5.0 | 6.9* |
| CPI-AL | 3.4 | -2.0 | 3.0 | 4.9 | 2.5 | 2.4 | 5.3 | 9.5 $ |
| CPI-RL | - | -1.6 | 3.0 | 4.8 | 2.5 | 2.4 | 5.3 | 8.9 $ |

*Note available.IW:* Industrial Workers; UNME: Urban Non-Manual Employees.
*AL:* Agricultural Labourers.RL: Rural Labourers,* As in December 2006.
*+:* As on February 10, 2007.$: As in January 2007.
*Source*: Annual Report and Handbook of Statistics on the Indian Economy, Various issues, Reserve Bank of India.

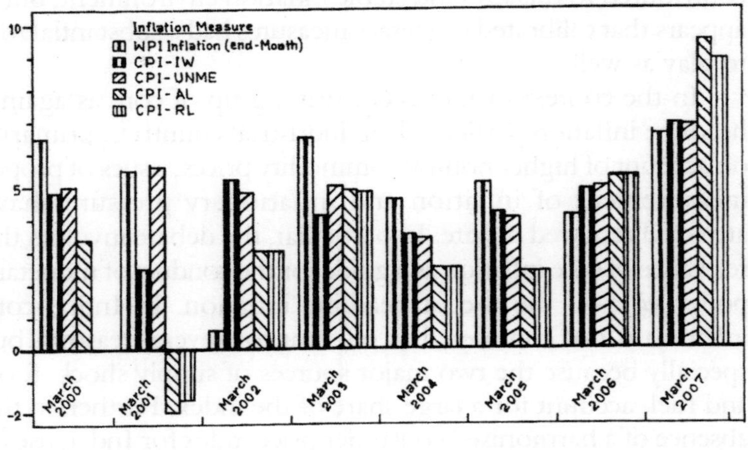


**Fig. 4.5 :** Wholesale Price Inflation (WPI) and Consumer Price Inflation (CPI)

How did monetary policy support the growth momentum in the economy? As inflation, along with inflation expectations, fell during the earlier period of this decade, policy interest rates were also brought down. Consequently, both nominal and real interest fell. The growth rate in interest expenses of the corporates declined consistently since 1995-96, from 25.0 per cent to a negative of 5.8 per cent in 2004-05 (Table 4.9). Such decline in interest costs has significant implications for the improvement in bottom lines of the corporates. Various indicators pertaining to interest costs, which can throw light on the impact of interest costs on corporate sector profits have turned positive in recent years.

**Table 4.9 :** Monetary Policy and Corporate Performance-Interest Rate Related Indication

| *Year* | *Growth Rate in Interest Expenses (%)* | *Debt Service to Total Uses of Funds Ratio** | *Interest Coverage Ratio#* |
|---|---|---|---|
| 1990-91 | 16.2 | 22.4 | 1.9 |
| 1991-92 | 28.7 | 28.3 | 1.9 |
| 1992-93 | 21.6 | 24.4 | 1.6 |
| 1993-94 | 3.1 | 20.9 | 2.0 |
| 1994-95 | 8.1 | 27.2 | 2.4 |
| 1995-96 | 25.0 | 21.5 | 2.7 |
| 1996-97 | 25.7 | 18.7 | 2.1 |
| 1997-98 | 12.5 | 8.1 | 1.9 |
| 1998-99 | 11.1 | 17.6 | 1.6 |
| 1999-00 | 6.7 | 17.6 | 1.7 |
| 2000-01 | 7.1 | 14.0 | 1.7 |
| 2001-02 | -2.7 | 19.4 | 1.7 |
| 2002-03 | -11.2 | 8.9 | 2.3 |
| 2003-04 | -11.9 | 12.7 | 3.3 |
| 2004-05 | -5.8 | 21.8 | 4.6 |

*— Represents ratio of loans and advances plus interest accrued on loan to total uses of funds.

#— Represents the ratio gross profit (i.e., earning before interest and taxes) to interest expenses.

*Source:* The data is based on selected non-government non-financial public limited companies, collected by Reserve Bank of India.

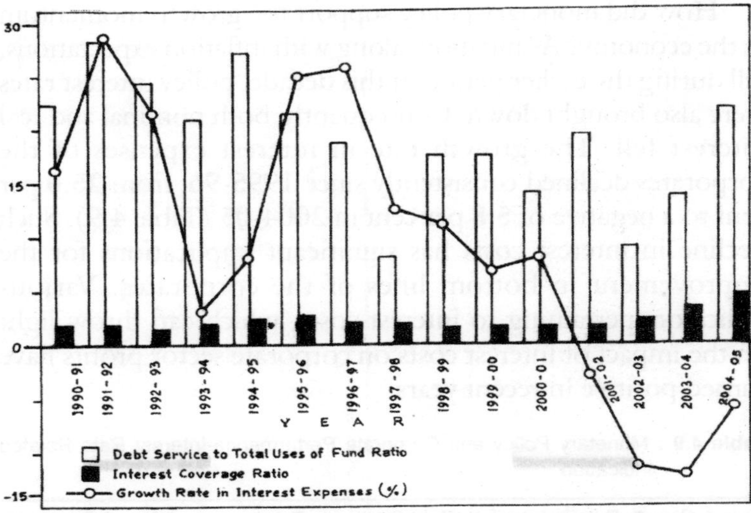


**Fig. 4.6 :** Monetary Policy and Corporate Performance-Interest Rate Related Indication

## What is Needed to Improve Monetary Transmission?

While the changes in policy rates are quickly mirrored in the money market rates as well as in government bond yields, lending and deposits rates of banks exhibit a degree of downward inflexibility. In this context, administered interest rates fixed by the Government on a number of small saving schemes and provident funds are of special relevance as they generally offer a rate higher than corresponding instruments available in the market as well as tax incentives (RBI, 2001: RBI, 2004a). As banks have to compete for funds with small saving schemes, the rates offered on long-term deposits mobilised by banks set the floor for lending rates at a level higher than would have obtained under competitive market conditions (Fig 4 7). In fact, this was observed to be a factor contributing to downward stickness of lending rates, with implications for the effectiveness of monetary policy (Table 4.10).

These small savings schemes administered by the government through the wide reach of post offices, and some

**Table 4.10** : Small Savings and Bank Deposits

*(Amount in Rupees Billion)*

| | *Average Interest Rate on Small Savings (%)* | *Small Savings Outstanding* | *Average Interest Rate on Banks' Term Deposits (%)* | *Bank Term Deposits Outstanding* | *Small Savings as % of Bank Deposits* |
|---|---|---|---|---|---|
| 1991-92 | 9.95 | 586 | 9.1 | 2,308 | 25.4 |
| 1992-93 | 9.48 | 609 | 9.6 | 2,686 | 22.7 |
| 1993-94 | 12.21 | 677 | 8.7 | 3,151 | 21.5 |
| 1994-95 | 13.20 | 833 | 7.0 | 3,869 | 21.5 |
| 1995-96 | 11.33 | 937 | 8.5 | 4,338 | 21.6 |
| 1996-97 | 13.03 | 1,061 | 9.4 | 5,056 | 21.0 |
| 1997-98 | 11.92 | 1,268 | 8.8 | 5,985 | 21.2 |
| 1998-99 | 10.34 | 1,553 | 8.9 | 7,140 | 21.7 |
| 1999-00 | 11.50 | 1,875 | 8.6 | 8,133 | 23.1 |
| 2000-01 | 11.60 | 2,251 | 8.1 | 8,201 | 27.4 |
| 2001-02 | 11.61 | 2,629 | 9.6 | 9,503 | 27.7 |
| 2002-03 | 11.56 | 3,138 | 8.7 | 10,809 | 29.0 |
| 2003-04 | 10.88 | 3,758 | 6.5 | 12,794 | 29.4 |
| 2004-05 | 9.37 | 4,577 | 6.2 | 14,487 | 31.6 |
| 2005-06 | 8.91 | 5,246 | — | 17,444 | 30.1 |

*Source:* Annual Report and Handbook of Statistics on the Indian Economy, various issues, Reserve Bank of India.

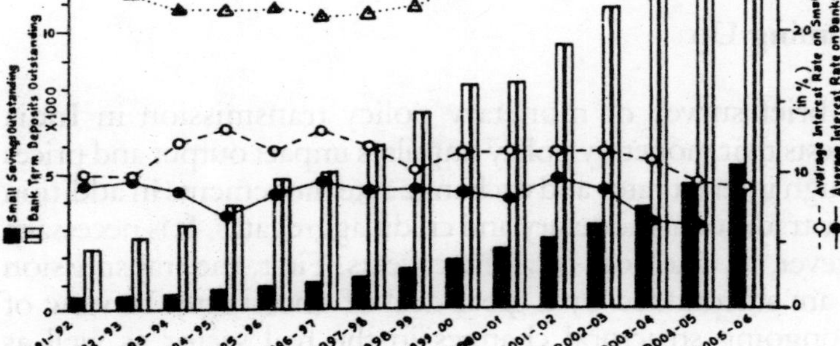


**Fig. 4.7** : Small Saving and Bank Deposits

through commercial banks, provide small savers access to tax savings instruments that are seen as safe and stable. Benchmarking these administered interest rates to market determined rates has been proposed from time to time. Whereas some rationalisation in such schemes has taken place, further progress in this direction will depend on the provision of better social security and pension systems, and perhaps easier access to marketable sovereign instruments (Mohan, 2006c).

In consonance with the objective of enhancing efficiency and productivity of banks through greater competition—from new private sector banks and entry and expansion of several foreign banks—there has been a consistent decline in the share of public sector banks in total assets of commercial banks. Notwithstanding such transformation, public sector banks still account for over 70 per cent of assets and income of commercial banks. While the public sector banks have responded well to the new challenges of competitions, this very public sector character does influence their operational flexibility and decision making and hence, interferes, on occasions, with the transmission of monetary policy impulses. Similar influence on monetary transmission is exerted by the priority sector directives in terms of allocation of 40 per cent of credit for specified sectors. The impact is, however, much limited now with the deregulation of lending rates and the rationalisation of the sectors for priority credit allocation.

## Summing Up

The brief survey of monetary policy transmission in India suggests that monetary policy impulses impact output and prices through interest rates and exchange rate movements in addition to the traditional monetary and credit aggregates. It is necessary, however, to take note of a few caveats. First, the transmission lags are surrounded by a great deal of uncertainly. In view of the ongoing structural changes in the real sector as well as financial innovations, the precise lags may differ in each business cycle. Second, the period was also marked by heightened volatility in the international economy, including developments such as the series of financial crises beginning with the Asian crisis. Third, the period under study has been marked by sharp reductions in customs duties and increasing trade openness which could have impacted the transmission process. The 1990s were also witness to global disinflation. Overall, the period has been one of substantial ongoing changes in various spheres of the Indian economy as well as in its external environment. Fourth, the period of study has been characterised by significant shifts in the monetary policy operating framework from a monetary-targeting framework to multiple indicator approach. Fifth, the size of interest rate pass-through has increased in recent years, with implications for transmission, finally, empirical investigation is constrained by the use of industrial production as a measure of output in the absence of a reasonably long time series on quarterly GDP of the economy. In view of the significant structural shifts towards the services sector and the inter-linkages between agriculture, industry and services, the result of these empirical exercises should be considered tentative and need to the ratified with a comprehensive measure of output, as also by considering alternative techniques.

On the whole, the Indian experience highlights the need for emerging market economies to allow greater flexibility in exchange rates but the authorities can also benefit from the capacity to intervene in foreign markets in view of the volatility observed in international capital flows. Therefore, there is a need to maintain an adequate level of foreign exchange reserves and this in turn both enables and constraints the conduct of monetary policy. A key lesson is that flexibility and pragmatism are required in the management of the exchange rate and monetary policy in developing countries rather than adherence to strict theoretical rules.

## Notes

### Developmental Measures

- Discontinuation of automatic monetisation through an agreement between the Government and the Reserve Bank. Rationalisation of Treasury Bill Market. Introduction of delivery *versus* payment system and deepening of inter-bank repo market.

- Introduction of Primary Dealers in the government securities market to play the role of market maker.
- Amendment of Securities Contracts Regulation Act (SCRA), to create the regulatory framework.
- Deepening of government securities market by making the interest rates on such securities market related. Introduction of auction of government securities. Development of a risk-free credible yield curve in the government securities market as a benchmark for related markets.
- Development of pure inter-bank call money market. Non-bank participants to participate in other money market instruments.
- Introduction of automated screen-based trading in government securities through Negotiated Dealing System (NDS). Setting up of risk-free payments and system in government securities through Clearing Corporation of India Limited (CCIL). Phased introduction of Real Time Gross Settlement (RTGS) System.
- Deepening of forex market and increased autonomy of Authorised Dealer.

**Institutional Measures**

- Setting up of Technical Advisory Committee on Monetary Policy with outside experts to review macroeconomic and monetary development and monetary developments and advise the Reserve Bank on the stance of monetary policy.
- Creation of a separate Financial Market Department within the Reserve Bank.

# 5 MONETARY POLICY AND GROSS NATIONAL PRODUCT (GNP)

Monetary economics is primarily concerned with the effects of individual decisions, monetary institutions, and policy actions to determine the demand for and the supply of money and its subsequent impact on the aggregate economy- with booms and recession, the growth of output, the rate of inflation, the nature of interest rates, the role of wages, the behaviour of exchange rates, amongst others.

A large share of the importance of monetary economics stems from the crucial intermediary role that money plays in most transactions taking place on today's market economies. No less is it due to the fact that a majority of analysts believe the monetary policies have an overwhelmingly important bearing on the economic well being of a nation.

Monetary economics, as it has to deal with some extremely challenging problems, often reduces complicated details of the economy to very manageable essentials. One of the most relevant essentials is the interaction between money, inflation, and growth. While doing so, it usually disregarded details of the behaviour of individual economic units that are basically the subject matter of micro-economics. In monetary economics, we deal with the money and asset market as a whole, abstracting from the differences between various markets. The cost of this abstraction is that omitted details sometimes matter, especially in LDCs. The benefit of abstraction is an increased understanding of the dynamic and stochastic aspects of economic behaviours, based upon which it is possible to draw reasonable conclusions regarding issues relating to the design and conduct of monetary policy.

The object of this chapter is to present a systematic treatment of monetary economics in a way that is clear, technical, and accurately reflective of certain important research development that have occurred in this field over the past 20 years. Such an endeavour, involving an econometric investigation based on Indian macro-economic data, is primarily directed towards obtaining a correct theoretical perspective of all these developments in order to prompt a realization of the relevance of monetary economics within the context to the Indian economic that is currently undergoing a radical metamorphosis.

We shall take up three principal topics here. Section I discusses the concept of the demand for real balances, and on the basis of empirically estimated short run and long run money derived functions for the Indian economy, highlights six of their essential characteristics. The phenomenon of money demand instability is then examined within the Indian context.

Section II studies in detail the mechanized of money supply determination. It then deals with the concept of appropriate targeting: in effect, the choice between money stock and interest rate targets. Alternative monetary control procedures are then developed formally and the econometric analysis focuses upon the relative stability of the money demand and supply functions.

Section III looks at the links between money, output, inflation, and interest rtes, besides providing empirical evidence to establish the proposition that inflation in India is primarily a monetary phenomenon. It attempts to measure the welfare costs of inflation and concludes with a brief summary of alternative methods to control inflation.

## DEMAND FOR MONEY

The purpose of this section is to develop an understanding of the determinants of the quantity of money demanded by individuals and to relate this to empirical estimates of the money demand function for the Indian economy.

We initiate the discussion on the topic of money demand with a review of the concept of real balance. One of the essentials of money demand is that individuals are interested in the purchasing power or their money holdings, *i.e.* the value of their cash balances in terms of the goods and services it will buy. They are not concerned with their nominal money holdings, i.e. the number of rupee notes they hold. This implies that: (i) real money demand should remain unchanged when the price level increase, but all real variables such as the interest rate, real income, and real wealth remain unchanged; and (ii) nominal money demand should increase in proportion to the increase in the price level, given the constancy of the real variables just specified.

An individual is said to be free money illusion if a change in prices, holding all real variables constant, leaves real behaviour unchanged. On the other hand, if such a change affects real behaviour, he is said to suffer from money illusion.

The empirical for India supports the theoretical argument that the demand for money is a demand for real balances or that the demand for nominal balances, with real variables constant, is proportional to the price level. Moreover, there is widespread agreement that the demand for real balances in India does, following accepted theory, increase as the level of real income rises and decrease as the nominal interest rate rises.

## The Demand for Real Balances Theory

The general approach in estimating money-demand functions for aggregate money stock or its individual components has been to explain the observed variability of real money holdings with reference to a few key variables that are assumed to play a strategic role in the behaviour of individuals.

The principal explanatory variables most commonly used in studies of real money demand, both for India and other countries, have been real income and the opportunity cost of holding money. It is assumed in such studies that money (M1) generally earns no interest or, at most, less interest than other assets. Thus, any one holding money is assumed to be giving up interest that could have been earned by holding some other asset. The opportunity cost is intended to capture the potential for substitution between money and competing financial and real assets. The relevant opportunity cost variables in these cases would be a measure of the rate of return on financial assets (proxied by the rate of interest) and measure of the rate of return on real assets (proxied by the expected inflation rate).

The expected inflation rate is derived from the hypothesis that individuals react to some concept of an anticipated inflation rate rather than to the current inflation rate. This expected inflation rate can be appropriately proxied by a weighted average of past rates of inflation. Empirical work in this area for other countries has proved that such proximate formations of expected inflation invariable tend to assign the highest weight to the last period's inflation rate, and this is well supported by the estimates obtained for the Indian economy.

## Empirical Evidence

### *Lagged Adjustment*

During empirical estimation, the usual distinction is made between long-run and short-run behaviour in the money market with a long-run function defined in terms of aggregate desired real money balances $(MD/P)^*$, and specified most generally as:

$$\frac{MD^*(t)}{P} = L[Y(t), r(t)] = AY(t)^{\alpha}\, r(t)^{\beta} \quad (1.1)$$

Where Y (t) is aggregate real income at time t; and r (t) is a long-term rate of interest at time t. The long-run elasticity's are expected to be: $\alpha > 0$ and $\beta < 0$.

An adjustment model of actual real money balances, (MD/P), towards this desired level, $(MD/P)^*$, is given by:

$$\ln \frac{MD\,(t)}{P} - \ln \frac{MD\,(t-l)}{P} = \theta \left[\ln \frac{MD^{*}\,(t)}{P} - \ln \frac{MD\,(t-l)}{P}\,(t-l)\right] \quad (1.2)$$

Which, in conjunction with eq. (1.1), yield the following general short run money-demand function used for estimation:

$$\frac{MD\,(t)}{P} \qquad \frac{A\ MD\,(t-l)^{(1-0)}}{P}\ Y\,(t)^{\alpha\theta}\ \ r\,(t)^{\beta\theta} \quad (1.3)$$

If $\theta = I$, there is no lag in adjustment. The closer to unity the value of $\theta$, the greater the proportion of any discrepancy between actual and desired real money balances that is made up in any time period. The use of such a partial adjustment mechanism for modelling the change in real money balances incorporates two possibilities for lags: one they occur because there are costs involved in adjusting money holdings and two, because the expectations of money holders are slow to adjust. Thus, given a change in real income, people may be unwilling to make a major adjustment in their real money holdings until they are sure that such a changes is permanent and not transitory.

Equation (1.3) is specified in logarithmic term because the income elasticity and interest elasticity of money demand can be obtained directly. Thus, while the short run effect are measured by the coefficients of equation (1.3), the corresponding long run coefficients are obtained by dividing these by the estimate of $\theta$ yielded by the coefficient of In MD (t-l)/P in equation (1.3).

The short-run money demand equation for the Indian economy was estimated using quarterly data over the period [1970-1 (1) to 1980-1 (IV)}. Whenever such quarterly data are used, it is essential to incorporate dummy variables to effect a seasonal adjustment of the data. The three dummies used were Q1, Q2, and Q3, which had the following form for any given representative year.

| Quarries | Q1 | Q2 | Q3 | Q4 |
|---|---|---|---|---|
| Rest: | 1 | 0 | 0 | 0 |
| Second: | 0 | 1 | 0 | 0 |
| Third: | 0 | 0 | 1 | 0 |
| Fourth: | 0 | 0 | 0 | 0 |

In order to avoid the dummy variable trap, the last quarter of a year is not represented by any dummy variable. Thus, if all the three seasonal dummies i.e., Q1, Q2, and Q3, are set at zero, we can infer that if refers to the fourth quarter of the year.

The quarterly estimates of real national income at 1970-1 prices were based on the study by Singh, Shetty, and Venkatachalam (1982). The rate of interest chosen to be the representative of the opportunity cost of holding narrow money was the three-year term deposits rate as the bulk of term deposits in India has been held in maturities of 3 years and above. The estimates of real money stock (M/P), assumed equal to real money demand (MD/P), were obtained by deflating quarterly averages of Ml by the wholesale price index (1970-1 = 1.00).

The estimated short-run money demand function was given by :

$$\text{In}\,(t)\frac{MD}{P} = \underset{(-2.8)}{-0.6632} + \underset{(7.8)}{0.6886}\,\text{Ln}\frac{MD}{P} + \underset{(3.6)}{0.4422}\,\text{Ln}\,Y(t)$$

$$-\underset{(-2.7)}{0.2516}\,\text{Ln}\,r(t) - \underset{(-4.2)}{0.2346}Q1 - \underset{(-7.0)}{0.1593}\,Q2 - \underset{(-4.0)}{0.1360}\,Q3$$

$R^{-2} = 0.93129$; S.E.E. = 0.0399; h-statistic = -1.37

Throughout the study, all equations were estimated using Ordinary Least Squares (OLS) along with a first-order Cochrane- Orcutt correction for serial autocorrelation. While reporting the results, the figures in parentheses indicate the t-values of the coefficients beneath which they appear. Also provided are the R-2, the standard error of estimate (S.E.E.) and the Durbin-Watson (D.W.) statistic (which is replaced by the corresponding h-statistic if the repressors include lagged dependent variables).

The coefficient of Ln Y is positive and provides an estimate of the short-run income elasticity of real money demand. The result imply that for every 1 per cent increase in real income, short-run real money demand would rise by about 0.44 per cent.

The coefficient of In r is negative and is consistent with the inverse relationship between money demand and the nominal interest rate. The coefficient estimate suggests that the short run interest elasticity of money demand is around -0.25 so that at 10 per cent increase in the interest rate center is paribus would decrease short run real money demand by about 2.5 per cent.

The coefficients of the seasonal dummies show clearly that money demand is well below its fourth-quarter value in all the other quarters, declining most severely in quarter 1. The t-values suggest that all the variables are very significant and the high $R^{-2}$ and the low S.E.E. confirm a good overall fit.

## The Long Run Money Demand Function

The long run income and interest elasticity's referred to in equation (1.1) i.e., the coefficients $\alpha$ and $\beta$, can be estimated from equation (1.4) by means of the following steps. From equation (1.3), we realize that the coefficient of ln MD (t-l)/P is equal to $(1\text{-}\theta)$ which, from the results provided in equation (1.4), yields $\theta = 0.3114$. As the coefficients of ln Y and ln r are $\alpha\theta$ and $\beta\theta$, respectively, in equation (1.3), we infer that $\alpha = 1.42$ and $\beta = -0.808$.

These results imply that the long run elasticities will exceed their corresponding short run elasticities by a factor, of nearly 3.2 $(-1/\theta = 1/.3114)$. The long run income elasticity of money demand is 1.42, which implies that real money balances rise more than proportionately to the rise in real income in the long run. This result may be interpreted as indicating that money can be viewed as a luxury asset in the Indian context (see Ghatak, 1981). The long run interest elasticity of money works out to be slightly more than 0.8, meaning that the recently announced decrease in the deposit rate from 13 per cent to 12 per cent, i.e., by about 7.7 per cent, would increase the demand for money by over 6 per cent in the long run.

How long does it take for the short- run elasticities to adjust towards their long run values just obtained/In theory, it takes forever for the full long run position to be reached. Table 3.1 shows these dynamic patterns of elasticities of the demand for real balances in response to changes in the level of income and the interest rater. It is seen that more than three-fourths of the adjustment is complete within the first year, and over 95 per cent of the adjustment is complete within the first two years.

**Table 5.1:** Dynamic Patterns of Elasticity's of Money Demand

| Quarters elapsed | Y | r |
|---|---|---|
| 1 | 0.44 | -0.252 |
| 2 | 0.75 | -0.425 |
| 3 | 0.96 | -0.544 |
| 4 | 1.10 | -0.626 |
| 8 | 1.35 | -0.767 |
| Long run | 1.42 | -0.808 |

In summary, we have so far described three essential properties of money demand in the Indian economy: (1) The demand for real money balances responds positively (negatively) to real income (the rate of interest), (2) long run money demand increases more than proportionately with real income, and (3) The short run responsiveness of money demand to changes in income and interest rates in considerably less than the long run response.

## India's Monetary Sector and Regression Analysis

For a causal observer, the Indian monetary sector is a blend of several forces. While there is a well-knit banking segment in the urban sector, in the rural areas the private money lenders dominate the lending business. Nonetheless, after independence, the Indian economy has witnessed a progressive network of small and large banks is urban and rural sectors despite the fact that in rural areas private money-lenders dominate. The number of bank branches after nationalization of major banks in 1936 has increased tremendously and have spread out to regions, which might not have been served by private profit seeking finançial institutions. However, while the number of deposits has increased in the last two decades, it is still uncertain how much of this credit should go to nationalization. The Indian monetary sector at present is bifurcated into a sophisticated urban sector and a crude but rapidly improving rural sector. The Reserve Bank of India formulates the monetary policy, though the Department of Finance of the central government has major say in it. The nationalized banks that control a large part of the total deposits (approximately 80 per cent in 1990) have to operate within the parameters of a consistently produced and distributed list of directives for their operations. The money supply is primarily controlled by making changes in the discount rate (or the bank rate as it is called in India), and the money supply changes are carried out freely and directly. It is, however, interesting to investigate if the change in money supply is carried out autonomously or whether it is a function of money demanded by the public.

Assuming that the unorganized rural sector would not yield biased estimates of regression coefficients (or by conveniently ignoring the presence of rural sector), several studies have estimated the demand for money function for India in a traditional form. Some of these are Samphath-Hussain (1981). Deadman-Ghatak (1981), Kulkarni (1986) and Singh (1984, 1990). Mr. Vasudevan surveyed related demand for money studies for India in 1977 (Vasudevan, 1977). Most of these studies have concluded that the demand for money in case of India is a stable function of set explanatory variables as expected by the traditional monetary theory. There is no evidence, however, of any study carrying out the New View mentioned in this chapter. This fact itself testifies the importance of our attempt to do so. For our estimation purposes the data was obtained from the International Financial Statistics Yearbook (IFS), an annual publication of the International Monetary Fund (IMF) in Washington D.C. The annual data of time period between 1960 to 1985 were used for the OLS estimation of Equation (1.3) coefficients. Two ways to define money supply ($M_1$ and $M_2$) and interest rate (the money market rate and government bond yield rate) are used for the sake of wider applicability of our analysis. Interest rate defined by the money market is the short-run borrowing rate among financial institutions. Conceptually, this is equivalent to the Federal Funds rate in the U.S. Government bond yield rate is the rate representing the yield rate at maturity of government bonds, hence it is a good proxy for the long-run interest rate. As usual, the real Gross Domestic Product (GDP) for India is defined by deflating the nominal values of GDP by the Consumer Price Index (CPI).

Table 5.2: Money Demand Estimation for India: 1960-1985

(1) $\text{Log } M_{lt} = -623 + .356 \text{ Log GDP}_1 + .145 \text{ Log GR}_1 + .599 \text{ Log } M_{lt-2}$

(-d. 183) (1.975) (.6711) (3.238)

R2 =.950, Standard Error of Regression=.057 Durbin-Watson Statistic = 1.968

(2) $\text{Log } M_{lt}\text{-=-}.667 + 441 \text{ Log GDP}_t + 0.57 \text{ Log Mr}_1 + .52 \text{ Log } M_{lt-1}$

(-2.365)(2.546) (1.19) (2.707)

Table 5.2 present the results of regression analysis for estimating Equation (1.3) of this section row 1 of this table is the estimated equation using government bond yield rate as the interest rate. Results show that value of (l – j) is .599, which implies that value of adjustment coefficient to desired and actual demand for money for two successive periods is .401. This also means that in one year, the Reserve Bank of India is able to close the discrepancy between desired and actual money demand by about 40 per cent. Hence, the test of endogenecity of money supply tells us that in the period observed here, about 40 per cent of changes in money supply were made as a response to increased demand for money by the economy. As mentioned before, another test of endogenecity of money supply is the effect of interest rate on the demand for money of the economy. If the money supply is even partly endogenous, then we expect that the interest rate does not have a significant effect on the money demand. This expectation has materialized in the actual estimation of Equation (1.3). A closer observation of estimated coefficient of log GR (vis $jb_1$) which represent the elasticity of demand for money with respect to the changes in interest rate is very small (-.145) and also when tested from it statistic is not very different from zero. Thus, in the period studied, the interest rate in the Indian economy did not influence the demand for money in a significant way.

The elasticity of demand for money with respect to the real GDP is measured by the estimated coefficient of log GDP. From its is statistic we can safely concluded that in the period between 1960 to 1985, the real GDP was a significant determinant of demand for money in India. In order to reaffirm the results of the first estimation, we decided to re-estimate Equation (1.3) by suing the second definition of interest rate. Row 2 of the above table preset these new results of estimation. The value of estimated coefficient of lagged money demand (l – j) in this case declined slightly to .52, making the value of j = .48. The estimated coefficient of income and interest rate logarithms is similar and therefore consistent with the first estimation. Due to low value of t statistic, log of interest rate again fails to have estimated coefficient that is significantly different from zero. This is not completely unexpected because as mentioned before when the Central Bank is pegging the interest rate (as the Reserve Bank of India has been in this period), the causation of interest rate to money demand becomes suspect. Other important indicators of estimation are very satisfactory. Both regressions show very high $R_2$ values, low standard errors of regression and Durbin-Watson statistics close to 2. Therefore, from these indicators also the estimation result are consistent.

## Money Illusion

There is one important question to be considered, and that is how the nominal demand for money (MD) responds to an increase in the level of prices (P). The estimated equation, using quarterly data over the period 1970-1 (1) to 1980-1 (IV), was:

$$\ln MD(t) = \underset{(3.3)}{1.1352} + \underset{(12.5)}{1.0607} \ln P9t) + \underset{(6.3)}{1.1557} \ln Y(t) \quad (1.4)$$

$$\underset{(-6.6)}{-0.9180} \ln r(t) \underset{(6.1)}{-0.4899} Q1 \underset{(-6.4)}{-0.2291} Q2 \underset{(1.5)}{-0.2916} Q3 \quad (1.5)$$

Thus we find strong evidence that an increase in prices raise the demand for nominal money balances in almost the same proportion. We therefore add a fourth conclusion to the earlier three. The demand for nominal balances is proportional to the price level. Thus, there is no money illusion; in other words, the demand for money is a demand for real balance.

## The Expected Rate of Inflation

It has however been argued that in many LDCs, including India, the interest rate is administered rather than market determined. This would imply that the effect of normal operations of the laws of demand and supply would not be fully reflected in the observed interest rates. Moreover, as Wong (1977) has argued, given the institutional pegging of interest rates, observed interest rates are unlikely to the linkage variables between holdings of alternative assets. This is the major reason for investigating the opportunity cost of holding money in terms of the expected rate of inflation, which has been observed to be an important variable in influencing the demand for money in LDCs. This is because wealth holders in LDCs can hold real commodities (e.g., buildings, land, gold, etc.) or money and, clearly, in such cases, the opportunity cost of money holdings must be given by the expected rate of inflation.

Under such circumstances, it is possible to understand why the demand for money in LDCs has usually been regarded as more a function of income and the expected rate of inflation rather than the interest rate. It is also clear, in such cases, why the transaction motive for holding money predominates over other motives for money holding. However, and this is important, to the extent that borrowing plays a role in financing economic activity and in so far as there is some relationship between the organized and unorganized money markets, as is clearly the case with India, the rate of interest should be used along with the expected rate of inflation in explaining money demand, although this could raise problems of multi-colinearity.

In other to obtain an empirical measure of the expected rate of inflation, we use the 'adaptive expectations' model, initially developed by Cagan (1956), which postulates that this expected rate of inflation in time period t, $\pi^*$ (t), is a weighted average of past observed values of the actual inflation rate, $\pi$ (t), with geometrically declining lags. This may expressed as follows:

$$\pi^*(t)=\varphi\,\pi(t\text{-}l)+\varphi(1\text{-}\varphi)\,\pi(t\text{-}2)+\varphi(1\text{-}\varphi)^2\,\pi(t\text{-}3)+...+...+\varphi(1\text{-}\varphi)^{r\text{-}1}\,\pi(0) \quad (1.6)$$

with $\pi$ ? $\pi$ ? 1, implying that the weights sum up to unity.

Equation (1.6) may also be written as:

$$\pi^*(t) = (;\text{-}\varphi)\,\pi^*(t\text{-}1) + \varphi\,\pi(t\text{-}1) \quad (1.7)$$

which yields

$$\pi^*(t) - \pi^*(t\text{-}1) = \varphi\,[\pi\,9t\text{-}l) - \pi^*\,(t\text{-}l) \quad (1.8)$$

Equation (1.8) states that expectations are revised (adapted) during each period by a constant fraction, $\pi$, of the difference between the last observed inflation rate, i.e. $\pi$ (t-l), and the rate was expected for that period i.e., $\pi^*$(t-l).

The rationale behind such a model is that people make predictions about the behaviour of future prices from their observations of past price movements and that their behaviour is determined by the rate of inflation which they expect to occur. The hypothesis is that a step-by-step process of adjustment corrects errors, i.e. discrepancies between expected and actual rates of inflation. It is an implication of the model that the longer a given rate of inflation persist, the more closely will people come to expect that rate. Moreover, the greater the weight assigned to recent events in the determination of expectations, the higher will be the value of $\varphi$.

Using quarterly data on $\pi$ (t), measured by the wholesale price index (1970-1 = 1.00), over the sample period 1970-1 (1) to 1980-1 (IV), and initializing the series by equating the expected inflation rate with the actual inflation rate in the first quarter of 1970-1, i.e. by setting $\pi^*$ (t), using equation (1.8), given alternative values of the adjustment coefficient, $\varphi$. For each of these sets, we computed its Mean-Squared – Error (MSE), over 44-quarter sample period, defined by:

$$J = \sum_{t=1}^{++} [\pi(t) - \pi^* + (t)]^{2/44}(1.9) \tag{1.9}$$

and the following equation, which minimized its corresponding MSE, was considered as the most appropriate formulation for estimating the expected rate of inflation:

$$\pi^* (t) = 0.617\ \pi^* (t\text{-}l) + 0.383\ \pi\ (t\text{-}l) \tag{1.10}$$

using the results series on $\pi^*$ (t), the following money demand function was estimated using quarterly data over the period 1970-1(1) to 1980-1(IV):

$$\ln \frac{MD\,(t)}{P} = \underset{(-3.6)}{-0.4835} + \underset{(8.1)}{0.7325} \ln \frac{MD\,(t\text{-}l)}{P} + \underset{(2.9)}{0.3758} \ln Y\,(t)$$

$$-0.2331 \ln r(t) - 0.0043 \ln \pi^{*}(t)$$
$$(-2.5) \qquad (-2.7)$$
$$-0.2086\, Q1 - 0.1543\, Q2 - 0.1214\, Q3$$
$$(-3.7) \qquad (-6.9) \qquad (-3.5)$$
$$R2 = 0.9350;\ S.E.E. = 0.390;\ h\text{-Statistic} = -0.41 \quad (1.11)$$

It is thus seen that the opportunity cost variables are significant and capture very well the potential for substitution between money and competing financial and real assets. We therefore add a fifth conclusion; an increase in expected rate of inflation reduces the demand for real money balances.

## Multicollinearity and First-Differenced Data

A complication arises in all the above formulations of the money demand function due to the widely held belief that the economy's transactions technology changes over time as a result of increased magnetization and the expansion in the number of bank branches. As such considerations are important in the Indian context, a money-demand relation like equation (1.3), so that its logarithmic form becomes:

$$\ln \frac{ND(t)}{P} = \theta \ln A + (1-\theta) \ln \frac{MD(t-1)}{P} + \alpha\theta \ln Y(t) + \beta\,\theta \ln r(t) + \Gamma\theta t + \varepsilon(t) \qquad (1.12)$$

Where $\varepsilon$ (t) is the stochastic disturbance term which, although implicit in the discussion, has not been made explicit in any of our earlier equations. Here, the variable t is time and $\Gamma\theta$ its coefficient. The value of $\Gamma$ should be positive, to reflect the need for more real money balances, for given Y (t) and r (t); as time passes and there is a greater acceptance of banking habits.

However, as it happens, coefficient estimates of the formulation described above in equation (1.12) could be unsatisfactory due to the presence of multicollinearity between income (Y) and the time trend (t), both of which enter as regressors in the specification of the money demand function. The simplest way of overcoming this econometric problem is to work with first-differenced data. Thus, if one uses equation (1.12) for period t-l, and subtracts the latter from former, result would be:

$$\delta \ln \frac{MD(t)}{P} = (1-\theta)\, \delta \ln \frac{MD(t-l)}{P} + \alpha\, \theta\, \delta \ln Y(t)$$
$$+ \beta\, \theta\, \delta \ln r(t) + \Gamma \varepsilon(t)$$

Where $\delta \ln Y(0) = \ln Y(t) - \ln Y(t-l)$, and so on. (1.13)

In the above equation, the θ ln a term, which was the intercept term in the original formulation, has dropped out of analysis and Γθ has entered in its place as it is equal to: Γθt-Γθ (t-l). More important is the fact that the disturbance term in equation (1.13) is δε (t) rather than ε (t) as in equation (1.12). It turns out in empirical investigations that the former suffers from less serial correlation in comparison to the latter, suggesting that the econometric estimates obtained with differenced data should be more reliable.

With equation (1.13) as our framework, the following equation was estimated using annual data on the Indian economy over the 20 year period 1970-I to 1990-I. The estimates were as follows:

$$\delta \ln \frac{Md(t)}{P} = 0.0956\, \delta \ln \frac{MD(t-l)}{P} + 1.0958\, \delta \ln Y(t)$$
$$\underset{(-1.9)}{-0.4771}\, \delta \ln r(t) + \underset{(2.1)}{0.0067}$$

$R2 = 0.4140$; S.E.E. = 0.0880; h-statistic = -0.83 (1.14)

Based upon these results, we add a sixth conclusion. The need for real balances increases with time ceteris paribus, indicating the spread of magnetization. Moreover, these values imply the following parameter estimates: $\theta$ = 0.9044, $\alpha$ = 1.2116, $\beta$ = -0.5275, $\Gamma$= 0.0074. However, the low explanatory power of the money-demand equation and the substantially reduced significance of the parameter estimates suggest that money demand is less responsive to movements in Y (t) and r(t) than would be expected to be the case. This is one of the several reasons for believing that attempts to provide reliable econometric evidence on money demand behaviour for the Indian economy have not yet been successful due to what is referred to as money demand instability.

## Money Demand Instability

The demand for real balances has always been considered to be one of the least understood and most highly unstable equations in the Indian macro-economy. This is because of perceived shifts in the money demand function, referred to earlier, exacerbated by frequent revisions carried out by the RBI in defining money supply. While, of late, these shifts have become less volatile, empirical evidence still contradicts the belief that we have entered a period of stability in the money demand function.

Moreover, the revisions in the money supply concepts in 1977 and the series of changes in the Indian financial system since then has fuelled greater speculation that the money demand function could have shifted once again in the 1980s, and the results set out below, by and large, substantiate this claim.

The point of the discussion can be seen from Table 5.2. Here we provide the percentage change in the determinants of real money demand between the 10-year period 1980-81 to 1990-91. We also show the percentage changes in real balances that are forecast by the percentage changes in these determinants.

To understand the table, consider for example the first row. Real income increased by 61.9 per cent from 1980-1 to 1990-1. With the long run income elasticity of 1.42 implied by equation

**Table 5.3 :** Actual and predicted change in Real Balances, 1980-91

| | *% age change in independent variables* | *% age change in real money demand using equations* | |
|---|---|---|---|
| | | *(1.4)* | *(1.11)* |
| Real income | 61.9 | +87.9 | +87.0 |
| 3-year term deposit rate | 20.0 | -16.2 | -17.4 |
| Expected inflation rate | -42.2 | – | +0.7 |
| Predicted change in real balances | – | 71.7 | 70.3 |
| Actual change | – | 102.0 | |

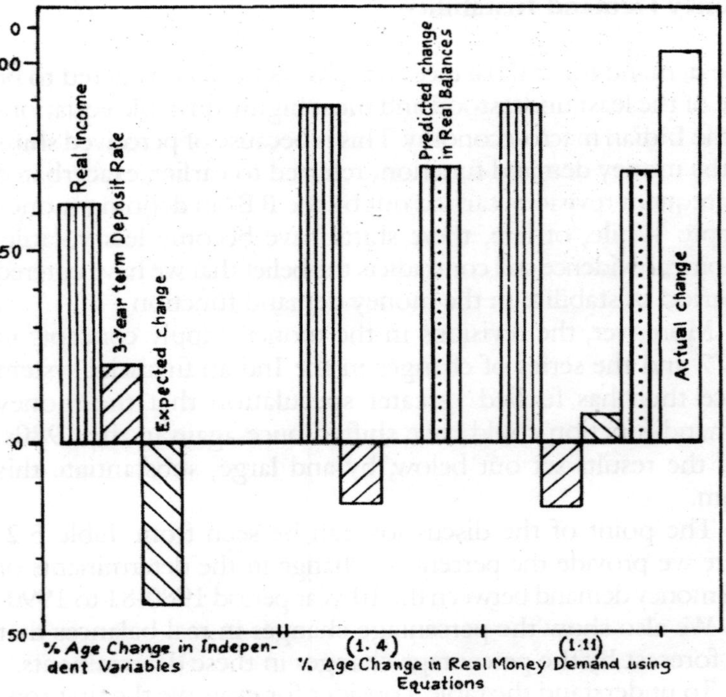


**Fig. 5.1 :** Actual and predicted change in Real Balanes, 1980-91

(1.4), money demand should have risen by 87.9 per cent (=1.42 × 61.9) over that period. The entries in the other rows are calculated accordingly. Altogether, the three factors should have caused real balances to rise by 71.7 per cent using equation (1.4) and 70.3 per cent using equation (1.11). In actuality, real balances increased by 102.0 per cent over this period. This discrepancy testifies to the inherent instability of the estimated money demand functions.

Most research on money demand for the Indian economy has ought to improve upon the rather simple specifications set out in this section. One way has been to estimate separate demand functions for currency and demand deposits using instantaneous adjustment for the latter variable in order to model the greater importance of institutional holders of demand deposits and the predominant use of such deposits as transactions balances. Doing so has invariably yielded a long-run income elasticity of less (more) than unity for currency (demand deposits). The later phenomenon reflects the continuing process of monetization, limited opportunities to economize on cash balances and the paucity of other financial assets in which to hold savings.

Other estimated variants of the money demand function replace current income by some concept of permanent income which seeks to disassociate elements of transitory income from the determination of money demand. Interested readers would do well to refer to Gupta (1983) for an exhaustive listing of the variables likely to affect money demand in the Indian economy.

## THE SUPPLY OF MONEY

### Basic Relationships

To kept the analysis simple without neglecting the essential issues, we begin with the basic definitions of M and H given by:

$$M = C + D \quad (2.1)$$
$$H = C + R \quad (2.2)$$

Where M is narrow money (M1) which is defined as the sum of currency © and demand deposits (D); and H is high-powered money which is defined as the sum of currency © and bank reserves (R).

The major objective of this section is to determine how the money stock is related to variables that are more directly under the control of the monetary authority (hence forth abbreviated to MA). To do so, let us focus attention on the relationship between M and H. From equation (2.1) and (2.2), it is evident that the money-multiplier (mm) which is defined as the ratio M/H is given by:

$$mm = (M/H) = (C + D)/(C + R) \tag{2.3}$$

Now dividing each of the components on the right-hand-side of equation (2.3) by D, yield:

$$mm = (M/H) = [(C/D) + 1]/[(C/D)] \tag{2.4}$$

We now have to decide what determines the money-multiplier so that we can specify a money-supply function of the form:

$$M = [\{(C/D) + 1\}/\{(C/D)\} H = mm (.) H \tag{2.5}$$

In this context, the determinant of the money multiplier (mm) must be studied with respect to the two behavioural parameters: the currency-deposit ratio (C/D) and the reserve-deposit ratio (R/D). From this perspective, the most important aspect is the bank's choice of its reserve-deposit ratio, and it is the behaviour of R/D in relation to mm that will be examined.

In analyzing the choice, it will be convenient to recognize two categories of reserve. The first of these if required reserves (RR), the quantity that a bank lust hold as required by law. This quantity depends on the bank's deposits (D): the greater its deposits, the greater the reserves it is required to hold. As an approximation, we shall assume that RR is proportional to D.

Letting k denote this proportionality factor, required reserves are then equal to kD, i.e., RR = kD. The other category of reserves is excess reserves (ER), the amount of reserves held above the required quantity. Thus, we have the decomposition:

$$R = RR + ER = kD + ER \tag{2.6}$$

Our principal behavioural hypothesis concerning banks is that the quantity of excess reserves chosen obeys a relation of the form:

$$ER/D = \varphi(r) \tag{2.7}$$

With φ being a decreasing function of r: $\delta\varphi/\delta r = \varphi'(r) < 0$.

The logic of this assumption is that banks may want to hold excess reserves beyond the required level so that unexpected demands on them for cash or payments to other banks can be facilitated without allowing total reserves to fall below the legally required minimum. However, these excess reserves are costly to hold as they earn no interest, and by reducing such reserves, a bank is able to increase its investments on which it earns interest. Consequently, the opportunity cost of holding excess reserves can be represented by the interest rate (r) and the higher this rate, the less will be the excess reserves held. This aspect of behaviour is reflected in our assumption that the derivative $\varphi'(r) < 0$. The role of D in equation (2.7) is to normalize by using total deposits as the relevant measure of bank size.

Together, equations (2.6) and (2.7) provide a simplified explanation of the reserve-deposit ratio R/D. To see this, divide each term in equation (2.6) by D and note that the result is:

$$R/D = k + \varphi(r) \tag{2.8}$$

Since $\varphi'(r) < 0$, we see immediately that R/D will be smaller, for a given value of the legally determined k, the higher the rate of interest (r).

Substituting equation (2.8) into equation (2.4) yields:

$$M/H = [(C/D) + 1]/(C/D) + k + \varphi(r))] \qquad (2.9)$$

Furthermore, we could express equation (2.9) as:

$$M/D = \mu(r; k; C/D) \qquad (2.10)$$

Where $\mu$ is a function with $\mu_1 > 0$, $\mu_2 < 0$, and $\mu_1 < 0$. That the signs of the first two partial derivatives, i.e. with regard to p and h, are as indicated follows from equation (2.9). For the partial with respect to C/D to be negative, we relay on the fact that:

$$k = \varphi(r) = R/D < 1 \qquad (2.11)$$

Therefore, if we express the right-hand-side of equation (2.9) as,

$$\begin{aligned} M/H &= [(C/D) + 1]/[(C/D) + (R/D)] \\ &= (C/D) + (R/D) - (R/D) + 1]/(C/D) + (R/D)] \\ &= 1 + [1 - (R/D)]/[(C/D) + (R/D)] \end{aligned} \qquad (2.12)$$

Then the second term on the right-hand-side of equation (2.12), which is positive, decreases with any increase in C/D, keeping R/D constant. This implies that mm is inversely related to C/D.

Equation (2.1) when written as:

$$M = \mu(r; k; C/D)\,H \qquad (2.13)$$

is called a money supply function as it describes how much money would be 'supplied' for specific magnitudes of H, r, k, and C/D. Since $\mu_1 > 0$, the money supply function is increasing in r as compared with a money demand function which is decreasing in r.

**Monetary Control**

The question to be posed now is what appropriate targets the

MA should aim for? A key distinction, in this context is between ultimate targets and intermediate targets. Ultimate targets are variables, such as the money growth rate whose behaviour really matters since it has a bearing on the inflation rate. The interest rate or the stock of high-powered money are intermediate targets of policy which the MA aims at only so that it can hit the ultimate targets more accurately.

There are two levels at which such a discussion can proceed. The first is at the technical level where the focus is narrower; Can a given target level of the money stock be attained more accurately by holding the interest rate fixed or by fixing high-powered money? The second is at the general level where the focus is broader: Can the MA make the economy more stable by aiming for a particular money stock or for a particular interest rate?

As the framework for evaluating both these questions is identical, well shall, as well are concerned more with the technical aspect, discuss only the first issue. The analysis indicates that the MA should adopt the following guidelines in order to ensure that hits its money stock target more closely: (1) If the demand-for-money function is stable (compared with the money supply function), then the MA should fix interest rates; (2) If the demand-for-money function is relatively unstable, then the MA should target high-powered money. This bring us to the central concept of determining the relative stability of the money demand and money supply function, and the peripheral concepts of monetary control and alternative control procedures.

## Alternative Control Procedures

### *Money-stock Targeting*

Suppose that, at the beginning of period t, the MA expects that the values of Y (t) and P (t) will be $Y^c$ (t) and $P^c$ (t). Now, if the nominal money stock that the MA wishes to achieve for time period t is $M^*$ (t), it can try to achieve its target by choosing H (t), which is appropriately assumed to be under its control.

For the purpose of this exercise, we treat both k and C/D as constants. Then given the money supply function, equation (2.13), we know that the actual value of M (t) will depend only on the value of H (t) set by the MA and on the interest rate r(t).
In this control process, treating k and C/D as constants, we can write the money supply function, equation (2.13), as:

$$[M(t)/H(t)] = \mu [r(t)] \qquad (2.14)$$

Solving the above equation in terms of r(t) yields:

$$r(t) = \mu^{-1} [M(t)/H(t)] \qquad (2.15)$$

where $\mu^{-1}$ is the inverse function of ì. We now substitute equation (2.15) into the money demand function, equation (1.1), to yield:

$$[MD(t)/P(t)] = L[Ye(t), \mu\text{-}1 \{M(t)/H(t)\}] \qquad (2.16)$$

We then set $MD(t) = M(t) = M^*(t)$; $P(t) = P^e(t)$ and $Y(t) = Y^e(t)$, in equation (2.16) to obtain:

$$\{M^*(t)/P^e(t)] = L[Ye(t), \mu^{-1} \{M(t)/H(t)\}] \qquad (2.17)$$

Since the values of all the other variables in the above equation are determined, equation (2.17) can be solved for H(t).
The resulting value will be the one that should realize the target value $M^*(t)$, given the anticipated value $Y^e(t)$ and $P^e(t)$. By choosing H(t) in this way the MA can attempt to track $M^*(t)$, even though it does not have any direct control over M(t).

### *Interest Rate Targeting*

In order to illustrate that alternative procedures could also be used if the MA desires to exert control over M(t), consider the following scheme: Suppose that at the start of period t, instead of committing itself to provide a value of H(t) that is expected to induce a money stock outcome of $M^*(t)$, the MA commits itself to maintaining a value of the interest rate r(t) that it expects to result in a money stock outcome of $M^*(t)$.

Such a control process would involve writing the money demand function, equation (1.1), in terms of r(t), i.e.,

$$r(t) = L^{-1}\,[Y(t), MD(t)/P(t)] \qquad (2.18)$$

where $L^{-1}$ is the inverse function of L. As before, we then set $MD(t) = M^*(t)$, P(t), $P^e(t)$, and $Y(t) = Y^e(t)$ in equation (2.18) to yield.

$$r(t) = L^{-1}\,[Y^e(t), M^*(t)/P^e(t)] \qquad (2.19)$$

Since all the values on the right-hand side of the above equation are assumed to be known, equation (2.19) can be solved for r(t). Given that value and treating, as before, k and C/D as constants, we would be able to determine mm(t) and, subsequently from the money supply relation, H(t). Under this control procedure, the extent of randomness affecting M(t) would be different to when H(t) was set and maintained by the MA. Terminologically, this procedure is said to be one in which the MA uses the interest rate as an instrument, whereas the instrument in the earlier control scheme was high-powered money.

Having shown that there are at least two distinct procedures for attempting to control the money stock, the next step is to consider which of the two is superior. In response to this question, we shall not develop a formal econometric analysis.

## Econometric Analysis

### *A Simple Stochastic Model*

To proceed econometrically, we will adopt specific forms

for the money demand function ($M^d$) and the money supply function ($M^s$). We assume that these relationships are linear in the logarithms of all variables, except that they are linear in r(t) itself. Thus, these functions will be given by:

$$M^d: \ln\frac{M(t)}{P(t)} = a(0) + (1)\ln Y(t) - a(2)\,r(t) + \delta(t) \quad (2.20)$$

$$M^s: \ln M(t) = b(0) + b(1)\ln H(t) - b(2)\,r(t) + \varepsilon(t) \quad (2.21)$$

By placing a minus sign before a (2) r(t), the coefficients a (1), a (2), b (1), b (2) will all be positive. The disturbances δ(t) and ε(t) are serially uncorrelated random processes, i.e. the probability distribution of δ (t) has mean zero and variance $\sigma_\delta^2$, while the distribution of ε (t) has mean zero and variance $\sigma_\varepsilon^2$.

Using annual data on the Indian economy over the period 1950-51 to 1990-91, the following system was estimated:

$$\ln\frac{M(t)}{P(t)} = -3.8948 + 1.2691\ln Y(t) - 0.0586\,r(t) + \delta(t)$$
$$(-2.8) \quad (14.8) \quad (-4.1)$$

$$R^{-2} = 0.9710;\ \text{S.E.E.} = 0.0745;\ \text{D.W} = 1.89 \quad (2.22)$$

$$\ln M(t) = 1.3168 + 0.8251\ln H(t) + 0.0690\,r(t) + \varepsilon(t)$$
$$(9.6) \quad (27.4) \quad (4.8)$$

$$R^2 = 0.9953;\ \text{S.E.E.} = 0.0866;\ \text{D.W.} = 1.95 \quad (2.23)$$

Thus, the estimates of the parameters are: â (0) = -3.8948, â (1) = 1.2691, â (2) = 0.0586, b (0) = 1.3168, b (1) = 0.8251, and b (2) = 0.0690.

Defining y(t) = Ln Y(t), p(t) = Ln P(t), m(t), and h(t) = Ln H (t), we can rewrite estimated system as:

$$m(t) = P(t) - 3.89948 + 1.2691\,y(t) - 0.0586\,r(t) + \delta(t) \quad (2.24)$$

$$m(t) = 1.1316 + 0.8251\,h(t) + 0.0690\,r(t) + \varepsilon(t) \quad (2.25)$$

## Optimal Choice of Monetary Policy Instruments

We begin the analysis by considering the control procedure with high-powered money as the instrument. Thus, we assume that at the start of period t, the MA uses its knowledge of the money demand-supply, equation (2.24)-(2.25), to set h(t) so as to make the expected value of m(t) equal to the target m*(t), with the target being formulated in terms of ln M(t) rather than M(t) itself. To do that the MA in effect, replaces y(t), p(t), δ (t), and ε(t) in equation (2.24) and (2.25) by their expected values, sets m(t) = m*(t) and, by eliminating r(t), solves for the appropriate value of h(t).

This implies that we can rewrite the system as:

$$m^*(t) = pe(t) - 3.8948 + 1.2691\ ye(t) - 0.0586\ r(t) + 0 \quad (2.26)$$
$$m^*(t) = 1.3168 + 0.8251\ h(t) + 0.0690\ r(t) + 0 \quad (2.27)$$

Equating the right-hand sides of equation (2.26) and (2.27), solving for r(t) and substituting the ensuing result into equation (2.27), we find that h(t) sould be set equal to:

$$h(t) = 2.6390m^*(t) - 1.4271\ [p^e(t) + 1.2691\ y^e(t)] + 3.9627 \quad (2.28)$$

Thus, equation (2.28) provides the optimal setting for h(t) if the objective of ensuring that m(t) = m*(t) is to be attained.

But, this target will typically not be attained precisely because, when the events of period t occur, δ(t) and ε(t) will usually not be equal to their mean values of zero, nor will p(t) and y(t) correspond to their expected values of $p^e(t)$ and $y^e(t)$. Consequently, the actually realized value of m(t) will diverge away from m*(t), even though h(t) has been set appropriately. The actual value of m(t) can be obtained from equations (2.24) and (2.25), which describe the system, with h(t) specified by equation (2.28).

Solving eqs. (2.24) and (2.25) simultaneously yields:

$$m(t) = 0.37889h(t) + 0.5408 \; [p(t) + 1.2691y(t)]$$

$$-1.5014 + 0.5408 \; d(t) + 0.4592 \; \varepsilon(t) \qquad (2.29)$$

Substituting the value of h(t), provided in equation (2.28), into equation (2.29) above yields:

$$m(t) = m^{*}(t) + 0.5408 \; [p(t) - p^{e}(t)] + 0.6863 \; [y(t) + y^{e}(t)]$$

$$+ 0.5408 \; \delta(t) + 0.4592 \; \varepsilon(t) \qquad (2.30)$$

From this we see that the control error [m(t) – M*(t)] is a liner combination of the random disturbances, δ (t) and ε(t), and the expectation errors, $[p(t)\text{-}p^{e}(t)]$. In order to simplify the ensuing discussion, I shall assume that the MA does not commit any expected errors, i.e., $p(t)\text{-}p^{e}(t) = 0$ and $y(t)\text{-}y^{e}(t) = 0$. Therefore control error in period t is given by:

$$m(t) - m^{*}(t) = 0.5408 \; \delta(t) + 0.4592 \; \varepsilon(t) \qquad (2.31)$$

implying that the control error is a weighted average of the money demand and the money supply disturbances, δ(t) and ε(t).

In order to comparè the merits of this control procedure involving high-powered money with the other one involving the interest rate which will be discussed shortly, we need a measure of the extent of which control errors will result from this procedure on average, over a large number of periods. The most appropriate measure in such cases in the mean-squared error (MSE) for m(t), which is defined as:

$$MSE \; [(t)] = E[m(t) - m^{*}(t)] \qquad (2.32)$$

Here, the symbol E indicates that the expected value of

$[m(t)\text{-}m^*(t)]^2$ is being computed, i.e. our measure is the mathematical expectation of the probability distribution of the random variable $[m(t) - m^*(t)]^2$. This is so as the control error is a random variable since both ä(t) and å(t) are random variables.

In order to compute the MSE value $E[m(t) - m^*(t)]^2$, we first note that since $[m(t) - m^*(t)]$ is a weighted average of two random variables with zero means, its mean is also zero. Therefore, $E[m(t) - m^*(t)]^2$ equals the variance of $[m(t) - m^*(t)]$, as well as the mean-squared value of that expression. Using basic probability theory, it is possible to compute the variance of a random variable that is a linear combination of other random variables. In particular, if $X_1$ and $X_2$ are random variables, while, while $\alpha_1 X_1 + \alpha_1 X_2$ is.

$$\text{var}(\alpha_1 X_1 + \alpha_2 X_2) = (\alpha_1^2 \text{ var}(X_1) + a_2^2 \text{ var}(X_2) + 2\alpha_1\alpha_2 \text{ cov}(S_1, X_2) \quad (2.33)$$

where cov $(X_1, X_2)$ is the covariance of those variables. Applying the above formula to our problem yields:

$$E[m(t) - m^*(t)]^2 = 0.2924\,\sigma_\delta^2 + 0.2109\,\sigma_\varepsilon^2 + 0.4967\,\text{cov}[\delta(t), \varepsilon(t)] \quad (2.34)$$

As $\delta(t)$ refers to disturbances to money demand, which involves the behaviour of (non-bank) money holders, while $\varepsilon(t)$ refers to disturbances to money supply, which involves bank behaviour, we assume that these two variables $\delta$ and $\varepsilon$, are independent of each other. Thus, the covariance term in equation (2.34) will equal zero and can be simplified to yield:

$$E[m(t) - m^*(t)]2 = \text{MSE}\,[m]^h = 0.2924\,\sigma_\delta^2 + 0.2109\,\sigma_\varepsilon^2 \quad (2.35)$$

Where MSE $[m]^h$ indicates the mean-squared error for m(t) using h(t) as the instrument. Equation (2.35) is a good approximation of the more complete version provided by equation (2.34), and we will use this simplified variant in order to measure the extent to which control errors will result on an average from the procedure of using high-powered money as an instrument to target money stock.

We now shift our attention to the other money stock control procedure alluded to earlier: the one with r(t) use as the MA's operating instrument. Our objective now would be to compute an MSE expression comparable with that obtained in equation (2.35).

In this case, the money supply equation (2.25), is not involved in the determination of m(t). instead the MA merely sets r(t) so as to make m(t) in eq. (2.24) equal to the target value $m^*(t)$, taking as given the anticipated values of p(t), y(t), and $\delta(t)$. This implies that it initially solves equation (2.26) for the appropriate value of r(t) and subsequently substitutes this result into equation (2.24) as the actual outcome will be governed by the latter equation. This yields:

$$m(t) = m^*(t) + [p(t) - p^e(t)] + 1.2691\ [y(t) - y^e(t) + \delta(t) \quad (2.36)$$

Assuming that the MA does not commit any expectational errors the control error in equation (2.36) can be simplified to:

$$m(t) - m^*(t) = \delta(t) \quad (2.37)$$

Consequently, the relevant MSE value is merely:

$$e[m(t) - m^*(t)]^2 = MSE[m]^e = \sigma_\delta^2 \quad (2.38)$$

Which is smaller than $\sigma_\delta^2$. Now if $\sigma_\varepsilon^2$ is smaller than $\sigma_\delta^2$, then it automatically follows that MSE $[m]^h$ obtained in equation (2.35) must be mush lower than the corresponding MSE $[m]^r$ obtained in equation (2.38).

Therefore, a sufficient condition for the procedure based on high-powered money as the instrument to be superior to that based on the interest rate as the instrument is that:

$$\sigma_\varepsilon^2\ ?\ \sigma_\delta^2 \quad (2.40)$$

For the Indian economy, based upon the results presented

in equations (2.22) and (2.23), it is seen that the money-demand equation has an S.E.E. of 0.0745, while the corresponding S.E.E. for the money-supply equation is 0.0866. This implies that:

$$\sigma_{\delta}^{2} = (0.0745)2 = 0.0056 \qquad (2.41a)$$
$$\sigma_{\varepsilon}^{2} = (0.0866)2 = 0.0075 \qquad (2.41b)$$

Substituting the above results into equations (2.35) and (2.28) yields the following MSEs with h(t) and r(t) as the instruments:

$$MSE[m]^{r}=0.2925\ (0.0056)+0.2109\ (0.0075)=0.0032 \qquad (2.42a)$$

$$MSE[m]^{e} = 0.0056 \qquad (2.42b)$$

It is thus seen that although $\sigma_{\varepsilon}^{2} > \sigma_{\delta}^{2}$, MSE $[m]^{h}$ < MSE $[m]^{c}$, implying that, within the Indian context, h(t) is a biter instrument for controlling the money stock than r(t).

The general type of analysis utilized here was initially developed by Poole (1970). It was first applied to the money stock control problem by Pierce and Thomson (1972), whose analysis was later on extended to a dynamic model with rational expectations by McCallum and Hoehn (1983).

The results indicate that while the RBI, which is de jure monetary authority in India, can influence the behaviour of the money stock, it cannot control it as precisely as it would want to. However, on the basis on the control it exerts over the money stock, it is reasonable to specify it as an ultimate target within the framework of monetary issues in the Indian context.

## MONEY, OUTPUT AND INFLATION

In this section, we concentrate on the long run effect of money growth on inflation and take up two major topics. First, we examine the monetarist proposition that due to money growth.

Then we look at the welfare costs of inflation to determine the circumstances under which inflation is of any consequence in terms of the society's individuals.

In attempting to explain the causes of inflation in LDCs, we find that the literature contains two major competing hypotheses. Firstly, there is the monetarist model which sees inflation as essentially a monetary phenomenon. The structuralist model, by contrast, argues that the causes of inflation must be sought in certain structural characteristics, especially the presence of bottlenecks in LDCs that made them particularly prone to inflation. This chapter, as it deals only with monetary economics, will attempt to illustrate and empirically test only the monetarist proposition and readers interested in understanding the basic underpinnings of the structuralist model of inflation are advised to refer to Ghatak (1981).

### Money and Inflation

We propose to establish a basic result in this section. The inflation is indeed primarily a monetary phenomenon, which cannot continue without continued money growth. In order to do so, we need to develop an analysis of the dynamic of inflation that attempts to explain the monetarist claim that inflation is always and everywhere a monetary phenomenon. To obtain a firm understanding of this, two distinctions have to be borne in mind. The first is between the short run and the long run. The second is the distinction between monetary and structural disturbance to the economy.

Monetarists tend to concentrate on the long run and on economies in which changes money growth are the primary disturbances. In such cases, they tend to be invariably right when they argue that money explains most of what is happening to inflation. But as we move away from the long run and from monetary disturbances towards short run inflation determination and alternative shocks, it becomes necessary to be much more eclectic. In the short run, disturbance other that changes in the money stock affect inflation and, conversely, changes in the money stock do have real effects. And even if the disturbances are purely monetary, it will still generally take a while before they are fully reflected only in inflation.

There is one principal proposition in the adjustment process towards long run equilibrium in the monetary model that I shall prove empirically: A sustained increase in the growth-rate of money will, in the long run when all adjustments have taken place, lead to an equal increase in the rate of inflation.

## The Money-Inflation Link

If the above monetarist proposition is to be vindicated then we should expect to find a tight link between inflation and growth in money. The statement that inflation is a money phenomenon is a direct implication of the quantity theory of money, which is the backbone of monetarist macroeconomics and needs to be examined very carefully within the Indian context.

The quantity theory relates the levels of the nominal money supply (M), the income velocity of money (V), the general price level (P) and real output (Y) in the following way:

$$M\,V = P\,Y \tag{3.1}$$

Rewriting eq. (3.1) in terms of natural logarithms, and specifying it in terms of the price level yields:

$$\ln P = \ln M \ln Y + \ln V. \tag{3.2}$$

we can also rewrite eq. (3.1) as follows:

$$(M/P)\,V = Y \tag{3.3}$$

Where (M/P) is real money stock which, in monetary equilibrium must equal real money demand (M/P), i.e.,

$$M/P = MD/P \tag{3.4}$$

Incorporating eq. (3.4) into eq. (3.3), rewriting it in logarithms, and stating the resultant in terms of velocity yields:

$$\ln V = \ln Y - \ln (MD/P) \quad (3.5)$$

If we now assume that in the long run, desired real balances adjust to actual real balances, i.e.,

$$(MD/P)^* = (MD/P)$$

We can rewrite eq. (1.1) in its logarithmic form as:

$$\ln (MD/P) = \ln A + \alpha \ln Y + \beta \ln r \quad (3.6)$$

Substituting eq. (3.6) above into eq. (3.5) yields:

$$\ln V = -\ln A + (l-\alpha) \ln Y - \beta \ln r \quad (3.7)$$

Substituting the above result into equation (3.2) yields:

$$\ln P = -\ln A \ln M - \alpha \ln Y - \beta \ln r \quad (3.8)$$

where $\alpha > 0$ and $\beta < 0$.

Equation (3.8) can be used to test the monetarist proposition as well as to account for the sources of inflation in India by specifying the following functional formal of the model:

$$\ln P(t) = a_0 + a_1 \ln M(t) - a_2 \ln Y(t) - a_3 \ln r(t) \quad (3.9)$$

Where the monetarist propositions imply the following parametric restrictions:

$$a_1 = 1; a_2 = \alpha \text{ and } a_3 = \beta.$$

If these restriction hold, then differentiating equation (3.9) with regard to time t yields:

$$\frac{I}{P}\frac{dp}{dt} = \frac{I}{M}\frac{dM}{dt} - \alpha\frac{I}{y}\frac{dy}{dt}\frac{I}{y} - \beta\frac{dr}{dt} \quad (3.10)$$

However, by definition:

$$\frac{dP}{dt} P_i \frac{dM}{dt} = M; \quad \frac{dY}{dt} = Y; \text{ and } \frac{dr}{dt} = r.$$

Therefore, we can rewrite equation (3.10) in terms of the percentage change over time of each of the variables as follows, recognizing the fact that $\pi = (P/)$:

$$\pi = (M/M)\ \alpha\ (Y/Y)\ t\ \beta\ (r/r) \quad (3.11)$$

At this point, it will be convenient, to introduce the hitherto ignored distinction between the nominal and the real interest rate. This distinction is important in the context of steady-state analysis because a steady-state equilibrium may feature a constant, but non-zero, inflation rte, i.e. $\pi$ (t) > 0. Since this non-zero inflation rate will be constant over time in a steady state, it is plausible to assume that individuals will recognize the existence of inflation and correctly anticipate that it will continue to prevail in the future. This would imply that:

$$\pi^*(t) = \pi(t) \quad (3.12)$$

Where $\pi^*(t)$ is the expected inflation rate.

The real rate of interest, R(t), is defined as the difference between the nominal rate of interest, r(t), and the expected inflation rate, $\pi^*(t)$, i.e.

$$R(t) = r(t) = V^*(t) \quad (3.13)$$

In conjunction with equation (3.13), this yields:

$$R(t) = r(t) = \pi(t) \qquad (3.14)$$

The distinction represented in the above equation reflects one of the most important ideas in monetary economics. Equation (3.14) can be rewritten as:

$$r(t) = R(t) + \pi^{*}(t) \qquad (3.15)$$

Now, in steady state equilibrium, both investment and capital must grow at the same are because of their relationship. Thus, capital must grow at the same rate as output, implying that the output-capital ratio must be constant. But this entails a constant marginal product of capital and the latter is, in equilibrium equal to the real rate of interest.

Now, if R(t) is constant, then changes in ð(t) are fully reflected in r(t) and the nominal interest rate would increase *pari passu* with the rate of inflation, i.e.

$$r(t) = \pi(t) \qquad (3.16)$$

However, in steady-state equilibrium, the inflation rate will be a constant, implying that $\pi(t) = 0$. Incorporating this result into equation (3.16) yields:

$$r(t) = 0 \qquad (3.17)$$

Consequently, equation (3.11) can be written as:

$$\Pi = (M/M - \alpha\, Y/Y) \qquad (3.18)$$

## Empirical Evidence

Using annual data on the India economy over the 40-year period 1650-1 to 1990-1, the following equation was estimated:

$$\ln P(t) = 6.004 + 0.945 \ln M(t) - 0.990 \ln Y(t) + 0.271 \ln r(t)$$
$$(3.1) \quad (10.3) \quad (-3.7) \quad (3.2)$$
$$R2 = 0.9919;\ S.E.S. = 0.0739;\ D.W. = 1.2872 \qquad (3.19)$$

Differentiating equation (3.19) with regard to time and them by assuming steady state equilibrium, setting r/r = 0, yielding the following long run link between inflation, money and output:

$$\pi = \frac{0.945\ M}{M} - \frac{0.990\ Y}{Y} \qquad (3.20)$$

This result immediately suggests that, for a constant level of real output, i.e., Y/Y = 0, the inflation rate is nearly equal to the growth-rate of nominal money supply (0.945 = 1). That is the basis for the view that inflation, in the long run, is a monetary phenomenon. Thus, the monetarist contention that a sustained increase in money growth will, in the long run, when all adjustment have taken place, lead to an equal increase in the rate of inflation is clearly borne out in the Indian context.

Comparing like coefficients in equations (1.18) and (3.20) leads to the conclusion that $\alpha$ = 0.990. Comparing this with the elasticity estimates provided in Table 3.1 reveals that it lies somewhere between the short run estimate of 0.44 and the long run estimate of 1.42, which indicates that the estimate of $\alpha$ obtained in equation (3.20) is the medium-term elasticity of real money demand with regard to real income. Indeed this value of 0.99 corresponds to the cumulative medium-term elasticity after 3-4 quarters have elapsed, indicating the approximate time taken for prices to respond to a positive supply shock.

### Inflation and Interest Rate

High interest rates in recent years have spurred researchers to seek to comprehend the theories of interest rate determination with special emphasis on the establishment of a relationship between inflation and interest rates. This is all the more relevant in the present Indian context where attempts are being made to free the interest rates and allow them to reflect market forces.

The classical theories of interest rates and the Fisherian theory, so named after Irving Fisher who was the first to draw attention to the inflation-interest rate linkage, on the interaction between the time preference of individuals and the marginal productivity of capital dealt with the determination of real interest rates. With the advent of money into the ensuring analysis, the loanable funds approach of Fisher and the liquidity preference or portfolio approach of Keynes were integrated into the literature. Rather than positing a definitional relationship between the nominal and the real rate of interest, as given in equation (3.13), Fisher sought to recognize the distinction between them by formulating a more general version given by:

$$r(t) = R(t) + b\pi^{*}(t) \qquad (3.21)$$

He then attempted to test the hypothesis that b = l in the above formation. When he observed a smaller than expected coefficient, he noted that this erratic behaviour of interest rates was due tot the 'instability of money.'

However, recent empirical work by Tanzi (1980), using the concept of the output gap, has vindicated the strict version of the Fisherian theory, implying thereby that the coefficient of $\pi^{*}$ in equation (3.21) is close to unity, as Fisher had anticipated.

## Economic Activity and Interest Rates

Let $\pi^{*}(t)$, $\pi(t)$, and r(t) indicate the expected rate of inflation, actual rate of inflation and nominal rate of interest; let Y(t) and Y(t) be the actual and potential levels of output; and let $R^{c}(t)$ and $R^{r}(t)$ denote the expected, realized and natural (long run) real rates of interest.

Rewriting Fisher's equation, equation (3.21), we have:

$$r(t) = R^e(t) + b\pi^*(t) \tag{3.22}$$

Under the twin Fisherian assumptions of: (1) $\pi^*$ is the only variable affecting r, and (2) changes in $\pi^*$ are fully reflected in r; the expected real rate $R^e(t)$ is implicity assumed constant and equal to $R^e(t)$ and b can be dropped from this equation.

However, because of random factors, the expected or ex- ante real rate, $R^e(t) = R(t) = \pi^*(t)$, can diverge from the realized or ex post real rate, $R^r(t) = r(t) - \pi(t)$. If we define:

$$R^e(t) - R^r(t) = \pi(t) - \pi^*(t) = D(t) \tag{3.23}$$

Then Fisher's theory requires that:

$$E[D(t)] = 0$$
$$E[D(t)D(t)] \ \sigma^2, \text{ fi } t = t$$
$$= \sigma, \text{ if } t \neq t$$

However, if business fluctuations have an impact of D(t), as they will, these conditions will not be satisfied, leading to a systematic divergence between $R^e(t)$ and $R^r(t)$. Thus, by ignoring the effect of business cycles on the divergence between $\pi$ and $\pi^*$, Fisher's theory fails to account for the possible effects of such deviations of $R^e$- thereby imparting a pseudo constancy to its long run behaviour which is unwarranted in view of the fact that expected real of interest can vary across the cycle.

For example, in a recession, firms will tend to liquidate inventories and postpone investment plans, so that as the demand for loanable funds falls more than supply, the credit market will turn more favourable to borrowers. In such circumstances, borrowers (lenders) will expect to pay (receive) lower rates of interest in comparison to better times. The net result should be a fall in the expected real rate of interest and, given inflationary expectations in the nominal rate of interest too.

We can formalize this relationship as follows:

$$Re(t) = R'' + 0[Y(t), \theta > 0] \qquad (3.24)$$

Substituting equation (3.24) into equation (3.22) yields:

$$r(t) = R'' + b\pi^{*}(t) + \theta[32^{*}y(t) - Y(t)] \qquad (3.25)$$

This was the revision of the Fisherian equation as envisaged by Tanzi (1980) and will form the basis of our empirical testing. This modification is still expressed in terms of inflationary expectations, as required by Fisher's theory, but it adds the level of economic activity as a basic explanatory variable in the determination of the nominal rate of interest.

Eqs. (3.24) and (3.25) together indicate that:

(1) When the output gap is zero, $Y(t) = Y(t)$, and no inflationary expectation, $\pi^{*}(t) = 0$, then $r(t) = R'' = R^{e}(t)$, implying that the nominal rate of interest would equal the (constant) natural real rate of interest which would equal the expected real rate.
(2) If $b = 1$ and $Y(t) = Y(t)$ then the nominal interest rate would increase *pari passu* with the expected rate of inflation.
(3) During an expansion (recession), the nominal rate of interest would increase by more (less) than inflationary expectations, thereby affecting the expected real rate of interest.

## Empirical Evidence

In order to obtain empirical estimates of equation (3.25), we require, both a measure of the expected rate of inflation, $\pi^{*}(t)$ and as a measure of the output gap, $G(t)$.

As we are now dealing with annual data, and not quarterly data as in Section 1.2.4, the estimates of the expected rate of inflation obtained by using equation (1.10) are no longer valid. In order to re-estimate ð*(t), we used annual data on ð(t), measured by the wholesale price index (1970-71 = 1.00), over the 30-year sample period 1960-61 to 1990-91. Initializing the series by setting ð*(1960-61) = ð(1960-61) = 6.58 per cent, we generated different sets of estimates of ð*(t), using the adaptive expectations model given by equation (1.7), for alternative values of the adjustment coefficient φ and the following most appropriate formulation, which minimized its corresponding MSE, was obtained:

$$\pi^*(t) = 0.899\ \pi^*(t\text{-}l) + 0.101\ \pi(t\text{-}l) \qquad (3.26)$$

The low level of φ (= 0.101) indicates that recent events have very little bearing on the determination of inflationary expectations in the Indian economy reflecting, in part, the volatile nature of inflation rates in India.

As far as the determination of the output gap is concerned, we have to remember that strictly speaking G(t) is the difference between actual real output, Y(t), and potential real output, Ÿ(t). However, in order to avoid difficulties with the logarithm of a negative number, a ratio specification of the output gap is employed analysis. Thus, we have:

$$G(t) = Y(t)/\ddot{Y}(t) \qquad (3.27)$$

Implying therefore that:

$$\ln G(t) = \ln Y(t) - \ddot{Y}(t) \qquad (3.28)$$

The potential output series computed by Rao, Fernandes, and Deshpande (1990) was used in order to derive estimates of the output gap for the Indian economy.

For estimation purposes, we used annual time series data on all the concerned variables, $\pi^*(t)$, ln G(t), and for the 30-year period 1960-61 to 1990-91, the empirical relationship, as suggested by equation (3.25), is shown below:

$$r(t) = 3.8956 + 0.9797\ \pi^*(t) + 8.2901\ \ln G(t)$$
$$(3.4) \qquad (6.0) \qquad (2.5)$$

$$\text{R-2} = 0.7157;\ \text{S.E.E. } 0.7903;\ \text{D.W.} = 2.013 \qquad (3.29)$$

The results uncover three pertinent facts regarding the behaviour of interest rate in India. These are: (1) the log run (natural ) real rate of interest in the Indian economy, obtained by setting $\pi^*(t) = \ln G(t) = 0$ in equation (3.29), is seen to be about 3.9 per cent which very closely corresponds to the long run real output growth rate 4.1 per cent for the Indian economy over the period 1960-61, thereby substantiating the theoretical arguments regarding the close correspondence between real interest rates and real output growth rates; (2) as the coefficient of $\pi^*(t)$ is seen to be almost unity ($0.9797 = 1$), the Fisherian that if the output gap is zero, then the nominal rate of interest increases *pari passu* with the expected rate of inflation; and (3) considering that the output gap has always been negative for the Indian economy, i.e., $Y(t) < \ddot{Y}(t)$, for all t, it implies that the nominal interest rate has always increased at a slower rate than inflationary expectations.

## The Welfare Cost of Inflation

The analysis of the preceding section suggests that the rate of inflation has little effect on the real rate of interest. However, from a practical perspective, actual inflation rate but, instead, takes on different values across alternative steady states with different rate of money creation and inflation. In particular, the level of real money balances depends negatively on the prevailing inflation rate because, as equation (3.29) indicated, the rate of interest must rise *pari passu* with the (expected) rate of inflation, thereby depressing the real demand for money, following equation (1.1).

This suggests that there are welfare costs of inflation, for a relatively lower level of real money balances implies a reduction in the transaction-facilitating services provided by money, and consequently an increase in the amount of time and energy that must be devoted to purchasing goods and services for any given level of spending. Since this must be at the expense of leisure that is desired by individuals, it follows that higher inflation rates lead to lower utility levels for individuals.

In the light of the foregoing conclusion, it is of considerable interest to develop a technique for measuring the magnitude of the welfare cost of a steady (anticipated) inflation. The approach we shall adopt is a modified form of the method that was first introduced into the literature by Bailey (1956), and it utilizes a type of reasoning that is usually associated with consumer surplus analysis in the area of public economics and applied microeconomics.

**Lump-sum Transfers**

One aspect of the above result needs to discussed. It is fairly easy to see that steady inflation reduces the volume of monetary services and decreases the welfare of money holders. But there are other costs that need to be considered. Essentially, it is necessary to recognize that the foregoing analysis assumes that newly created money is turned over by the monetary authority to the government, which then distributes it to households as transfers are paid in a lump-sum fashion, that is, in such a way that any household's behaviour has no influence on the amount it receives'. An alternative assumption regarding the way that money can enter into the economy will be considered in the next sub-section.

For the time being, we shall retain the assumption that money enters via lump-sum transfer and carry out an econometric exercise designed to illustrate the general magnitude of welfare losses arising from the currently rising inflation rate in India.

For this purpose, we use the Deaver's (1970) model which assumes that the demand for real balances (MD/P) depends upon the actual rate of inflation ($\pi$) and real income (Y). it is given by:

$$(MD/P) = A\,Y^{a}\,e^{-\beta\eta} \qquad (3.30)$$

Where α is the income elasticity of demand for real balances and β is the elasticity of demand for real balances with regard to inflation. Here, we represents the base of all natural logarithms. Thus, the money demand schedule, equation (3.30), represent the quantity of real balances demanded as a function of the rate of inflection, for a given level of real income.

Using annual data over the past decade, 1981-82 to 1990-91, which was a period of comparatively quiescent inflation, we estimated the following money demand function, whose theoretical form was suggested by equation (3.30), for the Indian economy.

$$\ln \frac{MD(t)}{P} = -8.3626 + 1.6241 \ln Y(t) - 1.2766\,\pi\,(t)$$

$$(-2.3) \qquad (26.4) \qquad (-3.0)$$

$$R\text{-}2 = 0.9904;\ S.E.E. = 0.0284;\ D.W. = 1.82 \qquad (3.31)$$

Now, assuming that NDP will grow at 2.5 per cent in 1991-92 (see Economic Survey 1991-92, Government of India), the level of real income in 1991-92 is projected at Rs. 81912 crores (at 1970-71 prices). Substituting Y= 81912 n equation (3.31) yields:

$$\ln m = 10.0115 - 1.2766\pi \qquad (3.32)$$

Where, for convenience, we have replace MD/P by m; and dropped the time index t. This implies that our calculated welfare loss will be expressed as a fraction of this income level in 1991-92.

Now the value of real money balances at a zero inflation rate, m°, is obtained by setting $\pi = 0$ in equation (3.32) this yields:

$$m^{\circ} = 22281 \qquad (3.33)$$

Let use now assume that the inflation rate in 1991-92 would be 13.2 per cent (which is the point – to point estimate of the inflation rate based on the wholesale piece index for December 1991 over its corresponding level for December 1990. Thus, the level of real money balances with a 13.2 per cent inflation rate, $m^1$, is obtained by setting $\pi = 0.132$ in equation (3.32). This yields:

$$m^1 = 18826 \tag{3.34}$$

In order to compute the welfare loss (L) resulting from this fall in real money balances because of inflation, we initially rewrite equation (3.32) in terms of the inflation rate, i.e.

$$\pi = 7.8423 - 0.7833 \ln m \tag{3.35}$$

and than evaluate its definite integral between the limits define in equation (3.34) and (3.33), i.e. $m^1 = 18826$ and $m^\circ = 22281$;

$$L = \int_{18826}^{22281} [7.8423 - 0.7833 \ln m]\, dm \tag{3.36}$$

The computation yield:

$$L = \int_{18826}^{22281} dm - 0.7833 \int_{18826}^{22281} \ln m\, dm$$

$$= 7.8423\,[22281 - 18826] - 0.7833\,[200785.0 - 166478.2]$$

$$= 222.6 \tag{3.37}$$

Thus, the social cost equivalent of the inflation rate of 13.2 per cent expected for the Indian economy in 1991-92 is about Rs. 223 crores which is just under three-tenth of 1 per cent of the NDP level (of Rs. 81912 crores) projected for that year.

This calculated cost is quite small in view of the low absolute order of magnitude of the inflation rate being experienced.

The other topic concerns the way in which money enters the economy implying the interaction of money with fiscal policy. Instead of our earlier assumption, let us now assume that the government used money creation as a source of revenue. This implies that the government uses newly printed money not to make lump-sum transfers payments, but to finance part of its purchases of goods and services. In such a case, the creation of money and its associated inflation, while imposing a cost of households by bringing about a reduction in their real money holdings, also yields some benefits since the extra revenue, termed inflation tax revenue, enables the government to reduce its tax collection without reducing government purchases.

## The Inflation Tax

The inflation-tax model has received considerable attention since it was first discussed by Gagan (1956). This model is based on the fact that inflation acts as a tax on money holding. While the original model emerged from a monetarist tradition, its application to LDCs can take a structuralist slant since it can be argued that if it is difficult to increase yields from other forms of taxation due to structural phenomena, the inflation tax can serve as a means of raising the share of the government in domestic product, enabling it to expand its expenditures.

It there is no real income growth, then the public will hold and constant level of real balances, however, since inflation erodes the real value of a given quantity of nominal money balances, it will become necessary for the public to save out of their income to obtain nominal balances sufficient to keep real balances constant. Inflation thus acts just like a tax because people are forced to spend less than their income and pay the difference to the government in exchange for extra money.

The amount of revenue produced is the product of the tax rate (the inflation rate) and the tax base (the real monetary base). Inflation tax revenue ® is thus given:

R = inflation rate (π) x real money base (MD/P-m). (3.38)

Substituting equation (3.30) into equation (3.38) yields:

$$R = \pi\ [A\ Ya\ e^{-\beta x}] \qquad (3.39)$$

It is seen for equation (3.39) that the following limits hold:

$$Lt\ R = 0\pi\ > o \qquad (3.40a)$$
$$Lt\ R = 0\pi > \infty \qquad (3.40b)$$

When the inflation rate is zero, the government gets no revenue from inflation. As the inflation rate rises, the amount of inflation tax received by the government initially increases as the rise in the inflation rate overwhelms the reduction in the real money base. Eventually, the real monetary base fall so much that the total amount of inflation tax revenue received by the government starts declining the finally fall back to zero.

Thus, there will exist a steady-state inflation rate, $\pi^*$, at which the corresponding inflation tax revenue ($R^*$) is at its maximum. To determine this revenue-maximizing rate of inflation, we differentiate equation (3.39) with respect to the inflation rate, π, and set the resultant equation to zero. This yields:

$$\delta R/\delta\pi = AY^{\alpha}\ [e^{-\beta\pi} + \pi\ (-\beta e^{-\beta\pi})] = 0 \qquad (3.41)$$

This provides a revenue-maximizing inflation rate given by:

$$\pi^* = 1/\beta \qquad (3.42)$$

Obviously, β is a crucial parameter and it is important to realize that a few generalization are possible about the likely magnitude of the inflation tax revenue that governments obtain normally from deliberate money creation leading to inflation.

To do so, we initially ascertain the size of the real money base in relation to the size of the economy at the normal rate of inflation. In India, the base in 1990-91 was about 24.3 per cent of NDP at factor cost. Given that the inflation rate is expected to be about 13.2 per cent in 1991-92. It would imply, from equation (3.38) that the government would have collected about 3.21 per cent of NDP (=0.132 × 0.243) in inflation tax revenue which is not a trivial amount. We now empirically estimate the maximum inflation tax revenue it could generate via the inflation tax.

The coefficient of $\pi$ in eq. (3.31) indicates that the revenue-maximizing rate of inflation is about 78 per cent year ($\pi^* = 1/\beta = 1/1.2766 = 0.7833$). The elasticity of demand for real balances (m) with regard to this rate of inflation ($\pi^*$) is:

$$[\delta m/\delta \pi]\ [\pi^*/m] = [-1.2766]\ [0.7833] = -1 \qquad (3.43)$$

To estimate the inflation tax revenue the Indian government could have obtained in 1991-92 at this rate, we rewrite eq. (3.31) in its original form given by eq. (3.30), i.e.,

$$MD/P = m = 0.00023344\ Y^{1.6241}\ e^{-1.2766\pi} \qquad (3.44)$$

And substitute this into eq. (3.39) along with the projected value of NDP in 1991-92, i.e., Y = Rs. 81912 crores. This yields:

$$R = \pi\ m = \pi\ [22281.10\ e^{-1.2766\pi}] \qquad (3.45)$$

Replacing $\pi$ in eq. (3.45) by $\pi^* = 0.7833$, yields:

$$R = 0.7833\ (8196.76) = \text{Rs. } 6420.52 \text{ crores}, \qquad (3.46)$$

Or about 7.48 per cent of NDP. At this inflation rate, however, the real money base, i.e., Rs. 8196.76 crores, would have shrunk to just 10 per cent of NDP and therefore, the social cost equivalent would be given by the following definite integral :

$$L = \int_{8179}^{22281} [7.8423 - 0.7833 \ln m] \, dm \qquad (3.47)$$

Which is Rs. 4615.73 crores, i.e. about 5.63 per cent of NDP.

Therefore, the government would be earning about Rs. 6420.52 crores at this revenue-maximizing rate of inflation and incurring about Rs. 4615.73 crores of social cost. Thus, the average cost works out to be approximately 72 paise ( = 4615.73/6420.52) per cent rupees earned from inflation tax revenue.

However, in such situation, the more appropriate way in which the formulate the cost-of-inflation question is as follows: The government must finance its purchases either by an explicitly tax or by money creation which yield inflation tax revenue. As each type of tax imposes a cost on society, the problem is to design a package of revenue sources that minimizes these distortions. Basic marginal reasoning indicates that a necessary condition for minimization is that, at the margin, the cost of society per rupee of revenue be identical across revenue sources.

It is possible to show that, for revenue from inflation, the marginal cost per rupee of revenue is given by the expression:

$$\frac{\delta \text{ cost}}{\delta \text{ rev}} = \frac{\pi\beta}{1-\pi\beta} \qquad (3.48)$$

where $\pi$ is the inflation rate and $\beta$ stands for the absolute value of the coefficient of ð in the money demand function, equation (3.30).

To show that the above expression is valid, note that since the cost of inflation is $\int \pi \, dm$, the marginal value is : $-\pi$ dm. The marginal revenue from a change in the steady state is given by: $\delta(\pi m) = \pi\delta m + m\delta\pi$. Thus, the rate, which given the marginal cost per unit of revenue is : $-\pi(\delta m/\delta\pi)$ divided by $\pi(m\delta/\delta\pi) + m$. Inserting $-\beta m$ for $\delta m/\delta\pi$ and simplifying, we obtain equation (3.34).

As the absolute value of $\hat{a}$ was 1.2766, as given in equation (3.31), the cost per rupee of inflation tax revenue raised by the current level of the inflation rate, i.e. $\pi = 0.132$ is given by:

$$\frac{\delta \text{ cost}}{\delta \text{ rev}} = \frac{(0.132)(1.2766)}{1-(0.132)(1.2766)} = 0.2027 \quad (3.49)$$

Thus, if the cost of raising government revenue is less than 20.27 paise per rupee for other sources of taxes then it would be inefficient to use the inflation tax as a source of revenue.

## The Control of Inflation

If the government tries to force the inflation rate any further beyond $\pi^* = I/\beta$, the fall in the real money base is more than the rise in the inflation rate and, thus, the inflation tax revenue starts to decline, leading to mounting budget deficits and an equally rapid money financing of such deficits. This fuels the inflation rate still further and the subsequent feedback lead to money growth-rates of almost the same order of magnitude as inflation rates. These features were ubiquitous in all of the hyperinflation that occurred in the mid-1980s in Latin America.

As Kiguel and Liviatan (1992) sum it up: In the absence of appropriate measures, countries with low (single digit) inflation typically find themselves in a moderate (low double-digit) or high (high double-digit) inflation, invariably as a result of external and, particularly, commodity price shocks. When the next inflationary shock hits, it takes explicit counter-inflationary policies to prevent inflation from rising to extreme (triple and quadruple-digit) inflation. Moderate inflation is, thus, not a state that economies can stay in indefinitely without a firm government commitment to prevent further increases in inflation-a point that needs to be underscored in the present Indian context where the inflation rate is already in the moderate phase.

In order to control inflation, two counter-inflationary packages have been recommended in the literature: the *orthodox* measures (which concentrate on fiscal and monetary contraction in terms of the budget deficit and money growth) and the *heterodox* measures (which add to the *orthodox* measures an income policy, including wage freezes, and a fixed exchange rate).

What, then, of the choice between *orthodox* and *heterodox* measures? According to Dornbusch (1992); Orthodox stabilization policies are very successful in stopping extreme inflation. Their success is usually much more limited, especially in the short run, in countries suffering chronic high inflation, where inflation is downwardly rigid and persistent. In these countries, the heterodox approach is more effective in bringing down inflation initially, although the cost of disinflation is not altogether avoided. These costs, typically in the forms of high unemployment, arise at a later stage, when the government tries to sustain the initial success as controls are phased out.

While income policies can do much in the high-inflation countries in fiscal adjustment programmes, the heterodox approach is not recommended for stopping inflation in countries that have traditionally experienced moderate and low inflation. These countries should rely as much as possible on orthodox measures.

In short: for low, moderate or extreme inflation, use *orthodox* measures; for high inflation, use *heterodox* measures.

A very important feature of such policies should be emphasized: Money growth following stabilization can afford to be high. Why? Because as the inflation rate falls, the demand for real balances increases. With a rising demand for real balances, the government can again create more money without generating inflation. Thus, at the beginning of successful stabilization, it can temporarily finance part of the deficit through the printing of money, without reigniting inflation. However, its theoretical relevance not withstanding, the ultimate success of such a post-stabilizations programme remains to be established.

## Current State of Monetary Policy

Strong winds of change are sweeping across the Indian financial landscape. We therefore have to adapt ourselves appropriately to update our understanding of these changes. All stakeholders are involved in this silent transformation. As actuaries, our stake is significant since we will shape the architecture of our part of the financial system that will emerge from these shifts. Fortunately, this time around, we are all aware of the changes taking place and considerable work is already underway into fashioning our response to the unfolding of the future. On the way forward, the role of actuaries will become critical in defining the best practices of tomorrow. The road ahead is challenging and will test the best skills in every aspect. It is in this context that we would share our perception of some of the challenges that are being faced in the conduct of monetary policy.

We seem to be living in a world of extraordinary developments with several remarkable features defining the surrounding environment. *First*, financial markets are unperturbed: with the flattening of yield curves, the compression of risk spreads and the search for yields continues unabated. *Second*, global imbalances have actually increased with no fears of hard landing, but with some sense of readying for a bumpy soft landing. Movements in major exchange rates are not reflecting fundamentals in an environment of generalised elevation in asset prices and abundant liquidity. *Third*, strong global economic growth could be accompanied by emerging pressures on core inflation. This could eventually pose a major challenge to monetary policy makers in terms of both direction and magnitude. By end-January, 2007, *i.e.,* at the time of formulating the Third Quarter Review of monetary policy, these dilemmas had become sharper and more testing than ever before. Taken together, global developments seemed in what could be described as a stable disequilibrium, and hence did not provide any definitive indication for a policy response. On the other hand, domestic developments seemed to dominate the outlook and clearly warranted closer scrutiny.

A distinctive feature of the Reserve Bank's communication strategy is to share its analysis with the public. Accordingly, we would like to highlight the analytical aspects of our assessment of the evolving scenario and the emerging issues that will condition the monetary policy response in the period ahead. The rest of my address is organised as follows: we will attempt to set out the environment in which we reviewed monetary policy. Against this backdrop, we will try to address the key issues that we had to grapple with as we fashioned the policy stance for the period ahead, we will conclude with a summary of the monetary policy stance and the measures taken in the Third Quarter Review.

**The Backdrop**

Perhaps the most distinguishing feature of recent domestic developments is the pace at which economic activity is expanding. On February 7, 2007 the advance estimates of the Central Statistical Organisation (CSO) placed India's real GDP at 9.2 per cent in 2005-06 and reaffirmed the robust optimism that has been building around India's macroeconomic performance. In retrospect, it is evident that there has been a pervasive sense of the gathering momentum of growth, reflected in the direction of revisions in projections by various forecasters during the year. For instance, real GDP growth projections of the Reserve Bank were raised from 7.5-8.0 per cent in the Annual Policy Statement of April, 2006 to 8.0 per cent in the Mid Term Review of October and further to 8.5-9.0 per cent in the Third Quarter Review. Similar revisions have also been made by various international observes and agencies. But actual growth has turned out to be ahead of all forecasts. Business confidence has been rising in successive rounds of surveys conducted by various agencies and there is considerable optimism on the outlook as reflected in order books, employment and profit margins. Viewed in an international perspective, the Indian economy seem to be well ahead of the synchronous global economic cycle that has enabled the world economy to record 4 per cent plus growth in an unprecedented run of five years to 2006.

There is growing evidence that the step-up in India's growth set in during 2000-04 is strengthening into an upward shift in the underlying trend. This acceleration of growth has been accompanied by a significant moderation of volatility, particularly in the period 2003-07. There are also indications of small but important shifts in the composition of growth. The services sector continues to be the main stay of the economy, contributing 73 per cent of overall growth: however, services led growth is getting reinforced by a sustained resurgence in industrial activity after a long hiatus of slow down and restructuring during the period 1996-2003. The buoyancy in industrial performance has been the most heartening feature of India's growth story. Accordingly, industry's contribution to overall growth has improved noticeably from the 1990s. While the services sector has been the most stable despite high growth, the recent acceleration in industrial growth has also displayed lower volatility than in preceding years (Table 5.4, Table 5.5 and Table 5.6).

Corporate balance sheets have strengthened considerably in an unprecedented run spanning seventeen quarters which began in the second half of 2002-03. Buoyant domestic demand and overseas markets have enabled corporates to scale up production and sales. Accordingly, profitability (net profits) has recorded growth consistently in the range of 25–60 per cent of on a year-to-year basis. Internally generated resources have powered a massive expansion in investments in existing capacity as well as in building up new capacity, while economising on borrowings from the banking system. Accordingly, interest burden (interest to sales ratio) has tended to fall (Table 5.4).

**Table 5.4:** Patterns of Growth: Average Growth Rates

*(Percentage)*

| | *Agriculture* | *Industry* | *Services* | *Overall* |
|---|---|---|---|---|
| 1970s | 0.6 | 4.7 | 4.1 | 2.9 |
| 1980s | 4.4 | 7.4 | 6.4 | 5.8 |
| 1990s | 3.0 | 5.9 | 7.4 | 5.8 |
| 2000-05 | 1.4 | 6.0 | 7.8 | 5.9 |
| 2005-06 | 6.0 | 8.0 | 10.3 | 9.0 |
| 2006-07 | 2.7 | 10.2 | 11.0 | 9.2 |
| Memo | | | | |
| 2000-03 | -0.2 | 5.2 | 6.6 | 4.6 |
| 2003-07 | 4.2 | 8.1 | 10.2 | 8.5 |

*Source:* RBI (2006) and CSO (2007a).

**Table 5.5 :** Patterns of Growth: Coefficients of Variation

(*Percentage*)

| | *Agriculture* | *Industry* | *Services* | *Overall* |
|---|---|---|---|---|
| 1970s | 13.65 | 0.80 | 0.53 | 1.42 |
| 1980s | 1.38 | 0.36 | 0.18 | 0.39 |
| 1990s | 1.30 | 0.71 | 0.27 | 0.32 |
| 2000-05 | 4.71 | 0.35 | 0.25 | 0.33 |
| Memo | | | | |
| 2000-03 | -23.21 | 0.47 | 0.13 | 0.22 |
| 2003-07 | 1.24 | 0.18 | 0.11 | 0.10 |

*Source :* RBI (2006) and CSO (2007a).

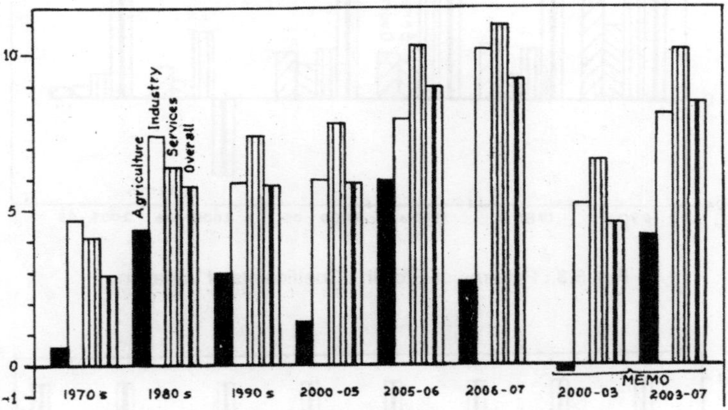


**Fig. 5.2 :** Patterns of Growth: Average Growth Rates

**Table 5.6 :** Patterns of Growth: Weighted Contribution

*(Percentage)*

| | *Agriculture* | *Industry* | *Services* | *Overall* |
|---|---|---|---|---|
| 1970s | 39.7 | 21.5 | 38.8 | 100.0 |
| 1980s | 19.5 | 27.0 | 53.5 | 100.0 |
| 1990s | 10.7 | 18.1 | 71.1 | 100.0 |
| 2000-05 | 0.1 | 21.5 | 78.3 | 100.0 |
| 2005-06 | 13.5 | 17.5 | 69.0 | 100.0 |
| 2006-07 | 5.8 | 21.4 | 72.7 | 100.0 |
| Memo | | | | |
| 2000-03 | -6.2 | 23.8 | 82.4 | 100.0 |
| 2003-07 | 9.7 | 18.7 | 71.6 | 100.0 |

*Source:* RBI (2006) and CSO (2007a).

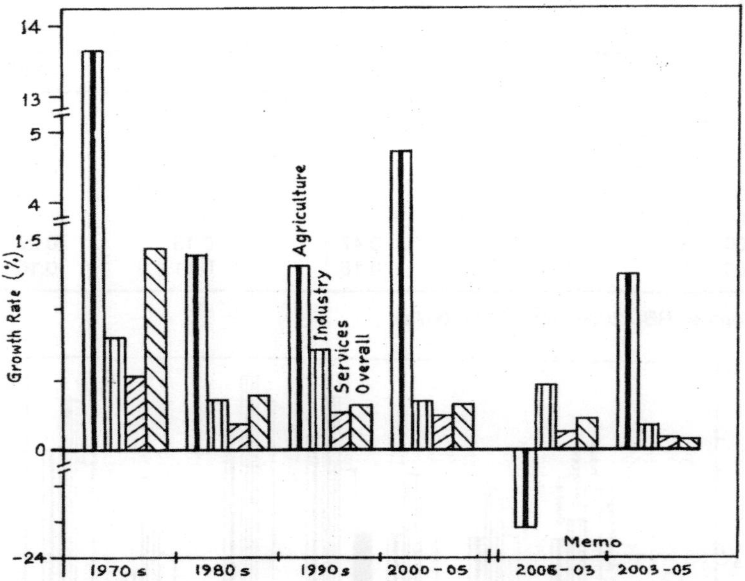


**Fig. 5.3** : Patterns of Growth : Coefficients of Variation

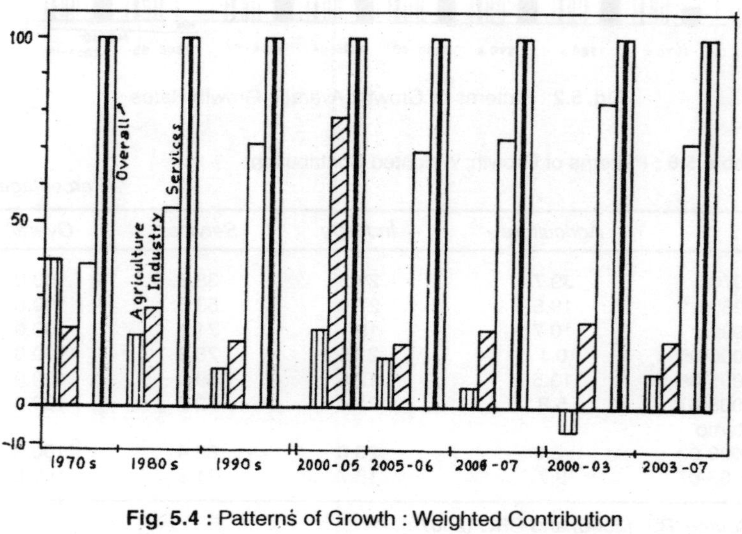


**Fig. 5.4** : Patterns of Growth : Weighted Contribution

**Table 5.7 :** Corporate Financial Performance

(Growth in per cent)

| *Item* | *2003-04* | *2004-05* | *2005-06* | *2005-06* | *2006-07* | *2005-06* | | | | *2006-07* | |
|---|---|---|---|---|---|---|---|---|---|---|---|
| | | | | *April-September* | | *Q1* | *Q2* | *Q3* | *Q4* | *Q1* | *Q2* |
| *1* | *2* | *3* | *4* | *5* | *6* | *7* | *8* | *9* | *10* | *11* | *12* |
| **Sales** | 16.0 | 24.1 | 16.9 | 17.2 | 27.4 | 18.5 | 16.4 | 13.2 | 19.5 | 25.6 | 29.2 |
| **Expenditure** | 14.4 | 22.9 | 16.4 | 16.6 | 25.6 | 18.0 | 16.3 | 12.7 | 18.9 | 24.6 | 26.6 |
| **Gross Profits** | 25.0 | 32.5 | 20.36 | 26.7 | 39.8 | 32.0 | 19.1 | 21.2 | 16.6 | 33.9 | 45.9 |
| **Interest** | -11.9 | -5.8 | 1.9 | -10.3 | 20.8 | -13.5 | -8.0 | 4.6 | 3.8 | 19.9 | 18.0 |
| **Profits After Tax** | 59.8 | 51.2 | 24.2 | 41.3 | 41.6 | 54.2 | 27.5 | 27.0 | 15.1 | 34.7 | 49.4 |
| **Memo** | | | | | | | | | | | |
| **Interest to Sales Ratio** | 3.4 | 2.6 | 2.0 | 2.2 | 2.2 | 2.2 | 2.1 | 2.1 | 1.7 | 2.2 | 2.0 |

*Notes:* 1. Growth rates are percentage change in the level for the period under reference over the corresponding period of the previous year.

2. Data in column (2) and (3) are based on audited balance sheets while those in column (4) onwards are based on the un-audited/audited abridged results of the non Government non-financial companies.

*Source:* RBI (2007a).

The optimism generated by India's recent macroeconomic performance has been somewhat marred by the setback to agriculture which has suffered substantial deceleration and instability. Shortfalls in key crops such as wheat (accompanied by depleting stocks), oilseeds and pulses have emerged and the supply situation in respect of these crops is further endangered on account of weather related adverse international conditions. The decline in the global production of wheat in 2006 has turned out to be the largest in ten years. Apart from poor harvests in key producing countries, their carry over stocks are declining and cereal acreage is losing out to the fast growing demand for bio-fuel production. Alongside, in the domestic economy, infrastructural bottlenecks are tightening. Managing the supply situation is emerging as a formidable challenge. In the current scenario, limitations on the supply response to the momentum of growth are showing up as excess demand pressures.

Monetary and financial conditions are reflecting these demand supply gaps as well as the onset of a durable pick-up in aggregate spending. Banks' non-food credit is expanding above 30 per cent for the fourth year in succession, driving up money supply. The growth of bank credit has favoured retail lending, particularly housing, real estate, trade transport and professional services and non-banking financial companies-sectors which hitherto were not priced into the credit market. While banks' exposures to these new sectors is still relatively small, given the low base, the high rates of growth have raised worries about the quality of these assets and potential non-performance. Default rates in regard to credit card receivables and personal loans have been rising. While buoyant deposit growth has, to an extent, alleviated the financial constraints on bank, credit deposit ratios remain high and investments in gilts have been drawn down to close to the statutory minimum of the SLR. These developments are likely to pose challenges to banks in managing liquidity.

Financial markets have, by and large, remained stable. Money markets experienced generally orderly conditions along with spells of tightening of liquidity in November and again from mid-December. During these episodes, contrasting conditions have often been observed when short-term interest rates have firmed up despite LAP absorptions but long-term rates have declined in the Government securities market. In December, there was an inversion of the yield curve and a narrowing of yield spreads. Forward premia have firmed up in November and December across the board in concert with the hardening of short-term interest rates in the domestic money market segments. On the other hand, asset prices, particularly equity prices, have risen to record highs.

Another significant feature of recent domestic developments is the firming up of inflation through the year. Currently hovering above 6 per cent, inflation, in terms of the wholesale price index, is ruling above indicative projections and represents a key concern in the evolving macroeconomic outlook. In terms of consumer prices, inflation is even higher in the range of 7-8 per cent.

**Table 5.8** : Wholesale Prices and Constituents

*(Year-on-year changes in per cent)*

| *Commodity* | *Weight* | *2005-06 (March 25)* | | *2005-06 (Jan. 14)* | | *2006-07 (Jan. 13)* | |
|---|---|---|---|---|---|---|---|
| | | *Inflation* | *WC* | *Inflation* | *WC* | *Inflation* | *WC* |
| 1 | 2 | 3 | 4 | 5 | 6 | 7 | 8 |
| All Commodities | 100.0 | 4.1 | 100.0 | 4.2 | 100.0 | 6.0 | 100.0 |
| 1. Primary Articles | 22.0 | 5.4 | 28.5 | 5.6 | 28.7 | 9.3 | 34.1 |
| Food articles | 15.4 | 6.6 | 24.2 | 7.4 | 26.5 | 8.5 | 22.0 |
| Non-Food Articles | 6.1 | -1.9 | -2.7 | -2.4 | -3.3 | 9.6 | 8.9 |
| Minerals | 0.5 | 45.6 | 6.8 | 34.8 | 5.7 | 2..6 | 3.0 |
| 2. Fuel, Power, Light and Lubricants | 14.2 | 8.9 | 47.9 | 7.9 | 41.1 | 3.7 | 14.0 |
| 3. Manufactured Products | 63.8 | 1.7 | 23.2 | 2.2 | 29.9 | 5.6 | 52.3 |
| Memo : | | | | | | | |
| Food Items (Composite) | 26.9 | 4.2 | 26.5 | 4.6 | 28.6 | 6.2 | 26.8 |
| WPI Excluding Food | 73.1 | 4.0 | 73.5 | 4.0 | 71.4 | 5.9 | 73.2 |
| WPI Excluding Fuel | 85.8 | 2.7 | 52.1 | 3.2 | 58.9 | 6.6 | 86.0 |

*WC:* Weighted contribution.
*Source* : RBI (2007a).

In crafting appropriate monetary policy in these conditions, it is important to undertake a careful assessment of the manner in which inflation is evolving. Primary articles, unlike in recent years, have contributed significantly to WPI during 2006-07. Accounting for a third of headline inflation, they can be interpreted to originate from supply side pressures. Furthermore, in 2006, there has been a surge in the international prices of cereals. International future prices of foodgrains have climbed to record levels due to substantial reductions in crop production estimates. At the same time, prices of manufactured products account for over half of current headline inflation (Table 5.8). Domestic prices are firming up in sympathy with international prices. Metal prices have risen by 53.6 per cent in 2006. Low stock levels and continuing demand has kept most metal prices high and elevated levels are likely to persist in the near term. In conjunction with emerging strains on capacity, elevated asset prices and the surging demand for bank credit, the rising prices of manufactures constitute the demand pressures on inflation.

The silver lining to the cloud is the improvement in public finances and the decline in international crude prices, and consequently in domestic prices of petroleum products. Excluding the beneficial effect of this softening of fuel prices results in inflation exceeding the headline in terms of wholesale prices. Globally too, headline inflation has been moderating mainly on account of the decline in international crude prices, while core inflation has generally remained firm and is likely to shape inflation expectations.

India's interface with the global economy has been another distinguishing feature of macroeconomic developments. The strength and resilience reflected in India's balance of payments has to be assessed in the context of global economic and financial developments. Global real GDP growth on a purchasing power parity basis is expected to have accelerated to above 5 per cent in 2006 but with a shift away from the US and towards Europe, Japan and the emerging world, all of which have distinctive features. In China.. for instance, there are concerns that high levels of growth might be unsustainable and that some parts of the economy are becoming overheated. In Korea, there are concerns about a relatively rapid growth in house prices along with a rise in household indebtedness. In Thailand, concerted efforts have been taken to stem strong capital inflows into the economy over the past few months.

Global financial markets have been reasonably stable while re-pricing risks. Short-term interest rates have firmed up since October, but long-term bond yield have fallen, translating into a steeper inversion of the yield curve. Foreign exchange markets have been recording lower levels of volatility in recent weeks than before. Global equity markets have posted steady gains. In line with developments in the major markets emerging equity markets in Asia and Latin America have continued to recover from the May-June sell-off. The markets which suffered the largest losses have more than recouped earlier losses.

Against this backdrop, India's merchandise export growth has resumed strongly from a dip in October, 2006. At the same time, imports of POL increased sizeably as in the previous year, but reflecting a sharp increase in import volume in the current year. Non-oil import growth, which remained subdued in the early months of 2006-07, has picked up during the third quarter in consonance with industrial activity. There are also reports of a substantial pick up in bullion imports in October-November. While the merchandise trade deficit has consequently widened, the sustained surplus on account of invisibles is expected to contain the current account deficit at well under 2 per cent of the GDP. The capital flows to India have recovered from the moderation during May-June 2006. Accordingly, the current account deficit is expected to be comfortably financed in the remaining part of the year.

To sum up the assessment, global growth continues to be strong but is exhibiting mixed patterns. In the global financial markets, current indications suggest that the risks remain underpriced and more diversified. Consequently, there is an increasing discomfort of the possibility of tail risk materializing.

Geo-political risks remain significant. There is a growing recognition of the need to contain extreme volatility in capital flows. More importantly, on the domestic front, demand pressures appear to have intensified alongside robust growth and there are increased supply side pressures in evidence. Macroeconomic management will be constrained by the lagged response of productive capacity and infrastructure to the ongoing expansion in investment.

## The Challenges

The foregoing analysis provides some evidence, though still formative, that a structural change could be taking place in the Indian economy. There is a gathering confidence that the economy is possibly poised on the threshold of a step-up in the growth trajectory. The central theme of the Third Quarter Review is the challenge of managing the transition to higher growth path, accompanied by low and stable inflation and well anchored inflation expectations. The objective is to firmly entrench potential output and productivity and thereby create the conditions for a further acceleration of growth. The role of monetary policy is to continue to maintain stability and so contribute to growth on an enduring basis.

It is in the context of sensitizing the public to the dilemmas and trade-offs involved in managing this change that the Mid-Term Review of October, 2006 explained the concept of overheating *i.e.,* a situation in which current output is running above potential output. In the current environment, and in the presence of structural change, the task of identifying overheating becomes difficult for the monetary authority. For the conduct of monetary policy, however, it is crucial to monitor all available information for signs of overheating with a view to keeping inflation expectations stable and ensuring that the gains from high growth are consolidated. Accordingly, sensing how close is the economy to its potential growth is the vital judgment that has to be made to set the timing and direction of monetary policy.

What is potential growth is thus the question that holds the key. There is general agreement among policy makers that the level and pace of potential growth is becoming increasingly difficult to diagnose. Open trade has expanded the supply potential of several economies. Moreover, for a country undergoing structural transformation with large unemployment/ underemployment of resources, the concept of potential growth become even more *fuzzy*. For instance, the *Economist* (February 3, 2007) observes: "India is undergoing a paradigm shift and so backward-looking historical data are now irrelevant for assessing future growth". Nevertheless, monetary policy decisions have to be made and the closest approximation of potential growth must be identified in terms of a rate of growth which is associated with non-accelerating inflation.

At the current juncture, the challenge facing us is to judge the compatibility of the current pace of growth with non-accelerating inflation. In this context, we would like to draw your attention to the new estimates of gross domestic saving and capital formation in India in 2005-06, released on January 31, 2007, the same day as the Third Quarter Review. Close analysis of these numbers reveals the underpinnings of the recent growth experience. The rate of Gross Domestic Saving (GDS), which was earlier estimated at 29.1 per cent of GDP in 2004-05, has been revised upwards by a clear 2 per cent of GDP. The rate of Gross Domestic Investment (GDI) for that year has also been raised by 1.4 per cent of GDP to 31.5 per cent. The significant improvement in GDS in 2004-05, is attributable mainly to a distinct increase in saving by the corporate sector. The revision is consistent with the observed improvement in corporate profitability and internally generated resources that has been sustained over the period 2003-07, and to which we have been drawing attention for some time. Corporate profitability has remained strong despite a sharp rise in input costs and in interest payments (Table 5.9). There is some evidence to suggest that the corporate sector performance is being powered by rising productivity. Accordingly, the increase in corporate saving during 2004-05 can be expected to be the onset of a longer trend, supporting high rates of GDS on a sustained basis.

Household saving remains the predominant component of domestic saving and would increase even further as incomes grow and social security reforms take shape. The improvement in GDS has particularly benefited form the turnaround in public sector saving. After turning negative between 1998-99 and 2002-03, public sector saving has turned positive from 2003-04 onwards, mainly reflecting the ongoing fiscal consolidation.

**Table 5.9 :** Non-Government Non-Financial Public Limited Companies

*(Percentage)*

| | *1990-95* | *1996-2000* | *2001-05* |
|---|---|---|---|
| Gross Profits to Total Net Assets | 10.00 | 8.54 | 8.62 |
| Gross Profits to Sales | 11.80 | 11.90 | 10.72 |
| Profits after Tax Net Worth | 12.04 | 8.68 | 10.14 |
| Tax Provision to Profits before Tax | 29.22 | 27.68 | 3.054 |
| Profits Retained to Profits after Tax | 63.74 | 6.10 | 53.3 |
| Dividends to Net Worth | 4.26 | 3.20 | 4.2 |
| Ordinary Dividends to Ordinary Paid-up Capital | 19.14 | 18.70 | 21.64 |

*Source : RBI Bulletin*, various issues.

Public sector saving will continue to have a significant role in further improvement in the GDS. The CSO's estimates for 2005-06 indicate that these signs are firming up with GDS placed above 32 per cent of GDP and GDI close to 34 per cent (Table 5.10 and Table 5.11). Against the background of these developments, it is plausible that GDS could rise to a range of 34-35 per cent of GDP by 2007-08. With a current account deficit of below 2 per cent of GDP, GDI could rise to a range of 36-37 per cent. Given an incremental capital output ratio—a summary measure of the productivity of capital of around 3.5 to 4.3, sustaining real GDP growth rates in the range of 8 to 9 per cent in the medium term appears eminently realisable.

**Table 5.10 :** Domestic Saving Rates in India

*(Percentage)*

| *Period/Year* | *Household Sector* | *Private Corporate Sector* | *Public Sector* | *Total* |
|---|---|---|---|---|
| | | Saving | | |
| 1970s | 12.2 | 1.6 | 3.7 | 17.5 |
| 1980s | 14.6 | 1.8 | 3.0 | 19.4 |
| 1990s | 18.5 | 3.7 | 1.0 | 23.2 |
| 2000-05 | 22.2 | 4.8 | -0.2 | 26.8 |
| Memo | | | | |
| 2004-05 | 21.6 | 7.1 | 2.4 | 31.1 |
| 2005-06 | 22.3 | 8.1 | 2.0 | 32.4 |

*Source :* RBI (2006) and CSO (2007b).

The Mid-Term appraisal of the Tenth Five Year Plan provides interesting estimates of assessed capacity of potential output in various sectors of the economy. The existence of high excess capacity in agriculture and allied activities, registered manufacturing, electricity, storage, public administration and other services suggests that the focus needs to shift from an 'investment only' approach to a more comprehensive one. In all these sectors capacity utilization has undoubtedly improved but there remains ample scope for high growth. Under capitalisation, which has traditionally characterized the services sector, is beginning to change with the emergence of more organised service activities.

**Table 5.11 :** Domestic Investment Rates in India

*(Percentage)*

| *Period/Year* | *Household Sector* | *Private Corporate Sector* | *Public Sector* | *Total* |
|---|---|---|---|---|
| | | Saving | | |
| 1970s | 7.6 | 2.4 | 8.2 | 17.6 |
| 1980s | 7.8 | 4.2 | 10.0 | 21.2 |
| 1990s | 8.5 | 6.7 | 7.8 | 24.5 |
| 2000-05 | 11.6 | 6.8 | 6.6 | 26.3 |
| Memo | | | | |
| 2004-05 | 11.4 | 9.9 | 7.1 | 31.5 |
| 2005-06 | 10.7 | 12.9 | 7.4 | 33.8 |

*Source :* RBI (2006) and CSO (2007b).

Yet another factor that needs to be taken into account in the assessment of potential growth is the trends in productivity. While the empirical evidence remains somewhat ambiguous, there are indications that trade liberalization has had a positive impact on total factor productivity since 1991. At the sectoral level, there is evidence of improved productivity for exporting sectors relative to non-exporting sectors. Some studies also throw up evidence of an increase in the growth of labour productivity (Goldman Sachs, 2007). Thus, it is clear that micro structural reforms undertaken over the years have enabled continuing productivity gains, particularly in the manufacturing sector, with enhanced access of Indian business to technology, increase competition, greater attention to research and development and other productivity enhancing activities. Widening and deepening of the financial sector, along with improved regulation and supervision, has also contributed to improvement in productivity.

An important challenge for the monetary policy authority is to judge the durability of the recent upsurge in growth. While there is some evidence, as documented, that the acceleration of growth has been supported by structural factors such as improvement in gross domestic saving and investment rates, productivity gains, the demographic dividend and capital accumulation including skill formation, it is important to disentangle the structural and cyclical components underlying the growth process. It is necessary to note that a cyclical upswing is also underlying India since 2003-04 after a prolonged through which began in 1996. There is also some sense that this upturn is part of a synchronized global economic cycle which has seen five consecutive years of accelerated global growth. In the event of a judgment that the current growth momentum is more cyclical than structural, the stance of monetary policy would need to reflect a sensitivity to the inevitability of a downturn. On the other hand, the judgment that structural factors predominate would warrant a different policy stance.

An overriding concern faced by the Reserve Bank is the persistently high growth of bank credit, with attendant worries relating to the quality of bank credit. In this context, the Reserve Bank has consistently emphasized diligent monitoring of the health of credit portfolios and non-performing assets, the need for counter-cyclical provisioning and sensitivity to risks. The sharp increase in credit to sectors such as housing, commercial real estate and retail loans have also been worrisome on account of the vulnerability of banks to credit concentration risks. The important question however relates to the sustainability of the credit expansion and its compatibility with the overall acceleration of growth. Credit penetration in India remains low even by emerging economy standards (Table 5.12). Consequently, growing financial intermediation could possibly be reflected in high credit growth. The Mid-Term Review of October 2006 reported empirical evidence of a structural break in the evolution of the elasticity of bank credit with respect to output with an upward shift since the end of the 1990s. Faster credit growth is also a reflection of the wider dispersal across the economy. Viewed in a holistic perspective, it is difficult to arrive at a clear judgment as to what rate of credit growth is too high is relation to potential growth.

**Table 5.12:** Cross Country Comparisons of Bank Credit Indicators

*(Percentage)*

| | *Average Growth Rate (Real)* | | *Domestic Credit as % of GDP* | | *Real Bank Credit Growth to Private Sector* | | |
|---|---|---|---|---|---|---|---|
| | *1995-99* | *2000-04* | *1999* | *2005* | *1995-99* | *2000-04* | *2005* |
| 1. Latin America | 3.6 | 4.5 | 42 | 45 | -0.2 | -1.1 | 18.4 |
| 2. China | 17.1 | 13.3 | 130 | 169 | 16.0 | 12.5 | 9.4 |
| 3. India | 6.1 | 14.6 | 51 | 65 | 6.9 | 13.5 | 30.0 |
| 4. Hong Kong SAR, Singapore | 1.4 | 3.4 | 130 | 122 | 0.6 | 2.2 | -3.2 |
| 5. Other Asia | -0.3 | 4.7 | 89 | 80 | 4.0 | 5.9 | 8.2 |
| 6. Central Europe | 9.6 | 8.1 | 40 | 42 | 8.8 | 3.8 | 8.0 |
| Total | 7.8 | 9.6 | 78 | 92 | 6.9 | 8.9 | 15.8 |
| Memo United States | 10.1 | 3.3 | 80 | 92 | 5.6 | 5.1 | 10.9 |

*Source:* Mohanty *et al* (2006).

In the presence of the kind of structural changes that I have described above, even when the macro availability of resources is adequate to fund the increase in demand arising from both consumption and investment, there could be micro imbalances that lead to observation of excess demand and overheating. It is in this context that monetary management has to also look at imbalances that could be transitional. The challenge before us at the present time is to manage the transition to a higher growth path, in the presence of some structural rigidities, in such a way that actual inflation and inflation expectations are contained and do not become mutually reinforcing.

Our assessment is that while expansion of capacity is underway, the realization, particularly in sectors like infrastructure could be constrained over the next two years. Indeed, the difficulties with improving the supply response are more complex and challenging than aggregate demand management. Supply management will need to encompass wide areas including labour markets, land laws and the content of regulation in each sector, as long as supply response are less than elastic, they could show up as excess demand, causing inflationary pressures and raising inflation expectations. To reiterate, managing structural change while keeping inflation low without dampening the growth momentum is the quintessential challenge to monetary policy in the period ahead.

Illustratively, given the growth in consumption demand, rising incomes and high growth in sectors such as information technology (IT), it is not surprising that there is a huge actual demand for housing, retail activity and office space from the burgeoning services sector. It is also not surprising that there would be associated problems on the supply side including availability of land, zoning and other land regulations, and social concerns about the conversion of land from agricultural purposes to other uses, therefore, monetary policy has to be creative in addressing these problems in a non-disruptive manner. It is in this context that prudential and other measures such as provisioning and risk weights on bank loans to specific sectors are being used so as to enhance the sensitivity to risks emanating from these sectors rather than standard monetary policy responses that address aggregate demand. The task before monetary policy is thus rendered complex, requiring that both macro issues and sectoral problems be addressed in a specific manner.

## The Monetary Policy Response

It is well known that monetary policy operates cumulatively with lags that can range between 12 to 18 months, depending on the specifics of the economy. It is in this context that beginning in mid 2003, the Reserve Bank started a graduated withdrawal of accommodation. Since September, 2004 repo/ reverse repo rates have been increased by 125/150 basis points, the CRR has been raised by 100 points, risk weights have been raised in the case of housing loans (from 50 to 75 per cent), commercial real estate (100 to 150 per cent) and consumer credit (from 100 to 125 per cent) and general provisioning requirement for standard advances in specific sectors has been raised to 1.0 per cent of standard advances.

At the time of the Third Quarter Review, the combination of macroeconomic developments embodied in high growth and firming inflation, escalating asset prices and the enduring strength of capital flows, a three-pronged approach was envisaged. A measured increase in policy interest rates to assuage demand pressures was considered necessary in conjunction with some modulation of capital flows and the need to fortify banks' balance sheets by precautionary provisioning and a greater sensitivity to underlying risks. Accordingly, in the Third Quarter Review, it was decided to increase the fixed repo rate under the Liquidity Adjustment Facility (LAF) of the Reserve Bank by 25 basis points to 7.50 per cent. The LAF reverse repo rate, the bank rate and the cash reserve ratio were kept unchanged. Furthermore, the provisioning requirement in respect of standard assets in the real estate sector, outstanding credit card receivables, loans and advances qualifying as capital market exposure, personal loans and systemically important non-deposit taking Non-Banking Financial Companies (NBFCs) was raised to 2 per cent. Risk weights for banks' exposure to such NBFCs was increased from 100 to 125 per cent. Interest rates on non-resident deposit schemes, which have been recording sizeable inflows, were reduced by 50 basis points for rupee deposits and by 25 basis points for foreign currency deposits. Banks were also restrained from granting fresh loans in excess of Rs. 20 lakhs against non-resident deposits.

The Reserve Bank has indicated that over the remaining part of the year, liquidity management would receive the highest priority. All policy instruments would be deployed to ensure appropriate modulation of liquidity. The stance of monetary policy was set out as:

- To reinforce the emphasis on price stability and well-anchored inflation expectations while ensuring a monetary and interest rate environment that supports export and investment demand in the economy so as to enable continuation of the growth momentum.
- To re-emphasis credit quality and orderly conditions in financial markets for securing macroeconomic and, in particular, financial stability while simultaneously pursuing greater credit penetration and financial inclusion.
- To respond swiftly with all possible measures as appropriate to the evolving global and domestic situation impinging on inflation expectations and the growth momentum.

It is important to note that monetary policy authorities all over the world are expressing similar sentiments in terms of an uncertain outlook, concerns about persistent underlying inflation and some nervousness about visitation of financial volatility. Accordingly, several central banks have shown a readiness to respond asymmetrically to any sings of price and financial instability. The ECB, the Bank of England, the Reserve Bank of Australia, the People's Bank of China and the Bank of Korea raised policy rates. In order to contain financial market volatility arising from large liquidity flows, several central banks have tended to tighten monetary policy, even at relatively low current inflation rates, as in Thailand, Turkey, Saudi Arabia and Iceland. On the other hand, some central banks have paused in their policy cycles, particularly the US Fed, the Bank of Canada, the Bank of Japan, Bank Negara Malaysia and the Banco de Mexico. Some other central banks have cut back their policy rates in recent months.

In India, it is recognised that inflation is a tax on the poor against which there are no hedges available. Consequently, ensuring price stability is a societal compulsion to which monetary policy as a arm of public policy must be committed. The measures taken in the Third Quarter Review needs to be seen as sustaining and supporting the growth process while ensuring a minimum social insurance by delivery of a tolerable rate of inflation.

## Banking in the Hinterland

Rural banking has great potential if banks adopt appropriate approach and suitable strategies-scale up to their business levels, achieve capacity utilisation and devise innovative ways to cater to the typical needs of the vast rural sectors.

We shall discuss it into three parts: (i) the rural urban divide in banking, (ii) important changes that are happening in the rural sector, and (iii) strategy for banking facilities/ development in the hinterland.

## The Rural Urban Divide

Analyses of certain indicators of banking penetration of scheduled commercial banks in the country, including RRBs, amply testify to the rural urban divide existing in their operations/business, as will be seen from the following:

## Average Population Per Branch Office (APPBO)

The average population served per branch office is an important indicator of banking penetration. The trend in this indicator ever since the last decade is as under (Table 5.13):

**Table 5.13 :** Average Population Per Branch Office

| | *1991* | *2001* | *2005* |
|---|---|---|---|
| Population per Branch | 13711 | 15209 | 15680 |
| Population per Rural Branch | 13462 | 15667 | 16650 |
| Population per Urban Branch | 14484 | 14137 | 13619 |

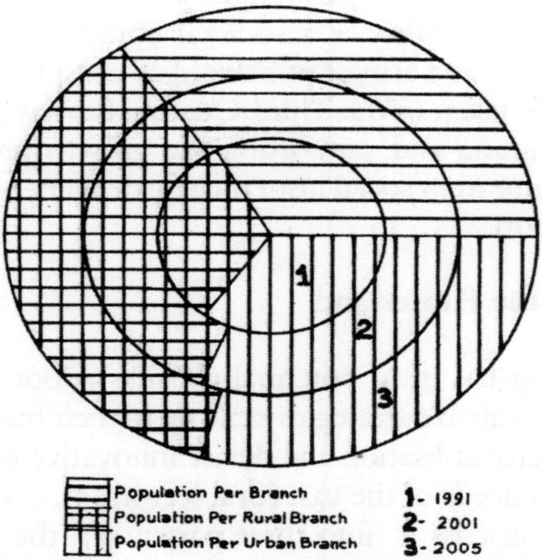


**Fig. 5.5 :** Average Population Per Branch Office

While the population per branch has decreased for urban areas, the same has increased for rural areas indicating that branch expansion has not kept pace with the population increase in the rural area.

## Number of Accounts Per 1000 Population

The number of deposit (current plus savings) and credit accounts per thousand population is given below:

**Table 5.14 :** Number of Accounts Per 1000 Population (March 2005)

| *Region* | *Deposit (C+S) Accounts* | | *Credit Accounts* | |
|---|---|---|---|---|
| | *Rural* | *Urban* | *Rural* | *Urban* |
| Northern Region | 338 | 652 | 55 | 71 |
| North Eastern Region | 186 | 281 | 35 | 41 |
| Eastern Region | 185 | 413 | 45 | 47 |
| Central Region | 242 | 375 | 45 | 49 |
| Western Region | 263 | 526 | 46 | 121 |
| Southern Region | 393 | 486 | 436 | 185 |
| All India | 270 | 483 | 64 | 104 |

C+S = Current + Savings.
*Source*: BSR 2005.

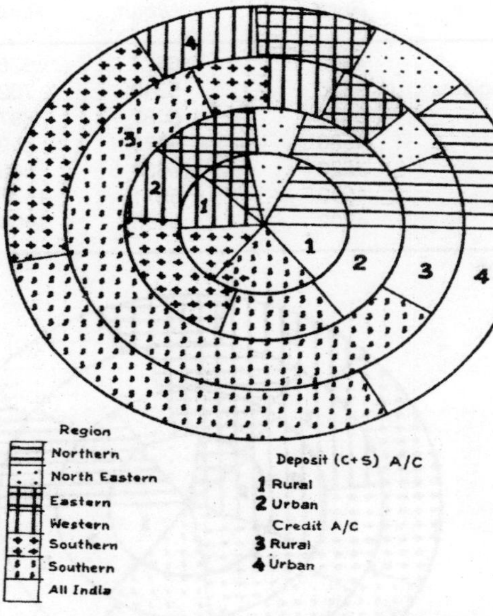


**Fig. 5.6 :** Number of Accounts Per 1000 Population (March 2005)

It is seen that the deposits (current plus savings) accounts per 1000 population in the rural areas as a whole, is about 60 per cent of the urban areas. North Eastern States, Orissa, Bihar and Chattisgarh have particularly low ratio. Similar position is generally evident even in terms of credit accounts per 1000 population. However, Southern states are relatively better off in this regard (Table 5.14: Annex 1 and Annex 2).

## Number of Account Per Branch

The number of deposit and credit accounts per branch in the rural areas is generally lower than the position in urban areas as shown under (Table 5.15):

**Table 5.15:** Region-wise No. of Accounts (March 2005)

| *Region* | *Deposit (C+S) Accounts* | | *Credit Accounts* | |
|---|---|---|---|---|
| | *Rural* | *Urban* | *Rural* | *Urban* |
| Northern Region | 4130 | 6677 | 675 | 771 |
| North Eastern Region | 3716 | 5340 | 702 | 781 |
| Eastern Region | 3676 | 6087 | 887 | 693 |
| Central Region | 4586 | 6075 | 859 | 797 |
| Western Region | 3826 | 6630 | 663 | 1530 |
| Southern Region | 4549 | 5571 | 1577 | 2121 |
| All India | 4202 | 6155 | 1000 | 1321 |

*Source* : BSR 2005.

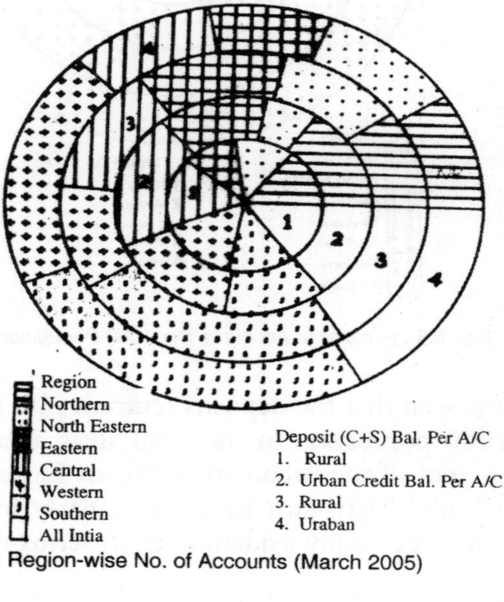


**Fig. 5.7 :** Region-wise No. of Accounts (March 2005)

## Outstanding Balances Per Branch

The deposits and credit outstanding per branch also reflect the rural urban divide. It is seen that deposits per branch in the rural areas is far lower than that in the urban areas, notably states in the North East, Northern and Western regions. In terms of credit per branch also, the difference is more pronounced in Northern and Western regions (Table 5.16).

**Table 5.16 :** Region-wise Size of Deposits and Credits (March 2005)

| *Region* | *Deposit (C+S) per Branch* | | *Credit per Branch* | |
|---|---|---|---|---|
| | *Rural* | *Urban* | *Rural* | *Urban* |
| Northern Region | 6.43 | 25.22 | 7.19 | 46.99 |
| North Eastern Region | 5.41 | 21.03 | 4.99 | 13.80 |
| Eastern Region | 4.99 | 18.80 | 3.99 | 23.62 |
| Central Region | 5.26 | 15.40 | 4.51 | 15.15 |
| Western Region | 4.67 | 26.51 | 7.72 | 63.77 |
| Southern Region | 4.01 | 14.41 | 8.73 | 32.68 |
| All India | 4.98 | 19.92 | 6.37 | 37.94 |

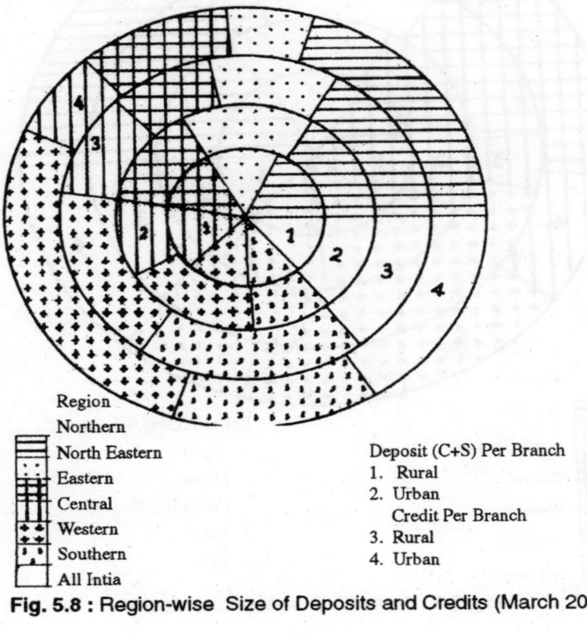


**Fig. 5.8 :** Region-wise Size of Deposits and Credits (March 2005)

## Outstanding Balances Per Account

The outstanding balances per account, both deposit as well as credit, reveals the much larger values in urban areas as evident at Table 5.17.

**Table 5.17 :** Size of Accounts (March 2005)

| *Region* | *Deposit (C+S) per A/C* | | *Credit per A/C* | |
|---|---|---|---|---|
| | *Rural* | *Urban* | *Rural* | *Urban* |
| Northern Region | 15.56 | 37.78 | 106.46 | 609.72 |
| North Eastern Region | 14.56 | 39.38 | 70.59 | 176.85 |
| Eastern Region | 13.57 | 30.88 | 44.58 | 341.00 |
| Central Region | 11.46 | 25.35 | 52.49 | 190.06 |
| Western Region | 12.19 | 39.99 | 116.42 | 416.71 |
| Southern Region | 8.82 | 25.87 | 55.39 | 154.08 |
| All India | 11.84 | 32.36 | 63.74 | 287.91 |

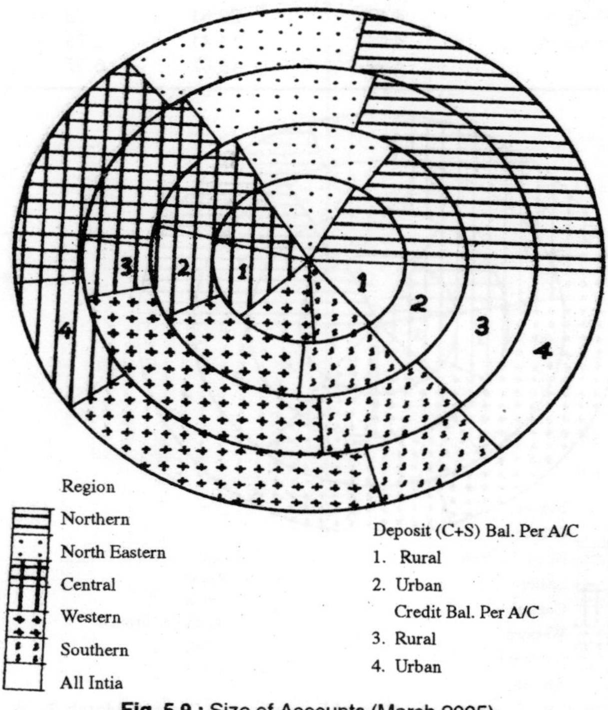


**Fig. 5.9 :** Size of Accounts (March 2005)

The average size of a deposit account in the rural areas is about one-third the size in urban areas and ranged from about Rs. 7,000 (in Andhra) to about Rs. 17,000 (in Punjab). The divide is as expected sharper in terms of Credit per account. The average credit account in rural areas ranged from Rs. 19,000 (in Tripura) to Rs. 1.31 lakh (in Haryana).

## Share of Different Credit Agencies in the Total Cash Dues of Households

The share of different agencies in the total cash dues of rural and urban households reveals the extent of penetration of formal financial sources.

This table clearly shows that the coverage of banks in the rural areas has fallen from 64 to 57 per cent while, significantly, the share of money lenders has increased from 17.5 to 29.6 per cent in these areas (Table 5.18).

**Table 5.18 :** Share of Different Agencies in Outstanding Debt of Households

*(Share in percentage)*

| *Credit Agencies* | *Rural Households* | | | *Urban Households* | | |
|---|---|---|---|---|---|---|
| | *1981* | *1991* | *2002* | *1981* | *1991* | *2002* |
| **Institutional of which** | **61.2** | **64.0** | **57.1** | **60.0** | **72.0** | **75.1** |
| Co-operative Soc/Bank | " | 21.6 | 27.3 | " | 17.2 | 20.5 |
| Commercial Banks | " | 33.7 | 24.5 | " | 21.6 | 29.7 |
| Government | " | 6.1 | 2.3 | " | 11.1 | 7.6 |
| **Non-Institutional of which** | **38.8** | **36.0** | **42.9** | **40.0** | **28.0** | **24.9** |
| Moneylenders* | " | 17.5 | 29.6 | " | 10.2 | 14.1 |
| **Total** | **100** | **100** | **100** | **100** | **100** | **100** |

* The category of moneylenders is the sum of agricultural moneylender and professional moneylender.

$ Cultivator households is defined as all rural households operating at least 0.002 hectare of land during the last 365 days preceding the date of survey.

*Source:* Computed from the various decadal All India debt and Investment Surveys.

## The Rural Sector Some Interesting Pointers

We would like to briefly dwell upon some facts, which bring home the potential of rural sector:

- The savings rate has increased to nearly 31 per cent in the recent period. Remittances from urban to rural areas are becoming more significant as migration increases. The need for banking facilities-savings, remittances and credit-has increased in rural areas.
- The share of agriculture in GDP has fallen from 43 per cent in 1970s to 20 per cent currently: within this, the share of foodgrains and cereals has declined from 31.7 to 240.1 per cent and that of commercial crops increased. Within the agricultural sector, the share of fishing and livestock has gone up from 20.3 to 29.3 per cent. Agriculture is getting increasingly diversified as floriculture, horticulture and other value added activities gain importance.
- The proportion of rural households, described as low income by National Council of Applied Economic Research (NCAER), has gone down from two third in early 1990 to 25 per cent currently and those with middle income from one third to 70 per cent. This represents increase of 50 million middle income households in rural areas.
- Retail credit has grown in the last four years by nearly 50 per cent per annum mostly at urban centres. As incomes increase, there is growing demand for retail credit in rural areas that is perhaps being met by the informal sector. Anecdotal evidence suggests that moneylenders in rural areas face more competition from other moneylenders rather than from the banks.
- With the growing rural connectivity and tele-density, a host of non-farm activities are mushrooming in the rural sector. Currently, the rural market accounts for 53 per cent of the Fast Moving Consumer Goods (FMCG) and

59 per cent of the durable market in India. The rural consumers represent more than 50 per cent of the country's 'consuming classes'.

## The Way Forward—Some Thoughts

Having discussed the rural urban divide in banking and the potential in rural banking, the question that remains to be addressed is – how can banks meet the challenges of banking in the hinterland?

(i) To start with, we believe, fuller utilization of existing capacity can itself given huge dividends. Given the existing number of nearly 48,000 rural and semi-urban branches, an increase of loans by rupees one crore per branch could imply additional profits of about Rs. 480 crore to the banking system.

(ii) Currently each rural branch services only around 1000 loan accounts. If we assume that a bank branch can serve at least 3000 households, it would imply at the minimum tripling of the business at rural branches. This might require redeployment and some increase in staff, especially field staff, and would be more than worth the effort considering the increase in business and profitability that it would result in.

(iii) Banks would need to decide the kind of delivery channels require for meeting the banking and remittance needs of the rural population. Today the branch is not the only way of delivering banking services. All options such a mobile and satellite offices, rural ATMs, smart card and mobile phone based banking, use of intermediaries including SHGs, including post offices need to be explored for penetrating into the rural markets. Several banks have tie-up arrangements with corporates engaged in contract farming. Information Technology solutions can take banking to the remotest corner and cut costs apart from providing valuable databases from furthering business strategies. Whatever be the mode of penetration, it is clear that unless there are well thought out strategies for marketing banking services in the hinterland, banks will be missing emerging opportunities. As mentioned earlier 50 million households in rural areas have moved from low income to high income giving rise to equal number of potentially bankable households. To look at the scope for branch banking and provision of banking services through other delivery channels in rural areas, banks can make use of the research already available on the monthly per capita expenditure centre-wise and district-wise, corroborated by data on consumption patterns for FMCG and mobile phones as also other indicators of expenditure patterns.

(iv) Banks need to have appropriate strategies for rural banking. Rural clientele need saving, remittances, loan and insurance product. When banks think of agricultural credit they generally think of crop loans especially, food crops. The needs of agriculture are, however, getting diversified and the required scale of finance is increasing. There is much more demand for allied activities such as dairy, fishing and livestock, cash crops, besides ancillary activities such as sorting, grading, processing, packaging and transporting to final destinations and markets. Other service sector activities that spin-off the main activities are also growing. This is giving rise to additional credit demand from a variety of new enterprises, besides demand for retail and consumer credit. Are banks geared for the surging credit demand in the rural areas in all sector, particularly allied agriculture and services sector?

The strategies of banks will need to focus on the following:

## Developing Products

A uniform banking/financial product for the entire country would obviously not work. Products need to be designed and packaged taking into account local culture, customs, language, literacy and social indicators. Also, rural households need to be provided credit in a composite way covering all-their needs, including life-cycle needs; the traditional crop loans, term loans, housing loans, consumption loans bouquet may not work. Regional offices of banks may need to be delegated with appropriate powers for product design, while ensuring consistency with Board policies. Banks need to look at the overall cash flow of rural households and fix general credit limits, which could be scaled up depending on new/additional activities taken up.

## Creating Awareness and Brand Building

Banks need to consciously evolve strategies for financial education in the rural areas. Products developed for the region will need to be actively marketed in a responsible and effective manner, with top priority at all times being accorded to transparency, customer education and satisfaction.

## Having the Right Staff for Marketing Products

In rural lending there is an imperative need for the marketing staff to be knowledgeable about agricultural practices and operations, besides being well acquainted with the features of the products and their suitability to the targeted category of customer. In a sense, providing financial services will also involve providing extension services as a risk litigant. Hence, banks will need proactive technical officers who can not only provide such services, but also train their field staff. Another very important requirement is relationship management in terms of face-to-face familiarity and continuity of contact. Surely, it is not without reason that the rural folk are comfortable with persons like the postmen and even the local moneylender, with whom they have occasion to regularly interact. Banks would do well to address this need for building up a relationship and rapport with the rural clientele.

## Use of Information Technology (IT)

There are a variety of ways in which IT can be used by banks.

Delivery of banking services through IT based solutions, such as mobile phones and smart cards, while keeping costs low, is one huge opportunity for increasing outreach afforded by modern technology that is rapidly innovating. Other uses of IT are in credit risk management and pricing, which require maintaining a comprehensive computerized data base – this can be used for a variety of purposes, such as marketing, credit scoring, pricing, credit monitoring including rating migration and devising appropriate internal control system, etc. There is clearly a need to have credit country: the huge externalities associate with having comprehensive credit records can be derived for more efficient financial intermediation. With appropriate IT solutions in place and suitable field staff, banks can also provide market insurance and capital market products for increasing their non funded business.

## Developing and Using Risk Mitigants

The three important risks identified in agricultural lending are yield risk (or input output risk), calamity risk and price risk. Banks will need to aim at minimizing these risks if they have to deliver affordable credit to agriculture. Extension work, including proper advice on use of fertilizer and pesticides, ensuring quality seeds and inputs are activities that minimize yield risk. Enterprises providing such services would need to be supported by banks and actively encouraged. Calamity risk minimisation involves insurance of crops and assets, including of livestock/cattle and fisheries. While restructuring of loans can provide more time for repayment, repeated rescheduling could lead to installments ballooning beyond the repayment capacity. Banks will have to evolve policies to address this issue while providing vulnerable groups opportunities to engage in activities that supplement the household income at times of natural calamities. Development of appropriately priced insurance products is obviously a challenge especially if such insurance has to be affordable and sustainable. Price risk in agriculture is inherent, having regard to the nature of agricultural operations where supply can not responds to prices immediately.

Hence, price support policies have been followed over the years. A more recent development is the future markets, which can provide opportunity to hedge risks. However, the players in these markets are mostly traders and speculators. There is a need to find ways in which commodity markets can be used to provide price support to farmers.

## Micro Finance

A separate strategy for micro finance may have to be evolved, as this involves providing low income families with access to banking. Invariably banks have found it advantageous to partner with community based organisations and NGOs working in the area for micro-finance. Promoting SHGs, nurturing them and transforming them from micro-finance to micro enterprise is something many banks are already engaged in Banks could explore the possibilities of working with the State Governments by offering them efficient technology solutions, such as smart cards for distribution of budgeted allocations for NREGP, pension payments and various other social sector expenditures. As some of your may be aware, a pilot project is under way in Andhra Pradesh (AP), where the AP government will tie up with banks, who will offer smart cards to BPL families/pension recipients/NREGP workers for disbursements of wages, pensions and other benefits. These smart cards can be operated at village level through village organisations-federated SHGs registered as cooperatives—that are eligible to be used as business correspondents by banks. It is expected that as the SHG members get used to the smart cards, there will be return flow of funds as they use their bank accounts for savings. The cards could also be used as normal debit cards at merchant establishments.

## Regional Rural Bank (RRBs) as Partners

One in every three rural/semi-urban branch in the country is an RRB branch. Moreover, the staff members of RRBs belong to the region and have knowledge of local language and customers.

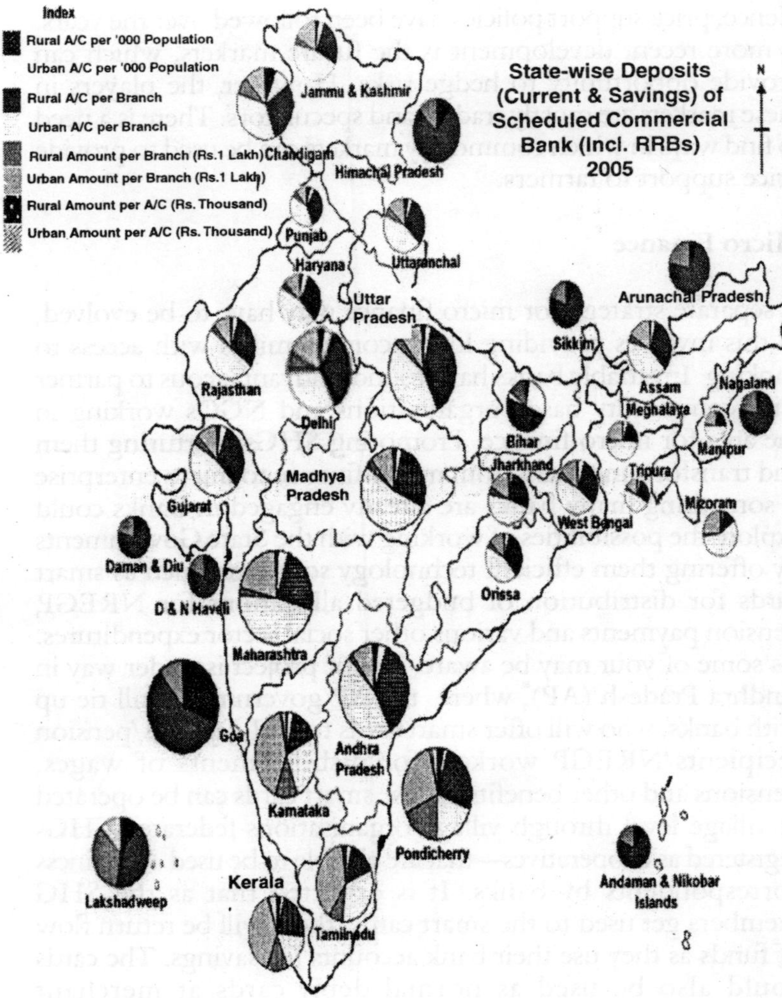


There are significant strengths and need to be leveraged by sponsor banks, who should view RRBs as their partners in rural banking. The initial costs for up scaling technology and skills in the RRBs will be amply rewarded by the benefits that would accrue in due course.

## Conclusion

Competition in urban areas is squeezing bank margins. Even though agriculture contributes only 20 per cent of GDP, the rural population constitutes 70 per cent of population and as reported accounts for 60 per cent of consumer durable market. This implies that there is an untapped business potential for aggressive banking in the rural areas. The challenge lies in locating these services through appropriate delivery channel and products. We are sure that the banks with their extensive network of branches in the rural areas will be able to leverage there presence and meet these challenges.

Our thanks to the Indian Banks Association and Rural Marketing Agencies Association of India for giving this opportunity for delivering the keynote address at this conference. We are sure that the day's deliberations will bring new insights to banking in the hinterland. We wish the conference every success.

***ANNEX-1***

**STATE-WISE DEPOSITS (CURRENT & SAVINGS) OF SCHEDULED COMMERCIAL BANKS (INCL. RRBS)**

| *Region/State* | *A/C per '000 population* | | *A/C per Branch* | | *Amt per Branch (Rs. Lakh)* | | *Amount per A/C (Rs. Thousand)* | |
|---|---|---|---|---|---|---|---|---|
| | *Rural* | *Urban* | *Rural* | *Urban* | *Rural* | *Urban* | *Rural* | *Urban* |
| **Northern Region** | **338.3** | **652** | **4130.3** | **6677** | **642.6** | **2522.4** | **15.6** | **37.78** |
| Haryana | 365.7 | 589 | 4752.0 | 6668 | 727.7 | 1749.2 | 15.3 | - |
| Himachal Pradesh | 487.8 | - | 3313.9 | - | 569.3 | - | 17.2 | |
| Jammu & Kashmir | 315.3 | 480 | 3523.6 | 6076 | 742.6 | 2116.5 | 21.1 | 34.83 |
| Punjab | 622.6 | 622 | 5290.5 | 5853 | 904.2 | 1463.9 | 17.1 | 25.01 |
| Rajasthan | 198.5 | 376 | 3287.3 | 5727 | 365.1 | 1241.3 | 11.1 | 21.68 |
| Chandigarh | 1006.7 | 1411 | 4416.1 | 5382 | 1215.2 | 1805.1 | 27.5 | 33.54 |
| Delhi | 720.7 | 1001 | 8570.0 | 7869 | 2034.2 | 4171.2 | 23.7 | 53.01 |
| **North Eastern Region** | **186.0** | **281** | **3716.3** | **5340** | **541.2** | **2102.7** | **14.6** | **39.38** |
| Arunachal Pradesh | 249.3 | 0 | 3184.4 | - | 974.9 | - | 3.6 | - |
| Assam | 197.7 | 333 | 4320.8 | 5427 | 541.9 | 2122.8 | 12.5 | 39.12 |
| Manipur | 71.6 | 203 | 2368.0 | 5044 | 321.2 | 2164.2 | 13.6 | 42.90 |
| Meghalaya | 170.6 | 380 | 2121.9 | 4776 | 428.3 | 2241.7 | 20.2 | 46.94 |
| Mizoram | 185.4 | 140 | 1209.3 | 5594 | 236.8 | 2384.4 | 19.6 | 42.62 |
| Nagaland | 133.7 | 0 | 2996.4 | - | 876.1 | - | 29.2 | - |
| Tripura | 184.2 | 365 | 3251.5 | 5510 | 509.6 | 1721.9 | 15.7 | 31.25 |
| **Eastern Region** | **185.2** | **413** | **3676.2** | **6087** | **498.8** | **1879.6** | **13.6** | **30.88** |
| Bihar | 15..0 | 341 | 3626.6 | 6234 | 483.5 | 1898.9 | 13.3 | 30.46 |
| Jharkhand | 222.1 | 282 | 3700.3 | 6623 | 695.6 | 2247.6 | 18.8 | 33.93 |
| Orissa | 189.5 | 277 | 3055.3 | 4133 | 383.5 | 1181.6 | 12.6 | 28.59 |
| Sikkim | 296.4 | 0 | 2589.7 | - | 684.2 | - | 26.4 | - |
| West Bengal | 205.7 | 511 | 4156.5 | 6372 | 497.2 | 1965.3 | 12.0 | 30.84 |
| A & N Islanc | 574.6 | 0 | 4176.6 | - | 1075.8 | - | 25.8 | - |
| **Central Region** | **241.8** | **375** | **4586.0** | **6075** | **525.7** | **1540.0** | **11.5** | **25.35** |
| Chattisgarh | 151.4 | 286 | 2968.3 | 5548 | 481.1 | 1844.9 | 16.2 | 33.25 |
| Madhya Pradesh | 174.7 | 315 | 2901.5 | 5675 | 368.2 | 1283.8 | 12.7 | 22.62 |

*(Contd...)*

**Annex-1:** *(Contd...)*

| | | | | | | | | |
|---|---|---|---|---|---|---|---|---|
| Uttar Pradesh | 266.2 | 412 | 5625.4 | 6323 | 579.0 | 1606.4 | 10.3 | 25.41 |
| Uttaranchal | 440.8 | 405 | 3763.3 | 5528 | 695.9 | 1629.4 | 18.5 | 29.48 |
| **Western Region** | **263.3** | **526** | **3826.4** | **6630** | **466.5** | **2651.3** | **12.2** | **39.99** |
| Goa | 2587.0 | 0 | 4976.0 | - | 930.7 | - | 18.7 | - |
| Gujarat | 294.8 | 448 | 3954.2 | 5861 | 528.2 | 1530.6 | 13.4 | 26.12 |
| Maharashtra | 215.2 | 572 | 3591.6 | 6960 | 362.9 | 3131.6 | 10.1 | 45.00 |
| D & N Haveli | 555.7 | 0 | 7871.8 | - | 1889.6 | - | 24.0 | - |
| Daman & Diu | 906.2 | 0 | 5705.5 | - | 1728.9 | - | 30.3 | - |
| **Southern Region** | **392.8** | **486** | **4548.7** | **5571** | **401.3** | **1441.4** | **8.8** | **25.87** |
| Andhra Pradesh | 309.6 | 518 | 4651.1 | 5764 | 324.8 | 1336.6 | 7.0 | 23.19 |
| Karnataka | 350.1 | 547 | 3738.0 | 52.88 | 324.2 | 1628.8 | 8.7 | 30.80 |
| Kerala | 683.1 | 427 | 5593.0 | 4835 | 548.0 | 985.6 | 9.8 | 20.38 |
| Tamil Nadu | 377.3 | 439 | 4406.1 | 5882 | 431.0 | 1524.5 | 9.8 | 25.92 |
| Lakshadweep | 729.7 | 0 | 2727.9 | - | 835.8 | - | 30.6 | - |
| Pondicherry | 792.7 | 529 | 6295.1 | 6997 | 843.0 | 1629.7 | 13.4 | 23.29 |
| **All India** | **269.6** | **483** | **4201.8** | **6155** | **497.6** | **1992.0** | **11.8** | **32.36** |

*Source:* Banking Statistical Returns, Reserve Bank of India, 2005.

## *ANNEX-2*

### STATE-WISE OUTSTANDING CREDIT OF SCHEDULED COMMERCIAL BANK (INCL. RRBS)

| *Region/State* | *A/C per '000 Population* | | *A/C per Branch* | | *Amt per Branch (Rs. Lakh)* | | *Amount per A/C (Rs. Thousand)* | |
|---|---|---|---|---|---|---|---|---|
| | *Rural* | *Urban* | *Rural* | *Urban* | *Rural* | *Urban* | *Rural* | *Urban* |
| **Northern Region** | **55.29** | **75.26** | **675.03** | **770.76** | **718.63** | **4699.53** | **106.46** | **609.72** |
| Haryana | 59.19 | 54.57 | 769.04 | 617.90 | 1011.18 | 2144.36 | 131.49 | 347.04 |
| Himachal Pradesh | 74.25 | - | 504.42 | - | 776.24 | - | 153.89 | - |
| Jammu & Kashmir | 35.33 | 57.23 | 394.79 | 724.17 | 431.56 | 2806.67 | 109.32 | 387.57 |
| Punjab | 76.12 | 60.57 | 646.88 | 570.10 | 759.66 | 2091.44 | 117.44 | 366.86 |
| Rajasthan | 47.75 | 46.54 | 790.63 | 708.09 | 517.97 | 2214.74 | 65.51 | 312.78 |

**Annex-2:** *(Contd...)*

| | | | | | | | | |
|---|---|---|---|---|---|---|---|---|
| Chandigarh | 136.02 | 172.08 | 596.67 | 656.50 | 2907.33 | 5390.61 | 487.26 | 821.12 |
| Delhi | 27.51 | 125.06 | 327.10 | 983.02 | 3332.30 | 8408.63 | 1018.74 | 855.39 |
| **North Eastern Region** | **35.16** | **41.04** | **702.48** | **780.58** | **495.90** | **1380.43** | **70.59** | **176.85** |
| Arunachal Pradesh | 40.88 | - | 522.13 | - | 529.49 | - | 101.41 | - |
| Assam | 30.28 | 47.72 | 661.70 | 777.58 | 461.82 | 1222.11 | 69.79 | 157.17 |
| Manipur | 15.57 | 38.85 | 514.76 | 963.57 | 320.60 | 1077.70 | 62.28 | 111.84 |
| Meghalaya | 41.04 | 51.15 | 510.54 | 643.08 | 1086.77 | 2798.33 | 212.87 | 435.14 |
| Mizoram | 56.79 | 29.89 | 370.39 | 1198.36 | 353.58 | 2020.55 | 95.46 | 168.61 |
| Nagaland | 24.44 | - | 547.73 | - | 417.74 | - | 76.27 | - |
| Tripura | 88.42 | 45.79 | 1561.01 | 690.83 | 303.29 | 875.14 | 19.43 | 126.68 |
| **Eastern Region** | **44.70** | **46.96** | **887.50** | **692.80** | **395.64** | **2362.43** | **44.58** | **341.00** |
| Bihar | 31.98 | 38.21 | 748.31 | 698.17 | 278.22 | 851.82 | 37.18 | 122.01 |
| Jharkhand | 45.54 | 28.29 | 758.66 | 664.25 | 308.94 | 1773.78 | 4.072 | 267.03 |
| Orissa | 71.76 | 66.03 | 1156.80 | 983.51 | 655.67 | 1949.31 | 56.68 | 198.20 |
| Sikkim | 61.66 | - | 538.65 | - | 672.55 | - | 124.86 | - |
| West Bengal | 45.86 | 51.02 | 926.71 | 635.97 | 375.96 | 2927.89 | 40.57 | 460.38 |
| A & N Island | 76.26 | - | 554.30 | - | 966.39 | - | 174.34 | - |
| **Central Region** | **45.26** | **49.23** | **858.50** | **797.14** | **450.66** | **1515.00** | **52.49** | **190.06** |
| Chattisgarh | 33.27 | 34.36 | 652.07 | 667.24 | 399.96 | 2261.93 | 61.34 | 339.06 |
| Madhya Pradesh | 42.06 | 55.30 | 698.56 | 996.06 | 497.44 | 1800.58 | 71.21 | 180.77 |
| Uttar Pradesh | 46.71 | 48.19 | 986.95 | 739.25 | 433.99 | 1340.68 | 43.97 | 181.36 |
| Uttaranchal | 69.16 | 49.34 | 590.47 | 673.42 | 480.46 | 1366.14 | 81.37 | 202.94 |
| **Western Region** | **45.61** | **121.36** | **662.81** | **1530.40** | **771.65** | **6377.29** | **116.42** | **416.71** |
| Goa | 218.78 | - | 420.82 | - | 1004.27 | - | 238.65 | - |
| Gujarat | 49.59 | 41.57 | 665.26 | 544.04 | 748.07 | 2894.39 | 112.45 | 532.01 |
| Maharashtra | 41.25 | 160.42 | 688.44 | 1953.17 | 747.42 | 7870.11 | 108.57 | 402.94 |
| D & N Haveli | 35.26 | - | 499.50 | - | 3370.58 | - | 674.79 | - |
| Daman & Diu | 61.38 | - | 386.44 | - | 2258.00 | - | 584.31 | - |
| **Southern Region** | **136.16** | **185.07** | **1576.88** | **2121.00** | **873.41** | **3267.98** | **55.39** | **154.08** |
| Andhra Pradesh | 135.11 | 93.22 | 2044.76 | 1037.07 | 926.50 | 2593.53 | 45.31 | 250.08 |

**Annex-2:** *(Contd...)*

| | | | | | | | | |
|---|---|---|---|---|---|---|---|---|
| Karnataka | 103.11 | 203.77 | 1100.83 | 1970.65 | 873.75 | 3138.45 | 79.37 | 159.26 |
| Kerala | 166.81 | 87.81 | 1365.75 | 994.38 | 780.39 | 2362.63 | 57.14 | 237.60 |
| Tamil Nadu | 148.10 | 273.86 | 1729.47 | 3666.07 | 897.28 | 4360.05 | 51.88 | 118.93 |
| Lakshadweep | 78.10 | - | 291.89 | - | 248.22 | - | 85.04 | - |
| Pondicherry | 187.07 | 90.17 | 1485.62 | 1192.90 | 1015.34 | 1667.06 | 68.35 | 139.75 |
| **All India** | **64.16** | **103.62** | **999.94** | **1320.99** | **637.41** | **3793.74** | **63.74** | **287.19** |

*Source:* Banking Statistical Returns, Reserve Bank of India, 2005.

# 6 FISCAL POLICY AND ECONOMIC GROWTH

The Eighties were a period of buoyant economic performance, the average growth rate for the decade being higher than that for any past decade.[1] Yet, when oil prices doubled within a few weeks following the Iraqi invasion of Kuwait in August 1990, the country very quickly slipped into the worst economic crisis that it has experienced since the mid-Sixties. This apparent paradox could not, however, have come as a surprise to anyone who was familiar with the fragility of the underlying fiscal condition.

## The Emergence of a Fiscal Imbalance

The state-dominated, heavy industries-based, Nehru-Mahalanobis strategy of protected industrialization, which India has pursued since the mid-Fifties, required not only a high rate of domestic savings and investments but also a large share for the public sector in total investment. While there may have been some deviation from time to time between the precise plan targets and actual performance, by and large these objectives have been satisfied.[2] Thus, the investment rate rose from only 10 per cent of the Gross Domestic Product (GDP) in the early Fifties to about 20 per cent by the mid-Seventies, finally reaching a plateau at around 23 per cent during the Eighties. The domestic savings rate also rose from around 10 to 21 per cent over the same period, with external capital inflows usually accounting for less than 2 per cent of total investment. The public sector share of total investment also rose from less than one-third in the early Fifties to about one-half during the Eighties.

However, the public sector's own savings performance has

been quite disappointing. Though public sector savings have been less than public investment throughout the planning period, this gap widened considerably during the Eighties. The share of the public sector in gross domestic savings declined from over 20 per cent at the beginning of the decade to only 8 per cent by 1989-90. In plan financing, while the Sixth Plan (1980-81 to 1984-85) envisaged that over 46 per cent of the public sector plan outlay would be financed by own resources of the public sector, the actual contribution turned out to be only 37 per cent. Similarly, during the Seventh Plan (1985-86 to 1989-90) only 27 per cent of the public sector plan outlay was financed from own resources as against a target of over 41 per cent.

Savings performance has fallen short of expectations both for public enterprises as well as the government. In the case of public enterprises, 236 central government enterprises yielded a net profit of Rs. 2,368 crores in 1990-91, implying a rate of return of only 2.3 per cent on Rs.101,797 crores capital employed. Of this, only Rs. 69 crores came from all the non-oil public enterprises put together. The record of the state level enterprises is worse. The departmental commercial undertakings of all states and union territories together reported a net loss of Rs. 1,885 crores in 1990-91. Of the two major type of non-departmental undertakings, the State Electricity Boards (SEBs) reported a combined loss of Rs. 4,169 crores while the State Road Transport Corporations (SRTCs) reported a loss of Rs. 470 crores. Thus, instead of generating a surplus, all public enterprises put together generated a net loss of some Rs. 4,176 crores.[3]

In the government proper, let alone financing any capital expenditure, revenue receipts have even fallen short of revenue expenditure during the Eighties. The budget of the central government has been showing a revenue deficit regularly since 1979-80 and now amounts to about 2.5 per cent of the GDP. The combined finance of all the states and union territories also started showing a revenue deficit from 1987-88 onwards, which now amount to over one per cent of the GDP.[4]

In other works, during the Eighties the government had to resort increasingly to borrowed funds to finance not only capital expenditure, which did not yield adequate returns but also a growing component of current expenditure. The consequent build up of public debt and the interest burden of the debt, which is now the largest and fastest growing item of expenditure, further fuelled the growth of revenue expenditure. This led to a vicious spiral of growing deficits. By 1989-90, the last year for which revised estimates are now available, the combined fiscal deficit of the Centre and States had risen to around 10 per cent of the GDP.

There are several consequences of this fiscal imbalance, which is now sought to be corrected by the on-going stabilization-adjustment programme. Most studies have shown that the present path of public debt expansion is not sustainable. In addition, the imbalance has also set the economy on a medium-term path of stagnlation along with a severe balance of payments problem. Growing revenue deficits combined with losses of public enterprises, have constrained the acceleration of public investment. At the same time, the large public draft of private savings has tended to push up even administered interest rates and crowd out private investment. This has limited the growth of productive capacity on the supply side, while the large deficits have continued to drive the high growth of aggregate demand. The widening gap between domestic absorption and domestic output has led to a growing trade deficit and aggravated the balance of payments problem arising from indiscriminate external commercial borrowing. To the extent these have been suppressed through import restrictions, excess demand in the home market has reinforced the cost push effects of administered price increases and exchange rate depreciation in pushing up the inflation rate.

The growing fiscal deficit should not, however, be taken to imply that the level of tax revenues is inadequate. The tax to GDP ratio rose from 6 per cent in 1950-51 to about 11 per cent by 1970-71 and further to about 17 per cent in the Eighties.

This seems quite high in comparison with other countries at similar levels of per capita income. As far as the Centre is concerned, the Long Term Fiscal Policy (LTFP) set a target that Central Government revenue should rises from 7.8 per cent to about 9.4 per cent of the GDP over the Seventh Plan period (1985-86 to 1989-90). These targets were exceeded by actual achievements in every year of the plan.

This is not; to suggest either that, the existing composition of taxation is appropriate or that the current tax structure is efficient. There are a number of serious anomalies which require urgent reform. These are discussed in the third part of this chapter. However, the principle factor underlying the fiscal imbalance described above is the runaway growth of public expenditure which is discussed below:

## The Growth of Government Expenditure

The accelerating growth of government expenditure is a relatively recent phenomenon. In the early Seventies, aggregate government expenditure was actually declining in real terms. It was only in the late Seventies, when nominal expenditure growth accelerated to over 13 per cent per annum, the real expenditure also started growing quite rapidly. After 1979, the nominal expenditure growth rate accelerated still further to 18.6 per cent. But by this time the trend inflation rate had also risen, not least because of the government's own expansionary policies. Hence, real expenditure growth remained stable. However, in the period after 1983, the rate of growth of real expenditure has also accelerated (Table 6.1).

**Table 6.1:** Growth Rates of Government Expenditure

| *Year* | *State and Central Governments* | | *Central Government* | |
|---|---|---|---|---|
| | *Nominal* | *Real* | *Nominal* | *Real* |
| 1971-74 | 7.6 | -6.5 | 4.1 | -10.1 |
| 1974-79 | 13.3 | 6.9 | 9.1 | 2.6 |
| 1979-83 | 18.6 | 6.9 | 20.1 | 8.1 |
| 1983-87 | 17.2 | 9.5 | 18.5 | 11.5 |

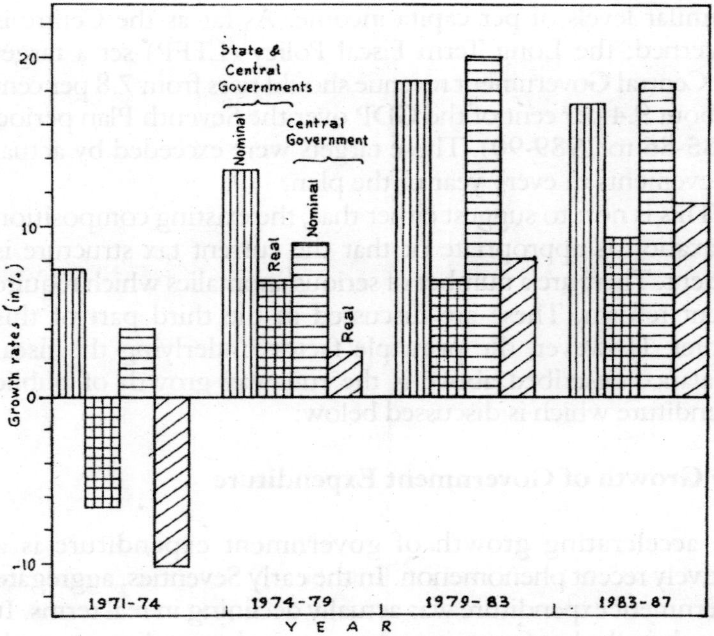


**Fig. 6.1 : Growth Rates of Government Expenditure**

It is this progressive acceleration in the growth of government expenditure which has led to the emergence of a fiscal crisis despite a steady increase in the tax: GDP ratio, which exceeded the LTFP targets in every year of the Seventh Five Year Plan. Strategies for resolving the fiscal crisis will therefore have to focus on compressing the growth of public expenditure. It is interesting to note in this context that during the past four decades of 'planned' economic development, much of the literate on public finance in India was preoccupied with questions of resource mobilization. Relatively little attention was paid to the growth, allocation or efficiency of public expenditure.

In addressing the question of expenditure growth and its containment, it is useful to proceed from trends as observable in the economic and functional classification of government expenditure. Mention was made earlier of the equity objective of fiscal policy. The burden of international experience suggests that this is best served through expenditure policies rather than revenue measures (Gillis, 1989). In India also, all evaluation, including those undertaken by reputed experts outside the government, show that despite the much talked about inefficiencies and leakages in anti-poverty programmes, these programmes have had a major role in reducing the incidence of poverty, especially during periods of drought and distress (Minhas, Jain and Tendulkar, 1991). However, these programmes are only short-term relief measures. In the long run it is the expenditure on primary education, health and related activitiesTwhich have a strong egalitarian impact. The anti-povetry programmes, together with the expenditure on these social services, constitute what may be called the redistributive package. How has our public expenditure pattern fared on this score?[5]

The functional classification of expenditure reveals that, measured at 1970-71 prices, the real per capita expenditure and allied activities, was only Rs. 3 in 1987-88 (Table 6.2). Adding to this about 40 per cent of the education expenditure which goes to primary education and the entire spending on health (even though only a part of this is spent on the poor), the real per capita expenditure on the total redistributive package amounted to only Rs. 29, as against Rs. 43 per cent spent of Defence and another a telling impact on the nation's infrastructure. The deteriorating condition of roads, widespread and frequent load shedding or tripping because of power shortage, bottleneck in rail transport and telecommunication have all combined into a formidable and binding supply side constraint on economic growth. The slow down in expansion of irrigation is now threatening the growth of food supply (Rao C.H.H., 1992) while the scarcity and deterioration of physical facilities such as hospitals and school buildings has led to a progressive decline in the quality of these critical social services.[6]

Clearly, while an attempt is made to contain the growth of total expenditure, the shares of the redistributive package and capital expenditure on essential infrastructure must be raise. The obvious candidates for overall expenditure compression are therefore the three main items of revenue expenditure which account for about 70 per cent of total government expenditure i.e. major subsidies, interest payments and compensation to government employees. Practical proposals as to how such compression might be achieved have been detailed elsewhere and need not be repeated here.[7] However, these may be briefly listed as follows:

- Phasing out of remaining export subsides with further progress towards convertibility and tariff rationalization which would make subsidy incentives unnecessary.
- Phasing out of the fertilizer subsidy over a three-year period along with increased allocation for capital expenditure in irrigation.
- Drastic cuts in fresh recruitment of government staff along with abolition of large numbers of posts which have proliferated in recent years. This measure, combined with the normal attrition of government employees every year would arrest the growth of wages and salaries and associated expenditure on consumption of goods and services. These now account for about a third of total government expenditure. It must be emphasized that these economies could be brought about without any harsh measures like retrenchment or a freeze on real wages.
- Reduction of budgetary support to public enterprises other than in key infrastructure sectors. Even key sector enterprises like the railways, SEBs and road transport undertakings should be systematically judged towards commercial viability based on improved efficiency and proper user charges.
- Reduction of the interest burden through quick retirement of a part of the public debt. This could be financed by the proceeds from the sale of public sector equity, instead of using such proceeds to finance the current expenditure of the government.

- Reduction of the interest changes payable on government debt to the RBI. This monetized debt has arisen out of seigniorage and should not be treated at par with other public debt.

A number of these measures have already been initiated in the July 1991 and March 1992 budgets and it may be expected that they would be sustained in the period ahead. However, while no serious effort has yet been made to compress government consumption expenditure, the share of redistributive expenditures like the employment programme, education and health has been reduced in the March 1992 budget. It was pointed out in the Finance Minister's budget speech that many of these redistributive programmes are in fact operated by the states. It remains to be seen whether the state budgets, which are still being finalized at the time of writing, make adequate provisions for such programmes.

## The Tax System: A Critical Evaluation

We now turn to the revenue aspects of fiscal policy, starting with an analysis of the tax system. This is important not so much to improve revenue productivity but to identify and rectify the sources of distortion and inequity. Terms of both the level of taxes and their growth, the performance of India's tax system has been quite satisfactory. The tax ratio rose from 9 per cent in the early Sixties to as much as 17 per cent in 1990-91. This is appreciably higher than the average rate of 12 per cent for countries at a comparable level of development. However, three disconcerting features must be noted.

- The tax ratio has been stagnant since the mid-Eighties. Even to maintain this ratio, substantial discretionary measures had to be resorted to every year.
- The increase in tax ratio has been accompanied by a significant increase in the share of indirect taxes, particularly import duties.

- The tax system has been inequitable and has caused serious distortions in the incentive structure and investment decisions.

The evolution of India's tax system is at variance with the general experience of other developing countries. Instead of increasing along with growth is income, the share of direct taxes has declined steadily from about 30 per cent in the early Sixties to just about 14 per cent in 1989-90. The share of customs duty, in contrast, increased from about 14 per cent in the early Sixties to over 23 per cent by 1989-90. This, too, is quite different from the usual pattern of a steadily declining share of international trade taxes as development proceeds (Hinrichs, 1966).

Like in other developing countries, the establishment of a broad bases, simple and neutral tax system in India is constrained by the existence of a large traditional economic sector, low literacy level, a weak information system and powerful distributional coalitions.[8] In addition to these, the requirement of large resources for plan financing, the pursuit of multiple objectives through tax policy and the tax arrangements of a federal setup have also had to be accommodated in the Indian tax structure. The resulting tax system is extremely complicated. It has a narrow base and has created considerable distortion in the relative price structure. Each of these issues is discussed in turn below.

The tax base is narrow for both direct and indirect taxes. In the case of personal income tax, the exclusion of tax on agricultural incomes, administrative difficulties of taxing the unorganized non-agricultural sector, provision of exemptions and rendered that tax base extremely narrow. Similarly, a generous deduction for depreciation and reinvestment and contributions to a wide variety of social purposes has eroded the corporate tax base. In the case of indirect taxes, most of the services are completely excluded from the base and even the retail general sales taxes have ceased to be either 'general' or 'retail', with the point of levy being shifted to the first stage of sale.

The narrowness of the tax base has accentuated the distortion effects of the Indian tax structure. These effects have been largely ignored because of the preoccupation with raising more and more revenue. Given that the tax bases are narrow, requirements of revenue have necessitated high average tax rates for both direct and indirect taxes. Additionally, the emphasis on equity had led to virtually confiscator levels of marginal tax rates in the case of personal income tax, though these have been moderated recently. The disincentive effects of such high marginal rates on work effort and investment were ignored.

In the case of indirect taxes, raising tax revenue at administratively convenient points has resulted in the imposition of a levy on inputs, outputs and capital goods alike at Central, State and even local levels, causing additional distortions in the tax structure. Similarly, high average rates of customs tariffs, combined with a large dispersion, have distorted the production structure. At the state level, tax competition to maximize revenue, generous schemes of sales tax incentives for promoting industrialization and inter-state tax exportation have been a further source of distortions. Finally, attempts by the central government to raise revenues from non-shareable sources like import duties and administered price increase have altered relative prices in unintended ways.

The tax structure in India has also become unduly complicated. A major reason for this is the pursuit of numerous objectives, apart from raising revenue, through the instrument of tax policy. Thus, equity considerations have led to minute rate differentiation in both direct and indirect tax structures, based merely on the policy makers' perception of what is desirable. The same instruments were also used to encourage savings, promote investment, particularly in 'desired' industries, maximize employment, promote inter-regional equity and promote several other social objectives. Not surprisingly, the resultant tax structure has turned out to be a formidable maze.

At the same time, it is doubtful whether this complicated tax structure has really served to promote the intended objectives.

With less than one per cent of the population paying personal income tax, the use of this instrument to promote equit is not very meaningful. In fact, international experience shows that active public expenditure policies aimed at raising the consumption of the poor are far more effective in promoting equity as compared to tax policies aimed at constraining the incomes of the rich (Gillis, 1989). Studies have also cast doubts on the effectiveness of tax concessions is enhancing the level of savings. While the inappropriateness of tax policy as an instrument for promoting employment, balanced regional development and a wide variety of other social objectives is well-known (Das Gupta, 1989; Bagchi and Nayak, 1990).

Many of these problems have been recognized by the Tax Reform Committee (TRC) which has recently submitted its interim report (Government of India, 1991). Lessons from tax reform experiences in various countries indicate that complex systems suggested in the optimal tax literature are impractical (Musgrave, 1987). The most successful tax reform experiences are those which have concentrated on broadening the tax base, levying lower and less differentiated tax rates, simplifying the tax structure, exempting taxes on inputs and strengthening tax administration and enforcement. These elements also characterize the philosophy underlying the interim report of the TRC.

In this report, rationalization is taken to be the main objective of the reform or direct and indirect taxes. Bringing various perquisites into the tax net, rationalization of tax incentives for savings, clubbing of non-wage incomes of the minor with parents' are some the direct tax aimed at this objective. In the case of domestic indirect taxes also, the emphasis of the report is on expanding the tax base by bringing important services into the tax net and extending the tax to the wholesale stage. In the case of import duty, however, the TRC has suggested that this be viewed primarily as an instrument for protection rather than raising revenue.

The TaxcReform Committee has also made recommendations regarding a gradual reduction in the rates of direct and indirect taxes, revenue sharing between the Centre and the States, tax harmonization and other measures for simplifying the tax system, which will have to be phased in over a period of time. However, given the complexity and inefficiency of the existing tax system, the recommendation of the TRC should only be viewed as a beginning of the tax reform process in India.

**Subsidies, User Charges and Non-Tax Revenue**

The tax reform measures discussed above are aimed at simplifying and rationalizing the tax system, not necessarily raising additional resources. However, an altogether different kind of rationalization is required in the pricing of public services which could lead to considerable additional flow of revenue.

There is a large class of publicly provided services which are in the nature of pure public goods. Defence, general administration and the maintenance of law and order are obvious examples. Such services, characterized by non-rivalry and non-excludability in consumption, cannot be easily priced or 'sold' to individual consumers (Samuelson, 1954 and 1955). They, therefore, have to be financed out of general revenues. All other publicly provided services could, in principle, be priced so as to recover the cost of delivering such services. However, whether such user cost pricing is desirable or not is quite another matter. There may be large externalities in the consumption of some of these goods and services. In such cases, the privately optimal level of consumption may be socially sub-optimal. The government may, therefore, decide to introduce and subsidy in order to support the socially optimal level of consumption. Again, there may be cases where the consumption of a 'merit' good like, say, primacy education by the poor is considered essential or socially desirable. The government may deliberately subsidize the consumption of such goods and services for certain target groups.[9]

Except in the case of such 'merit goods', 'public goods' and goods or services with large externalities, it would be desirable for the government to change 'user fees' sufficient to recover cost. It turns out, however, that the recovery rates are not only remarkable low across the board but even declining over time. As a consequence, there is a huge volume of subsidies involved in the delivery of virtually all goods and services being provided by the government. These include, of course, the explicit subsidies on food, fertilizer or exports already discussed above in the context of expenditure control. There is also the much large flow of implicit subsidies by way of unrecovered cost in a whole range of social and economic services. If these services were properly priced so as to recover costs, except where the subsidies are deliberately introduced to support particular largest groups, this would very substantially augment the total flow of non-tax revenues.

Our estimates show that between 1987-88, the total volume of government subsidies rose from about Rs. 8,000 crores to over Rs. 44,000 crores, i.e., from 8.2 per cent of the GDP to over 15 per cent. In economic services, the average recovery rate declined from about 55 per cent of cost in 1977-78 to below 41 per cent in 1987-88, implying an increase in the total subsidy on economic services from about Rs. 4,500 crores to over Rs. 27,500 crores over the decade (Table 6.4). The lowest rate of recovery is seen in industry, where there was a steep decline in the recovery rate from just under 40 per cent in 1977-78 to less than 17 per cent in 1987-88. The recovery rate in agriculture and irrigation is not much better at around 20 per cent. In power, only about a third of the cost is recovered while in communications, which was generating a 14 per cent recovery over cost in 1977-78, over 30 per cent of the cost now remains unrecoverd. Transportation is the only sector where cost recovery actually improved over the decade. But even here, as much as 25 per cent of the cost still remains unrecovered.

Since many of these economic services are delivered by departmental or non-departmental government enterprises and cooperatives, it is not surprising that a large part of the subsidy in economic services actually flows in the form of budgetary support to offset the poor cost recovery of these public enterprises. Out of a total subsidy of about Rs. 28,000 crores on economic services in 1987-88, around Rs. 15,000 crores flowed through the public enterprises. Of this, about Rs. 9,000 crores flowed through central public enterprises with an average recovery rate of only 41 per cent. In terms of their institutional classification, departmental enterprises had an average recovery rate of 67 per cent as against 31 per cent for non-departmental enterprises and only 20 per cent for cooperatives.

In other words, far from contributing a net surplus to the revenues of the government, public enterprises, have constituted a major source of resource drain. In the context of the present fiscal crisis, this calls for urgent reforms in this area. Ways must be found of imposing a hard budget constraint on these enterprises in order to at least stop the drain of government resources, even if large surpluses are not immediately forthcoming. That is itself would release thousands of crores in financial resources. A part of the resources so released could be deployed to augment the quantity of some subsidized services, or, where such subsidized services are desirable, improve their quality. The rest would significantly reduce the size of the deficit.

Turning to social services, the required course of action is less abvious. Recovery rates are much lower here, amounting to less than 4 per cent of the cost on an average. In other words, social services are being delivered virtually free of cost. Also, these services are being delivered largely though the state government. Hence, the large bulk of subsidy on social services, estimated at close to Rs. 17,000 crores in 1987-88, flows through the state government. This is in addition to the state' share of subsidize in economic services, which added up to about Rs. 13,000 crores in 1987-88, thus leaving the states with a total subsidy burden of about Rs. 30,000 crores in that year alone.

Clearly, the states cannot continue to subsidize public services on such a vast scale, given that their financial situation is even more stringent than that of the Centre. On the other hand, social services like education and health are precisely the services which ought to be subsidized on equity or 'merit good' consideration. Hence, the pruning of subsidies here will have to be very carefully calibrated in order to ensure that budgetary pressures do not subvert these larger social objectives. What can be said quite categorically, however, is that there is need for much closer targeting of subsidies in social services. This would help to filter out unnecessary or unintended subsidies. The resources saved through such improved cost recovery could then be deployed to actually raise the level of subsidy to deserving target groups, while at the same time, reducing the total volume of subsidy.

A good illustration of this is the education sector. The total subsidy to this sector in 1987-88 was almost Rs. 9, 600 crores. However, the subsidy to primary education amounted to only around Rs. 4,200 crores, the balance going to secondary and higher levels of education. In a country with around 60 per cent of the population still illiterate, anyone who has reached a secondary level of education is already a privileged person. To subsidize persons at that level, indeed at a much higher per student rate than at the primary level, is clearly iniquitous. The argument that higher levels of education must be subsidized because of externalities is also not sustainable since the private returns to education are very high in some lines of specialization and there is already a large surplus of manpower in others. Introduction of proper user charges could raise, at a conservative estimate, over Rs. 5,000 crores annually, from this sector alone.

## A Review of State Finances in India

This review of fiscal policy would remain incomplete if it did not address some of the critical issues pertaining to the 'States' Finances. The Constitution assigns the responsibility of providing major social and economic services to the states. As a consequence they incur almost 60 per cent of total spending and raise 35 per cent of the revenues. The revenue deficit attributable to budgetary operations of the states constitute over on per cent of the GDP and the fiscal deficit on states' account is about 3.5 per cent of the GDP.

In some respects, the fiscal condition of the states is even more critical than that of the Centre. As in the case of the Centre, their expenditure is more income elastic than revenue receipts, thereby generating a built-in tendency towards deficits. However, they do not have the same ability to finance their deficits. The States do not have independently powers to borrow from the market, nor can they take recourse to borrowing from the central bank because of the overdraft regulation scheme.[10] Given these constraints on debt financing for bridging the gap between expenditure and revenue at the state level, the burden of adjustment has tended to fall on capital and maintenance expenditure, with rather serious long-term implications for growth. Moreover, the squeeze on capital expenditure has been sharper in the less developed states, thereby aggravating interregional growth imbalances.

The trends in expenditure, classified into economic a functional categories, show quite clearly that the different elements of current expenditure have grown much faster than overall expenditure (Rao and Tulasidhar, 1991). While aggregate expenditure has grown at about 7 per cent in real terms during the Eighties, items like interest payments and visible subsidies have been growing at close to 13 per cent. Other current account items such as transfer payments and compensation to employees have also grown at a relatively high rate of around 8 per cent.[11] Interestingly, the only item of current expenditure which has grown relatively slowly is the on goods and services, which are largely spent of the maintenance of capital assets.

The rapid growth of revenue expenditure has outstripped even the growth of the tax revenue and central transfers, which have themselves grown at a high rater of over 16 per cent per annum in nominal terms. Meanwhile, the growth of non-tax revenues has been sluggish because of poor cost recoveries from various public services provided by the states. As a consequence of both uneconomic pricing as well as low efficiency of departmental and non-departmental enterprises, most of them have been reporting substantial losses. In irrigation, total losses, including depreciation, in 1987-88 amounted to Rs. 5,200 crores. As regards non-departmental enterprises, the several 'promotional' corporation, which seem to serve no purpose other than providing political patronage, claimed a budgetary support of over Rs. 500 crores in the fourteen major states. The two major non-department commercial enterprises, the SEBs and the SRTCs have continued to drain states' exchequers. The average loss of the SEBs was 14.4 per cent that of the SRTs 12 per cent of the capital invested in 1990-91.

Given the poor flow of non-tax revenues, the growth of total revenue has failed to keep pace with revenue expenditure. It has also been pointed out above that, unlike in the case of the centre, the expenditure revenue gap could not be easily financed through borrowing by the states. Therefore, the entire burden of adjustment of this imbalance between expenditure and its financing has fallen on capital and maintenance expenditure. Both capital expenditure as well as expenditure on the maintenance of capital assets, usually shown as spending on goods and services, have been growing at less than 5 per cent per annum in real terms, while total expenditure increased at over 7 per cent. Consequently, the share of capital expenditure in total state government expenditure declined fairly sharply from 35 per cent in 1980-81 to 28 per cent in 1987-88. The situation is likely to deteriorate further in the next few year with the significant deceleration in central transfers to states as a part of the country's fiscal adjustment programme.[12] The long-term growth implications of the slow growth of capital stock in the state government sector and its poor maintenance are quite obvious. These have been compounded by efficiency losses due to various distortions in relative prices introduced by the structure of sales tax, inter-state competition in terms of this tax and tax exportation.

What is especially disturbing is that the squeeze on capital and maintenance expenditure has been much sharper in the less developed states (Rao, 1992). The growth of capital expenditure in these state has been significantly lower than that of high income states. The ratio of maintenance expenditure vis-à-vis compensation of employees has also been lower in the poorer states. This has considerably aggravated inter-regional growth disparities. The poorer states have also suffered on account of inter-state exportation of taxes from the consuming to the producing states on account of the central sales tax. This should be obvious since production is concentrated in the more developed states.

A similar disparity is also noticed in the distribution of social expenditure such as health and education (Rao and Mundle, 1991). Thus, in their various dimensions, state finances have tended to reinforce rather than reduce inter-regional disparities. This could have been avoided if the central transfers were designed to offset the inherent fiscal disadvantages of the poorer states. Unfortunately, both statutory and plan transfers are given mainly on the basis of general economic indicators, with dominant weight being assigned to population rather than fiscal disadvantage (Rao and Aggarwal, 1991).

It follows from the foregoing review of the states' finances that reform in this areas should focus on compression of current expenditure, rationalization of the tax system and better targeting of implicit subsidies. Furthermore, central transfers should henceforth be explicitly directed at offsetting the fiscal disadvantage of the poorer states. Hopefully, this issue will be addressed by the Tenth Finance Commission. As far as the states themselves are concerned, specific measures which they could introduce have been discussed in some detail elsewhere (Rao, 1992) and are briefly listed here.

- A freeze on fresh recruitment over the next few years, identification of surplus staff and their redeployment in order to moderate the growth of the wages and salaries' bill.
- A cut-back on perquisites like leave-travel concession, bonus and leave encashment would also help to decelerate the growth of staff related expenditure.

- Expenditure on redistribute activities such as elementary education, basic health facilities and poverty alleviation should be enhanced. The Centre should also suitably rationalize the centrally sponsored schemes to facilitate enhancement of expenditure on such items.
- A part of the enhanced social expenditure should be financed through higher cost recoveries in services like irrigation, supply of electricity, road, transport and post-primary education.
- The major reforms on taxes relate to sales tax including value addition at the post-manufacturing stages should broaden the base. However, taxation of inputs should be avoided. The number of rate categories should also be reduced and the tax structure simplified. The practice of using sales tax concession for industrialization should be avoided. Measures are also needed to avoid excessive tax competition among the states and to reduce taxation of inter-state sale.

## A Final Remarks

The foregoing review is necessarily selective. It has dealt with only some of the more urgent issues in fiscal policy such as the deficit, expenditure control, reform of the tax system, subsidies and user charges. Some institutional questions, particularly relating to the states' finances and Centre-State financial relations have also been addressed. But fiscal policy is more than the mere arithmetic of budgets or even the formal processes of financial management in government. It is, in the main, an outcome a political process. Such questions about the political economy of fiscal policy have not been dealt with in this chapter as they have been addressed elsewhere in this volume (Bardhan, 1992). But it has to be said in conclusion, that to lose sight of the underlying political power relations which drive fiscal policy is to miss the central point about the roots of India's current fiscal crisis.

## Fiscal Situation

### *Combined Government Finances: 2007-08*

Combined Government finances were budgeted to ratios placed 0.7-0.9 percentage points of GDP lower than in 2006-07, reflecting the improvement in the finances of both the Central and State Governments. The improvement was envisaged to be achieved through a reduction in expenditure (as percentage of GDP), particularly in the revenue account. The combined debt-GDP ratio was budgeted to decline from 77.1 per cent at end-March 2007 to 73.8 per cent at end-March 2008 (Table 6.2).

**Table 6.2 :** Key Fiscal Indicators

| *Year* | *Primary Deficit* | *Revenue Deficit* | *Gross Fiscal Deficit* | *Outstanding Liabilities** |
|---|---|---|---|---|
| *1* | *2* | *3* | *4* | *5* |
| 2002-03 | 1.1 | 4.4 | 5.9 | 63.5 |
| 2003-04 | -0.03 | 3.6 | 4.5 | 63.0 |
| 2004-05 | -0.04 | 2.5 | 4.0 | 63.3 |
| 2005-06 | 0.4 | 2.6 | 4.1 | 63.1 |
| 2006-07 | -0.2 | 1.9 | 3.5 | 61.2 |
| 2007-08 BE | -0.2 | 1.5 | 3.3 | 58.5 |
| 2007-08 RE | -0.6 | 1.4 | 3.1 | 61.7 |
| 2008-09 BE | -1.1 | 1.0 | 2.5 | 57.7 |
| | | **States** | | |
| 2002-03 | 1.3 | 2.3 | 4.1 | 32.0 |
| 2003-04 | 1.5 | 2.3 | 4.4 | 33.2 |
| 2004-05 | 0.7 | 1.2 | 3.4 | 32.7 |
| 2005-06 | 0.2 | 0.2 | 2.5 | 32.6 |
| 2006-07 RE | 0.4 | 0.1 | 2.7 | 30.6 |
| 2007-08 BE | 0.1 | -0.3 | 2.3 | 29.4 |
| | | **Combined** | | |
| 2002-03 | 3.1 | 6.7 | 9.5 | 80.3 |
| 2003-04 | 2.0 | 5.9 | 8.4 | 81.4 |
| 2004-05 | 1.4 | 3.7 | 7.4 | 81.3 |
| 2005-06 | 1.0 | 2.8 | 6.7 | 80.4 |
| 2006-07 RE | 0.8 | 2.1 | 6.4 | 77.1 |
| 2007-08 BE | 0.1 | 1.3 | 5.5 | 73.8 |

RE : Revised Estimates. BE: Budget Estimates.

* : Includes external liabilities at historical exchange rates.

*Note:* The fiscal ratios are based on CSO's estimates of GDP, except for the Centre for the years 2007-08 and 2008-09 which are as per the Union Budgets, 2008-07.

The combined fiscal deficit during 2007-08 was budgeted to be financed primarily from domestic resources. Market borrowings were budgeted to finance 53.5 per cent of the Gross Fiscal Deficit (GFD) during 2007-08 (49.1 per cent a year ago), while other liabilities (small savings, provident funds, reserve funds and deposits and advances) were budgeted to finance 42.9 per cent (47.9 per cent in 2006-07). External assistance was budgeted to finance 3.6 per cent of the combined fiscal deficit during 2007-08 as compared with 3.0 per cent in 2006-07.

**Centre's Fiscal Situation: 2007-08**

The process of fiscal correction and consolidation under the Fiscal consolidation under the Fiscal Responsibility and Budget Management (FRBM) framework continued during 2007-08; the revised estimated for the year placed the revenue deficit and fiscal deficit lower than budget estimates, both in absolute terms and relative to GDP. Revenue deficit at Rs. 63,488 crore in 2007-08 was lower by Rs. 7,990 crore than the budget estimates. This reflected significant increase in the tax and non-tax revenue which more than offset the increase in the revenue expenditure on account of higher provision for interest payments and subsidies. The GFD at Rs. 1,43,653 crore in 2007-08 was lower by Rs. 7,295 crore than the bgudget estimates on account of the lower revenue deficit coupled with a decline in capital expenditure. As a result, gross primary surplus in the revised estimates at Rs. 28,318 crore was significantly higher than the budget estimates by Rs. 20,271 crore.

The reduction in GFD and revenue deficit by 0.4 per cent and 0.5 per cent of GDP, respectively, during 2007-08 (RE) over 2006-07 met the stipulated minimum threshold levels of 0.3 per cent and 0.5 per cent of GDP for GFD and revenue deficit, respectively, under the FRBM Rules, 2004.

Revenue receipts in the revised estimates increased by 8.0 per cent over the budgeted level and were placed at 11.2 per cent of GDP (Table 6.3). This was mainly on account of higher than budgeted net tax revenue, particularly under personal income tax, corporation tax, customs duties, service tax and securities transaction tax. However, collections under excise duties in the revised estimates were lower than the budget estimates.

**Table 6.3 :** Receipts of the Centre

| *Item* | *2006-07* | *2007-08* | *2007-08* | *Variation (4 over 3)* | |
|---|---|---|---|---|---|
| | *(Accounts)* | *(BE)* | *(RE)* | *Amount* | *Per cent* |
| *1* | *2* | *3* | *4* | *5* | *6* |
| 1. Total Receipts (2+3) | 5,83,387 (14.1) | 6,80,521 (14.5) | 7,09,373 15.1) | 28,852 | 4.2 |
| 2. Revenue Receipts (i + ii) | 4,34,387 (10.5) | 4,86,422 (10.4) | 5,25,098 (11.2) | 38,676 | 8.0 |
| (i) Tax Revenue (Net) | 3,51,182 (8.5) | 4,03,872 (8.6) | 4,31,773 (9.2) | 27,901 | 6.9 |
| (ii) Non-Tax Revenue | 8.,205 (2.0) | 82,550 (1.8) | 93,325 (2.0) | 10,775 | 13.1 |
| 3. Capital Receipts | 1,49,000 (3.6) | 1,94,099 (4.1) | 1,84,275 (3.9) | -9,824 | -5.1 |
| Of which: | | | | | |
| Market Borrowings | 1,14,801 | 1,10,827 | 1,10,727 | -100 | -0.1 |
| Recoveries of Loans | 5,893 | 1,500 | 4,497 | 2,997 | 199.8 |
| Disinvestment Proceeds | 534 | 41,651 | 36,125 | -5,526 | -13.3 |
| *Memo Items: Net of transactions relating to transfer of Reserve Bank's stake in SBI* | | | | | |
| Total receipts | 5,83,387 (14.1) | 6,40,521* (13.6) | 6,75,065# (14.4) | 34,544 | 5.4 |
| Disinvestment proceeds | 5,893 | 1,651* | 1,817# | 166 | 10.1 |

RE– Revised Estimates. BE–Budget Estimates.

* : Adjusted for an Amount of Rs. 40,000 crore on account of transactions relating to transfer of Reserve Bank's stake in State Bank of India (SBI) to the Central Government.

#: Net of transfer of profit from the Reserve Bank to the Central Government on Account of sale of Reserve Bank's stake in SBI amounting to Rs. 34,308 crore.

*Note:* Figures in parentheses are percentages to GDP.

The collections under non-tax revenues were also higher than the budget estimates on account of dividends and profits which were higher by 6.4 per cent than the budget estimates. Among the capital receipts, recoveries of loans and advances were higher than budgeted. The aggregate expenditure (adjusted for acquisition) cost of Reserve Bank's stake in (SBI) in the revised estimates for 2007-08 was 5.2 per cent higher than the budget estimates on account of higher revenue expenditure, particularly in interest payments and subsidies (Table 6.4). Increase in interest payments was mainly due to higher interest outgo in market loans, securities issued under market stabilisation scheme (MSS) and compensation and other bonds.

**Table 6.4:** Aggregate Expenditure of the Centre

| *tem* | *2006-07 (Accounts)* | *2007-08 (BE)* | *2007-08 (RE)* | *Variation (4 over 3) Amount* | *Per cent* |
|---|---|---|---|---|---|
| *1* | *2* | *3* | *4* | *5* | *6* |
| 1. Total Expenditure (2+3=4+5) | 5,83,387 (14.1) | 6,80521 (14.5) | 7,09,373 (15.1) | 28,852 | 4.2 |
| 2. Non-Plan Expenditure | 4,13527 (10.0) | 4,75,421 (10.1) | 5,01,849 (10.7) | 26,428 | 5.6 |
| Of which: | | | | | |
| Interest Payments | 1,50,272 (3.6) | 1,58,995 (3.4) | 1,71,971 (3.7) | 12,976 | 8.2 |
| Defence Expenditure | 85,510 (2.1) | 96,000 (2.0) | 92,500 (2.0) | -3,500 | -3.6 |
| Subsidies | 57,125 (1.4) | 54,330 (1.2) | 69,742 (1.5) | 15,412 | 28.4 |
| 3. Plant Expenditure | 1,69,860 (4.1) | 2,05,100 (4.4) | 2,07,524) (4.4) | 2,424 | 1.2 |
| 4. Revenue Expenditure | 5,14,609 (12.4) | 5,57,900 (11.9) | 5,88,586 (12.5) | 30,686 | 5.5 |
| 5. Capital Expenditure | 68,778 (1.7) | 1,22,621 (2.6) | 1,20,787 (2.6) | -1,834 | -1.5 |
| *Memo Items: Net of transactions relating to reserve Bank's stake in SBI* | | | | | |
| Total Expenditure | 5,83,387 (14.1) | 6,40,521* (13.6) | 6,73,842# (14.4) | 33,321 | 5.2 |
| Non-Plan Expenditure | 4,13,527 (10.0) | 4,35,421* (9.3) | 4,66,318# (9.9) | 30,897 | 7.1 |
| Capital Expenditure | 68,778 (1.7) | 82,621* (1.8) | 85,256# (1.8) | 2,635 | 3.2 |

RE : Revised Estimates. BE— Budget Estimates.

* : Excludes an Amount of Rs. 40,000 crore on account of transactions relating to transfer of Reserve Bank's stake in (SBI) to the Government.

#: Excludes acquisition cost of Reserve Bank's stake in SBI at Rs. 35,531 crore.

*Note:* Figures in parentheses are percentages to GDP.

The expenditure on subsidies at Rs. 69,742 crore (1.5 per cent of GDP) in the revised estimates for 2007-08 was 28.4 per cent higher than the budgeted amount mainly on account of food and fertiliser subsidies exceeding the budget estimates by Rs. 5,850 crore (22.8 per cent) and Rs. 8,050 crore (35.9 per cent), respectively. Food subsidies increased to Rs. 31,546 crore in the revised estimates mainly due to higher minimum support price and carrying cost. Fertiliser subsidies increased to Rs. 30, 501 crore mainly on account of increases in input cost of indigenous fertilisers and the cost of imported fertilisers.

Under capital expenditure, while defence capital expenditure declined, non-defence capital outlay adjusted for transactions relating to transfer of Reserve Bank's stake in State Bank of India increased by Rs. 3,358 crore or 10.1 per cent. Plan expenditure did not show much variation from the budget estimates, although Central assistance for State and Union Territories (UT) plans increased markedly in the revised estimates.

## Financing of the Union Budget

Gross and net market borrowings (dated securities and 364-day Treasury Bills excluding allocations under the Market Stabilisation Scheme) or the Centre for 2007-08 were budgeted at Rs. 1,87,769 crore and Rs. 1,10,827 crore, respectively. In the revised estimates, net market borrowings were placed marginally lower at Rs. 1,10,727 crore, financing 77.1 per cent of GFD.

Apart from market borrowings, short-term borrowings (14-day, 91-day and 182-day Treasury Bills) financed 17.7 per cent of GFD in the revised estimates as compared with 0.3 per cent of GFD in the budget estimates. In the public account, deposits and advances, state provident funds and reserve funds financed 5.4 per cent, 3.3 per cent and 2.4 per cent, respectively, of GFD.

**Table 6.5 :** Central Government Securities Issued during 2007-08

*(Amount in Rupees crore/Maturity in years/Yield in per cent)*

| ***Borrowings as per issuance Auction Calendar*** | | | ***Actual Borrowings*** | | | |
|---|---|---|---|---|---|---|
| *Period of Auction* | *Amount* | *Residual Maturity* | *Data of Auction* | *Amount* | *Residual Maturity* | *Yield* |
| *1* | *2* | *3* | *4* | *5* | *6* | *7* |
| April 5-12, 2007 | 6,000 | 5-9 | Apr 12,2007 | 6,000 | 8.39 | 8.16 |
| | 4,000 | 20 and above | Apr 12,2007 | 4,000 | 29.15 | 8.58 |
| April 20-27, 2007 | 6,000 | 10-14 | Apr 27,2007 | 6,000 | 9.71 | 8.16 |
| May 4-11, 2007 | 6,000 | 10-14 | May 11,2007 | 6,000 | 9.92 | 8.31 |
| | 4,000 | 20 and above | May 11,2007 | 4,000 | 29.06 | 8.64 |
| May 18-25, 2007 | 5,000 | 5-9 | May 25,2007 | 5,000 | 8.26 | 8.24 |
| | 3,000 | 15-19 | May 25,2007 | 3,000 | 14.96 | 8.40 |
| June 1-8, 2007 | 6,000 | 10-14 | Jun 5,2007 | 6,000 | 9.86 | 8.18 |
| | 3,000 | 20 and above | Jun 5,2007 | 3,000 | 29.00 | 8.52 |
| | | | Jun 12,2007* | 5,000 | 9.84 | 8.44 |
| June 15-22, 2007 | 6,000 | 10-14 | Jun 15,2007 | 6,000 | 9.83 | 8.35 |
| July 6-13, 2007 | 6,000 | 10-14 | Jul 6,2007 | 6,000 | 10.00 | 7.99 |
| | 4,000 | 20 and above | Jul 7,2007 | 4,000 | 28.91 | 8.45 |
| July 20-27, 2007 | 6,000 | 5-9 | Jul 20,2007 | 6,000 | 6.10 | 7.59 |
| | 3,000 | 20 and above | Jul 20,2007 | 3,000 | 25.10 | 8.34 |
| August 3-10, 2007 | 6,000 | 10-14 | Aug 3, 2007 | 6,000 | 9.93 | 7.93 |
| | 4,000 | 20 and above | Aug 3, 2007 | 4,000 | 24.87 | 8.45 |
| August 17-24, 2007 | 5,000 | 5-9 | Aug 24,2007 | 5,000 | 6.02 | 7.87 |
| | 2,000 | 10-14 | Aug 24,2007 | 2,000 | 9.89 | 7.91 |
| September 7-14, 2007 | 4,000 | 10-14 | Sept 7, 2007 | 4,000 | 14.43 | 8.16 |
| | 3,000 | 20 and above | Sept 7, 2007 | 3,000 | 28.74 | 8.41 |
| October 5-12, 2007 | 6,000 | 10-14 | Oct 12, 2007 | 6,000 | 9.73 | 7.91 |
| | 4,000 | 20 and above | Oct 12, 2007 | 4,000 | 25.20 | 8.45 |
| October 19-26, 2007 | 4,000 | 5-9 | Oct 26, 2007 | 4,000 | 5.84 | 7.74 |
| | 4,000 | 15-19 | Oct 26, 2007 | 4,000 | 14.54 | 8.13 |
| November 2-8, 2007 | 5,000 | 10-14 | Nov 8, 2007 | 5,000 | 14.26 | 8.26 |
| | 3,000 | 20 and above | Nov 8, 2007 | 3,000 | 28.57 | 8.39 |
| November 16-23, 2007 | 3,000 | 10-14 | Nov 23,2007 | 3,000 | 9.62 | 7.90 |
| | 4,000 | 15-19 | Nov 23, 2007 | 4,000 | 14.47 | 8.20 |
| December 7-14, 2007 | 5,000 | 10-14 | Dec 14,2007 | 5,000 | 9.56 | 7.92 |
| | 2,000 | 20 and above | Dec 14, 2007 | 2,000 | 28.47 | 8.26 |
| January 4-11, 2008 | 6,000 | 10-14 | Jan 11, 2008 | 6,000 | 9.49 | 7.55 |
| | 4,000 | 20 and above | Jan 11, 2008 | 4,000 | 28.40 | 7.89 |
| February 1-8, 2008 | 4,000 | 20 and above | Feb 8, 2008 | 4,000 | 28.32 | 7.77 |
| | 5,000 | 15-19 | Feb 8, 2008 | 5,000 | 14.01 | 7.62 |
| **Total** | **1,51,000** | | | **1,56,000** | | |

*Memo:*

| *Year* | *Weighted Average Maturity* | *Weighted Average Yield* |
|---|---|---|
| 2003-04 | 14.94 | 3.71 |
| 2004-05 | 14.13 | 6.11 |
| 2005-06 | 16.90 | 7.34 |
| 2006-07 | 14.72 | 7.80 |
| 2007-08 | 14.90 | 8.12 |

*: Not scheduled.

*Source:* Reserve Bank of India.

Account to the Reserve Bank records, gross and net market borrowings (including 364-day Treasury Bills) during 2007-08 amounted to Rs. 1,88,205 crore and Rs. 1,09,504 crore, respectively, accounting for 99.7 per cent and 99.9 per cent of the estimated borrowings for the year. Gross market borrowings through dated securities by the Central Government during 2007-08 amounted to Rs. 1,56,000, crore as against Rs. 1, 51,000 crore scheduled in the issuance calendar for the year (Table 6.5). All auctions were re-issuances of existing securities, barring one new issue (10-year security) for Rs. 6,000 crore on July 9, 2007. During 2007-08, an amount of Rs. 957 crore devolved on Primary Dealer (PDs). The weighted average maturity of dated securities issued during 2007-08 at 14.90 years was higher than that of 14.72 years during the previous year. The weighted average yield of dated securities issued during 2007-08 was 8.12 per cent as compared with 7.89 per cent during 2006-07.

**Cash Management: Central Government**

Higher than anticipated speeding and a decline in investments in Treasury Bills by the States on account of lower collections under the National Small Saving Fund (NSSF) resulted in the recourse to Ways and Means Advance (WMA) during the greater part of the first quarter of 2007-08 by the Central Government, even as the year commenced with a surplus cash balance of Rs. 50,092 crore. The Central Government also resorted to overdraft during this period. A surplus was, however, built up in June 2007, ahead of acquisition of Reserve Bank's stake in SBI, which was used up by the month-end to meet this expenditure and the Central Government reverted to WMA. With the transfer of surplus from the Reserve Bank on August 9,2007, the Centre's cash balance returned to a surplus mode and remained so thereafter. The cash surplus surpassed Rs. 1,00,000 crore on March 19, 2008 on the strength of buoyant advance tax collections. As on March 31,2008 the surplus cash balance was placed at Rs. 76,686 crore. During 2007-08, the Centre took recourse to WMA for 91 days as compared with 39 days during 2006-07. The average utilisation of WMA/OD during 2007-08 was Rs. 4, 255 crore as compared with Rs. 402 crore in the previous year.

## Extra-Budgetary Items

The Union Government has recognised that revenue deficit and GFD are understated to the extent the Government incurs liabilities on account of oil, food and fertiliser bonds which are recorded blow the line. Therefore, as a step towards bringing about greater transparency in fiscal accounting, the Budget has reported in its revised estimates for 2007-08 the issuance of special securities aggregating Rs. 18,757 crore to a oil marketing companies (Rs. 11,257 crore) and fertiliser companies (Rs. 7,500 crore) in lieu of subsidies. During 2007-08, the actual issuance of special bonds to oil companies as compensation for under-recoveries and for settlement of contingent liabilities amounted to Rs. 20,333 crore and Rs. 221 crore, respectively. Special bonds issued to fertiliser companies as compensation for fertiliser subsidy amounted to Rs. 7,500 crore. The Central Government also issued special bonds worth Rs. 9,996 crore to State Bank of India as subscription towards State Bank of India's rights issue of equity shares.

## State Finances: 2007-08

The State Governments budgeted a revenue surplus of 0.3 per cent of GDP in 2007-08 as against a revenue deficit (RD) of 0.1 per cent in 2006-07 (RE). The Gross Fiscal Deficit (GFD) was budgeted at 2.3 per cent of GDP in 2007-08, lower by 0.4 percentage points over the previous year (see Table 6.7). The progressive enactment of Fiscal Responsibility Legislation (FRL) by 26 States has enabled them to usher in a rule-based fiscal regime. The efforts of the State Government towards reducing fiscal imbalances were aided by larger devolution and transfers from the Centre based on the recommendations of the Twelfth Finance Commission (TFC) along with the improvement in tax buoyancy on the strength of macroeconomic fundamentals. Furthermore, all States have implemented Value Added Tax (VAT) in lieu of sales tax, which has been an unqualified success in raising the tax revenue for the States. The State Governments while presenting their budgets for 2007-08 took into account the priorities as laid down in the Eleventh Five-Year Plan (2007-12). In order to ensure the quality of human resource development, social sector expenditure was proposed to be raised by higher allocations in 2007-08. In view of the priority given to infrastructure development in the Eleventh Five-Year Plan, the State Governments have envisaged implementation of various projects, especially power and roads. Several State Governments have proposed to implement the infrastructure projects through the framework of public-private partnership (PPP). The State Governments have also undertaken development of urban infrastructure under the Jawaharlal Nehru National Urban Renewal Mission (JNNURM).

The correction in the revenue account during 2007-08 has been envisaged to be achieved primarily through enhancement in revenue receipts by 14.2 per cent of top of 23.3 per cent growth recorded in the previous year. Revenue receipts as a per cent of GDP have been estimated to increase by 0.1 percentage point to 12.9 per cent in 2007-08, mainly on account of own tax revenue and devolution and transfers from the Centre. The improvement in revenue account would also be facilitated by deceleration in revenue expenditure to 10.8 per cent during 2007-08 from 22.6 per cent growth in the previous year. As a per cent of GDP, the revenue expenditure was placed at 12.7 per cent in 2007-08 (BE) as compared with 13.0 per cent in 2006-07 (RE).

The decomposition of consolidated GFD of all State Governments based on their budget documents reveals that the surplus in the revenue account would partly finance capital expenditure in 2007-08, in contrast to the previous year when RD constituted 4.9 per cent of GFD. Accordingly, the share of capital outlay in GFD was budgeted to increase from 92.1 per cent to 109.7 per cent in 2007-08. Securities issued to NSSF would continue to be the major financing item of GFD, though its share was budgeted to decline due to expected shortfall in net collections in keeping with the recent trends and the policy decision to reduce the minimum obligation of the States to borrow from the NSSF to 80 per cent of net collections from 100 per cent. Market borrowings would correspondingly finance a higher proportion of GFD during 2007-08 at 24.3 per cent as compared with 16.8 per cent during the previous year (Table 6.6).

**Cash Management and State Governments' Market Borrowings**

The net allocation (provisional) for the market borrowings of the State Government during 2007-08 was placed at Rs. 28,781 crore. Taking into account repayment of Rs. 11, 555 crore during the year, and additional allocation of Rs. 40,234 crore (of which Rs. 35,780 crore was on account of allocation made by the Centre Government in view of expected shortfall in NSSF collection), the gross allocation of market borrowings was placed at Rs. 80,570 crore for the year 2007-08. During 2007-08, the States (including the Union Territory of Ponducherry) raised market loans amounting to Rs. 67,779 crore (84.1 per cent of gross allocation) through auctions, as compared with Rs. 20,825 crore (78.3 per cent of gross allocation) during the previous year. The cut-off yield ranged between 7.84-8.90 per cent. The weighted average yield on market loans firmed up to 8.25 per cent during 2007-08 from 8.10 per cent in the previous year (Table 6.7).

The average daily utilisation of WMA and overdraft by States during 2007-08 was Rs. 648 crore, as against Rs. 248 crore During 2006-07. The average daily utilisation of WMA since December 2007 has been lower than the corresponding months of the preceding year. During 2007-08, eight States availed of WMA for a period of 1-184 days, of which three States resorted to overdraft for a period ranging between 3-65 days.

The cash surplus position of the States, as reflected in their

**Table 6.6 :** Decomposition and Financing Pattern of GFD of States

| *Item* | *1990-95 (Average)* | *1995-2000 (Average)* | *2000-05 (Average)* | *2005-06 (Accounts)* | *2006-07 (RE)* | *2007-08 (BE)* |
|---|---|---|---|---|---|---|
| 1 | 2 | 3 | 4 | 5 | 6 | 7 |
| Decomposition (1+2+3-4) | 100.0 | 100.0 | 100.0 | 100.0 | 100.0 | 100.0 |
| 1. Revenue Deficit | 25.2 | 47.1 | 54.6 | 7.8 | 4.9 | -11.1 |
| 2. Capital outlay | 55.4 | 43.1 | 40.5 | 86.1 | 92.1 | 109.7 |
| 3. Net Lending | 19.4 | 10.0 | 4.9 | 6.1 | 5.7 | 10.7 |
| 4. Non-debt Capital Receipts | - | 0.2 | - | - | 2.7 | 9.3 |
| Financial (1 to 11) | | | | | | |
| 1. Market Borrowings | 16.1 | 16.4 | 26.4 | 17.0 | 16.8 | 24.3 |
| 2. Loans from Centre | 48.8 | 39.7 | 4.3 | 0.0 | 1.8 | 6.0 |
| 3. Special Securities issued to NSSF/ Small Savings | - - | 28.9* | 40.2 | 81.9 | 51.5 | 49.6 |
| 4. Loans from LIC, NABARD, NCDC, SBI & Other Banks | 1.8 | 2.9 | 4.0 | 4.5 | 5.6 | 6.8 |
| 5. Small Saving, P.F., etc. | 17.6 | 16.2 | 10.1 | 11.6 | 9.6 | 11.4 |
| 6. Reserve Funds | 6.8 | 5.6 | 5.0 | 5.8 | 4.2 | 3.9 |
| 7. Deposits & Advances | 9.9 | 9.9 | 4.2 | 8.1 | 1.6 | 1.4 |
| 8. Suspense & Miscellaneous | 4.3 | 2.8 | -0.8 | 8.8 | 0.0 | -1.3 |
| 9. Remittances | -1.4 | -3.7 | 0.7 | 0.1 | 0.3 | 0.0 |
| 10. Others | 0.7 | 1.4 | 4.7 | -37.7 | 11.6 | -1.1 |

RE: Revised Estimates. BE: Budget Estimates. -: Nil Negligible/Not applicable.

NSSF: National Small Savings Fund.

*: Pertains to 1999-2000 as it was introduced from that year only. The sum of items for 1995-2000 (Average) will, therefore, not add up to 100.

*Note:* 1. Owing to the change in the accounting procedure form 1999-2000, loans the Centre excludes States 'share in small saving collections which is shown under securities issued to the NSSF under internal debt. Accordingly, repayments of small saving collections included under repayments of loans to Centre is shown under discharge of Internal Debt in order to have consistent accounting for receipts and expenditure.

2. 'Other' include Compensation and Other Bonds, Loans from Other Institutions. Appropriation to Contingency Fund. Inter-state Settlement and Contingency Fund.

3. Figures in respect of Jammu and Kashmir and Jharkhand relate to revised estimates.

4. All financing items are on a net basis.

*Source:* Budget Documents of the State Governments.

investments in Treasury Bills (14-day and auction Treasury Bills), remained sizeable, increasing from Rs.73,403 crore at end-March 2008. The average investment by the States in Treasury Bills during 2007-08 amounted to Rs. 73,680 crore as against Rs. 63,718 crore during the previous year.

**Table 6.7 :** Market Borrowings of State Government 2007-08

| *Item* | *Date* | *Cut-off Rate (Per cent)* | *Tenor (Years)* | *Amount Raised (Rupees Crore)* |
|---|---|---|---|---|
| *1* | *2* | *3* | *4* | *5* |
| ***Auctions*** | | | | |
| First | April 19, 2007 | 8.30 | 10 | 1,837 |
| Second | May 10, 2007 | 8.34 | 10 | 350 |
| Third | May 17, 2007 | 8.40 | 10 | 1,400 |
| Fourth | June 19, 2007 | 8.45-8.57 | 10 | 3,566 |
| Fifth | July 26, 2007 | 8.00-8.25 | 10 | 1,389 |
| Sixth | August 16, 2007 | 8.30-8.90 | 10 | 3,485 |
| Seventh | September 20, 2007 | 8.14-8.50 | 10 | 3,074 |
| Eighth | October 4, 2007 | 8.20 | 10 | 590 |
| Ninth | October 8, 2007 | 8.31-8.40 | 10 | 4,672 |
| Tenth | November 13, 2007 | 8.39-8.69 | 10 | 5,300 |
| Eleventh | November 30, 2007 | 8.45-8.50 | 10 | 5,212 |
| Twelfth | December 18, 2007 | 8.39-8.58 | 10 | 2,963 |
| Thirteenth | January 7, 2008 | 8.03-8.12 | 10 | 5,833 |
| Fourteenth | January 24, 2008 | 7.84-7.98 | 10 | 7,778 |
| Fifteenth | February 15, 2008 | 7.93-8.02 | 10 | 7,776 |
| Sixteenth | February 22, 2008 | 8.12-8.48 | 10 | 4,975 |
| Seventeenth | March 7, 2008 | 8.28-8.45 | 10 | 4,349 |
| Eighteenth | March 26, 2008 | 8.35-8.70 | 10 | 3,229 |
| **Grand Total** | | | | **67,779** |

***Memo***

| *Year* | *Weighted Average Yield (per cent)* |
|---|---|
| 2003-04 | 6.13 |
| 2004-05 | 6.45 |
| 2005-06 | 7.63 |
| 2006-07 | 7.10 |
| 2007-08 | 8.25 |

*Source:* Reserve Bank of India.

## Fiscal Outlook: 2008-09

The Union Budget for 2008-09 proposed to continue the Fiscal consolidation process, with the key deficit indicators, *viz.*, revenue deficit and GFD, budgeted to be lower by 0.4-0.6 percentage points and primary surplus higher by 0.5 percentage points of GDP in 2008-09 than in the previous year (Table 6.8).

While the FRBM targets relating to GFD are set to be achieved in accordance with the mandate, the Budget proposed to reschedule the stipulated target of zero revenue deficit by 2008-09 under FRBM Rules, 2004. Primarily on account of a shift in plan priorities in favour of revenue expenditure-intensive programmes and schemes. The Budget envisaged a revenue-led fiscal consolidation along with reprioritisation of expenditure to augment allocations for improvement in social and physical infrastructure, particularly in rural areas so as to achieve a 'faster and more inclusive' growth.

**Table 6.8 :** Union Budget 2008-09 at Glance

| *Item* | *2007-08* | *2008-09* | *Growth are (per cent)* | |
|---|---|---|---|---|
| | *(RE)* | *(BE)* | *2007-08* | *2008-09* |
| 1 | 2 | 3 | 4 | 5 |
| 1. Revenue | 5,25,098<br>(11.2) | 6,02,935<br>(11.4) | 20.9 | 14.8 |
| (i) Tax Revenue (Net) | 4,31,773<br>(9.2) | 5,07,150<br>(9.6) | 22.9 | 17.5 |
| (ii) Non-Tax Revenue | 93,325<br>(2.0) | 95,785<br>(1.8) | 12.2 | 2.6 |
| 2. Non-Plan Expenditure of which | 4,66318<br>(3.7) | 5,07,498<br>(9.6) | 12.8 | 8.8 |
| (i) Interest Payments | 1,71,971<br>(3.7) | 1,90,807<br>(3.6) | 14.4 | 11.0 |
| (ii) Defence Expenditure | 92,500<br>(2.0) | 105,600<br>(2.0) | 8.2 | 14.2 |
| (iii) Subsidies | 69,742<br>(1.5) | 71,431<br>(1.3) | 22.1 | 2.4 |
| 3. Plan Expenditure | 2,07,524<br>(4.4) | 2,43,386<br>(4.6) | 22.2 | 17.3 |
| 4. Revenue Expenditure | 5,88,586<br>(12.5) | 6,58,119<br>(12.4) | 14.4 | 11.8 |
| 5. Capital Expenditure | 85,256*<br>(1.8) | 92,765<br>(1.7) | 24.0 | 8.8 |
| 6. Total Expenditure | 6,73,842*<br>(14.4) | 7,50,884<br>(14.2) | 15.5 | 11.4 |
| 7. Revenue Deficit | 63,488<br>(1.4) | 55,184<br>(1.0) | -20.9 | -13.1 |
| 8. Gross Fiscal Deficit | 1,43,653<br>(3.1) | 1,33,287<br>(2.5) | 0.8 | -7.2 |
| 9. Gross Primary Deficit | -28,318<br>(-0.6) | -57,520<br>(-1.1) | 267-8 | 103.1 |

*: Net of acquisition cost Reserve Bank's stake in SBI at Rs. 35,531 crore.
*Note:* Figures in parentheses are percentages to GDP.

The procedural reforms aimed at expanding the tax base, improving efficiency in tax collections and providing certain concessions for investments, which have led to the remarkable improvement in tax collections in recent years, are expected to continue in 2008-09. As a result, the gross tax-GDP ratio, which has been rising since 2002-03, is budgeted to improve form 12.5 per cent in 2007-08 (RE) to 13.0 per cent in 2008-09 (BE) (Table 6.9).

**Table 6.9** : Gross Tax Revenues of the Centre

| *Year* | *Direct* | *Indirect* | *Total* |
|---|---|---|---|
| 1 | 2 | 3 | 4 |
| 1990-91 | 1.9 | 8.2 | 10.1 |
| 1991-92 | 2.3 | 8.0 | 10.3 |
| 1992-93 | 2.4 | 7.5 | 10.0 |
| 1993-94 | 2.4 | 6.4 | 8.8 |
| 1994-95 | 2.7 | 6.5 | 9.1 |
| 1995-96 | 2.8 | 6.5 | 9.3 |
| 1996-97 | 2.8 | 6.6 | 9.4 |
| 1997-98 | 3.2 | 6.0 | 9.1 |
| 1998-99 | 2.7 | 5.5 | 8.2 |
| 1999-00 | 3.0 | 5.8 | 8.8 |
| 2000-01 | 3.2 | 5.7 | 9.0 |
| 2001-02 | 3.0 | 5.2 | 8.2 |
| 2002-03 | 3.4 | 5.4 | 8.8 |
| 2003-04 | 3.8 | 5.4 | 9.2 |
| 2004-05 | 4.2 | 5.5 | 9.7 |
| 2005-06 | 4.6 | 5.8 | 10.4 |
| 2006-07 | 5.3 | 6.1 | 11.4 |
| 2007-08 RE | 6.5 | 6.0 | 12.5 |
| 2008-09 BE | 6.9 | 6.1 | 13.0 |

Aggregate expenditure (adjusted for acquisition cost of Reserve Bank's stake in SBI in 2007-08) is budgeted to increase by 11.4 per cent in 2008-09 as compared with 15.5 per cent in the preceding year. Revenue expenditure in 2008-09 is budgeted to increase by 11.8 per cent as compared with 14.4 per cent in 2007-08 on account of containment of subsidies and deceleration in the growth of interest payments. The growth in grants to States and Union Territories is, however, budgeted to be higher at 16.3 per cent than 15.7 per cent a year ago. The capital expenditure comprising capital outlay and loans and advances is budgeted to decline by 23.2 per cent

The financing pattern of GFD reveals that the share of net market borrowings (excluding allocations under MSS) decline to 74.3 per cent of the GFD in 2008-09 from 77.1 per cent in 2007-08. On the other hand, the share of external assistance is budgeted to increase to 8.2 per cent from 6.9 per cent in 2007-08. Investments by the National Small Savings Fund (NSSF) in the special Central Government securities are budgeted to finance 7.4 per cent of GFD, as against a negative contribution of 1.3 per cent last year. During 2008-09, the budget expects draw drown of cash balances to finance 5.4 per cent of GFD, as against build up of cash balances amounting to 12-7 per cent of GFD in 2007-08.

**Indian Financial Sector Reforms**

The banking system in India has undergone significant changes during last 15 years. There have been new banks, new instruments, new windows, new opportunities and, along with all this, new challenges. While deregulation has opened up new vistas for banks to augments revenues, it has also entailed greater competition and consequently greater risks. The traditional face of banks as mere financial intermediaries has since altered and risk management has emerged as the defining attribute.

Financial sector reforms introduced in the early 1990s as a part of the structural reforms have touched upon almost all aspects of banking operations. For a few decades preceding the onset of banking and financial sector reforms in India, banks operated in an environment that was heavily regulated and characterised by sufficient barriers to entry, which protected them against too much competition. This regulated environment set in complacency in the manner in which banks operated and responded to the customer needs. The administered interest rate structure, both on the liability and the assets sides, allowed banks to earn reasonable spread without much efforts. Despite this, however, bank's profitability was low and NPLs level was high, reflecting lack of efficiency. Although banks operated under regulatory constrains in the form of statutory holding of Government securities (statutory liquidity ratio or SLR) and the Cash Reserve Ratio (CRR) and lacked functional autonomy and operational efficiency, the fact was that most banks did not operate efficiently.

While the broad objectives of the financial sector reforms, thus, were to enhance efficiency and productivity, the process of reforms were initiated in a gradual and properly sequenced manner so as to have a reinforcing effect. The approach has been to consistently upgrade the financial sector by adopting the international best practices through a consultative process. Financial sector reforms were carried out in two phases. The first phase of reforms was aimed at creating productive and profitable financial institutions operating within the environment of operational flexibility and functional autonomy. The focus of the second phase of financial sector reforms starting from the second-half of 1990s has been on strengthening the financial system consistent with the movement towards global integration of financial services.

## Financial Sector Reforms in India

The deregulation of interest rates constituted an integral part of financial sector reforms. The interest rate regime has been largely deregulated with a view to achieving better price discovery and efficient resource allocation. Banks now have flexibility to decide their deposit ad lending rate structures and manage their assets and liabilities accordingly. At present, apart from interest rates on savings deposits and NRI deposits on the deposit side, and export credit and small loans up to Rs. 2 lakh on the lending side, all other interest rates have been deregulated.

Indian banking system operated for a long time with high reserve requirements both in the form of CRR and SLR. This was mainly to accommodate the high fiscal deficit and its monetisation. The efforts in the recent period have been to lower both the CRR and SLR. The SLR has been gradually reduced from a peak of 38.5 to 25 per cent. The CRR was reduced from its peak level of 15.0 per cent maintained during 1989 to 1992 to 4.5 per cent of net demand and time liabilities (NDTL) in June 2003. Although the Reserve Bank continues to pursue its medium-term objective of reducing the CRR, in recent years, on a review of macroeconomic and monetary conditions, the CRR has been revised upwards to 6.0 per cent (to be effective from March 3, 2007).

It has been the endeavour of the Reserve Bank to establish an enabling regulatory framework with prompt and effective supervision, and development of legal, technological and institutional infrastructure. Persistent efforts, therefore, have been made towards adoption of international benchmarks, as appropriate to Indian conditions. In 1994, a Board for Financial Supervision (BFS) was constituted comprising select Members of the Reserve Bank Board with a variety of professional expertise to exercise 'undivided attention to supervision' and ensure an intergrated approach to supervision of commercial banks and financial institutions. The Reserve Bank had instituted a state of-the-art off-site Monitoring and Surveillance (OSMOS) system for banks in 1995 as part of crisis management framework for Early Warning System (EWS) and as a trigger for on-site inspections of vulnerable institutions. The scope and coverage of off-site surveillance has since been widened to capture various facets of efficiency and risk management of banks.

As a part the financial sector reforms, the regulatory norms with respect to capital adequacy, income recognition, asset classification and provisioning have progressively moved towards convergence with the international best practices. These measures have enhanced transparency of the balance sheet of the banks and infused accountability in their functioning. Besides sub-standard assets, provisioning has also been introduced for the standard assets. Measures to reduce the levels of NPAs concentrated on improved risk management practices and greater recovery efforts facilitated by the enactment of Securitisation and Reconstruction of Financial Assets and Enforcement of Security Interest (SARFAESI) Act, 2002. Several other channels of NPA management have also been instituted, *including Debt Recovery Tribunals, Lok Adalats* (People Court) and corporate debt restructuring mechanism with separate schemes for small and medium industries.

The minimum capital to risk weighted assets ratio (CRWAR), which was earlier stipulated at eight per cent was revised to 9 per cent in 1999, which is one percentage point above the international norm. As some banks in the public sector were not able to comply with the CRWAR stipulations, there was a need to recapitalise them to augment their capital base. Banks were allowed to raise capital from the market. In line with the amendment to incorporate market risk in Basel I, separate capital charge from market risk was also introduced in 2004.

Accounting standards and disclosure norms were strengthened with a view to improving governance and bringing them in alignment with the international norms. The disclosure requirements broadly covered capital adequacy, asset quality, maturity distribution of select items of assets and liabilities, profitability, country risk exposure, risk exposures in derivatives, segment reporting, and related party disclosures. In April 2005, commercial banks were advised to put in place business continuity measures, including a robust information risk management system within a fixed time frame.

In view of the increasing degree of deregulation and exposure of banks to various types of risks, the Reserve Bank initiated measures for further strengthening and fine-turning risk management systems in banks. The guidelines on asset-liability management and risk management systems in banks were issued in 1999 and Guidance Notes on Credit Risk Management and Market Risk Management in October 2002 and the Guidance Note on Operational Risk Management in 2005. In the Reserve

Bank the risk-based approach to supervision has been adopted since 2003 and about 23 banks supervision (RBS) on a pilot basis. On the basis of the feedback received from the pilot project, the RBS framework is being reviewed.

As part of the reform programme, due consideration has been given to diversification of ownership of banking institutions for greater market accountability and improved efficiency. The public sector banks expanded their base by accessing the capital market, which diluted the Government ownership. To provide banks with additional options for raising capital funds with a view to enabling smooth transition to the Basel II, the Reserve Bank in January 2006, allowed banks to augment their capital funds by issue of additional instruments.

With a view to enhancing efficiency and productivity through competition, guidelines were laid down for establishment of new banks in the private sector and the foreign banks have been allowed more liberal entry. Since 1993, 12 new private sector banks have been set up. As a major step towards enhancing competition in the private sector banks is now allowed up to 74 per cent, subject to conformity with the guidelines issued from time to time. The regulatory framework in India, in addition to prescribing prudential guidelines and encouraging market discipline, is increasingly focusing on ensuring good governance through 'fit and proper' owners, directors and senior managers of the banks. Transfer of shareholding of five per cent and above requires acknowledgement from the Reserve Bank and such significant shareholders are required to meet rigorous 'fit and proper' requirements. Banks have also been asked to ensure that the nominated and elected directors are screened by a nomination committee to satisfy 'fit and proper' criteria. Directors are also required to sign a covenant indicating their roles and responsibilities. The Reserve Bank has issued detailed guidelines on ownership and governance in private sector banks emphasizing diversified ownership.

The Reserve Bank released a roadmap for foreign banks articulating a liberalised policy consistent with the WTO commitments in March 2005. The roadmap is divided into two phases. During the first phase, between March 2005 and March 2009, foreign banks wishing to establish presence in India for the first time could either choose to operate through branches or set up 100 per cent Wholly Owned Subsidiaries (WOS), following the one-mode presence criterion. For new and existing foreign banks, it is proposed to go beyond the existing WTO commitment of 12 branches in a year. During this phase, permission for acquisition of shareholding in Indian private sector banks by eligible foreign banks will be limited to banks identified by the Reserve Bank for restructuring. The second phase is scheduled to commence from April 2009 after a review of the experience gained and after due consultation with all the stakeholders in the banking sector. In this phase, three interconnected issues would be taken up. First, rules for the removal of limitations on the operations of the WOS and treating them at par with domestic banks, to the extent appropriate, would be designed and implemented. Second, the WOS of foreign banks, on completion of a minimum prescribed period of operation, may be allowed to list and dilute their stake so that, consistent with the guidelines issued on March 5, 2004, at least 26 per cent of the paid-up capital of the subsidiary is held by resident Indians at all times. Third, during this phase, foreign banks may be permitted to enter into merger and acquisition transactions with any private sector bank in India, subject to the overall investment limit of 74 per cent.

In recent years, comprehensive credit information, which provides details pertaining to credit facilities already availed of by a borrower as well as his payment track record, has become critical. Accordingly, a scheme for disclosure of information regarding defaulting borrowers of banks and financial institutions was introduced. In order to facilitate sharing of information related to credit matters, a Credit Information Bureau (India) Limited (CIBIL) was set up in 2000.

The Banking Ombudsman Scheme was notified by the Reserve Bank in 1995 to provide for a system of redressal of grievances against banks. The scheme sought to establish a system of expeditious and inexpensive resolution of customer complaints. The scheme was revised twice, first in 2002 and then in 2006. At present, the scheme is being executed by Banking Ombudsman (BO) appointed by the Reserve Bank at 15 centres covering the entire country. The BO scheme covers all commercial banks and scheduled primary cooperative banks. The scheme was revised recently which brought more grounds of complaints within its ambit.

An independent Banking Codes and Standards Board of India was set up on the model of the UK in order to ensure that comprehensive code of conduct for fair treatment of customers is evolved and adhered to. With a view to achieving greater financial inclusion, since November 2005, all banks need to make available a basic banking 'no frills' account either with 'nil' or very low minimum balances as well as charges that would make such accounts accessible to vast sections of population. Banks were urged to review their existing practices to align them with the objective of 'financial inclusion'.

The smooth functioning of the payment and settlement system is a pre-requisite for financial stability. The Reserve Bank, therefore, has taken several measures from time to time to develop the payment and settlement system in the country along sound line. The Board for Regulation and Supervision of Payment and Settlement Systems (BPSS), set up in March 2005 as a Committee of the Central Board of the Reserve Bank, is the apex body for giving policy direction in the area of payment and settlement systems. Real Time Gross Settlement (RTGS) was operationalised on March 26, 2004. Its usage for transfer of funds, especially for large values and for systemically important purposes, has increased since then. With introduction of RTGS, whereby a final settlement of individual inter-bank fund transfers is effected on a gross real time basis during the processing day, a major source of systemic risk in the financial system has been reduced substantially.

A risk free payments and settlements system in government securities and foreign exchange was established by the Clearing Corporation of India Limited (CCIL), which is set up by banks. CCIL, acts as the Central Counter Party (CCP) fro mall the transactions and guarantees both the securities and funds legs of the transaction. Under the DvPIII mode of settlement that has been adopted, both the securities leg and the fund leg are settled on a net basis. The settlement through CCIL has thus reduced the gross dollar requirement by more than 90 per cent. A screen-based negotiated quote-driven system for dealings in the call/notice and the term money market (NDS-CALL) has been launched by the CCIL in September 18, 2006. The introduction of NDS-CALL helps in enhancing transparency, improving price discovery and strengthening market microstructure.

**Impact of Financial Sector Reforms in India**

Banks have been accorded greater discretion in sourcing and utilisation of resources, *albeit* in an increasingly competitive environment. The outreach of the Indian banking system has increased in terms of expansion of branches/ATMs. In the post-reform period, assets/liabilities of banks have grown consistently at a high rate. The financial performance of banks also improved as reflected in their increased profitability. Net profit to assets ratio improved from 0.49 per cent in 2000-01 to 1.13 per cent in 2003-04. Although it subsequently declined to 0.88 per cent in 2005-06, it was still significantly higher than that in the early 1990s. Banks have been successful in weathering the impact of upturn in interest rate cycle through increasing diversification of their income. Though banks had to incur huge expenditures on up gradation of information technology, the restructuring of the workforce in public sector banks helped them cut down the staff cost and increase in business per employee.

Another welcome development has been the sharp reduction in non-performing loans (NPLs). Both gross and net NPLs started to decline in absolute terms since 2002-03. Gross NPLs as percentage of gross advances, which were above 15 per cent in the early 1990s, are now less than 3 per cent. This distinct improvement in asset quality may be attributed to the improved recovery climate underpinned by strong macroeconomic performance as well as several institutional measures initiated by the Reserve Bank/Government such as debt recovery tribunals, *Lok Adalats*, scheme of corporate debt restructuring in 2001, the SARFAESI Act in 2002.

Since 1995-96, the banking sector, on the whole, has been consistently maintaining CRAR well above the minimum stipulated norm. the overall CRAR for scheduled commercial banks increased from 8.7 per cent at end-March 1996 to 12.3 per cent at end-March 2006. The number of banks not complying with the minimum CRRA also declined from 13 at end-March 1996 to just two by end-March 2006. Improved capital position stemmed largely from the improvement in profitability and raising of capital from the market, though in the initial stages the Government had to provide funds to recapitalise weak public sector banks.

Even though public sector banks continue to dominate the Indian banking system, accounting for nearly three-fourths of total assets and income, the increasing competition in the banking system has led to a falling share of public sector banks, and increasing share of the new private sector banks, which were set up around mid-1990s. It is clear that we are at the beginning of this new phase in the Indian banking with competitive pressure, both domestic and external, catching up and the need for banks to continuously reassess and reposition themselves in their business plans.

**Future Challenges for Indian Banks**

A few broad challenges facing the Indian banks are: (1) threats of risks from globalisation, (2) implementation of Basel II, (3) improvement of risk management systems, (4) implementation of new accounting standards, (5) enhancement of transparency and disclosures, (6) enhancement of customer service, and (7) application of technology.

### Globalisation – A Challenge as well as An Opportunity

The waves of globalisation are sweeping across the world, and have thrown up several opportunities accompanied by concomitant risks. Integration of domestic market with international financial markets has been facilitated by tremendous advancement in information and communications technology. There is a growing realisation that the ability of countries to conduct business across national borders and the ability to cope with the possible downside risks would depend, *inter alia*, on the soundness of the financial system. This has necessitated convergence of prudential norms with international best practices as well consistent refinement of the technological and institutional framework in the financial sector through a non-disruptive and consultative process.

### Opening up of the Capital Account

The committee on Fuller Capital Account Convertibility (Chairman: Shri S.S. Tarapore) observed that under a full capital account convertibility regime, the banking system would be exposed to greater market volatility, and this necessitated enhancing the risk management capabilities in the banking system in view of liquidity risk, interest rate risk, currency risk, counter-party risk and country risk that arise from international capital flows. The potential dangers associated with the proliferation of derivative instruments credit derivatives and interest rate derivatives also need to be recognised in the regulatory and supervisory system. The issues relating to cross-border supervision of financial intermediaries in the context of greater capital flows are just emerging and need to be addressed.

## Basel II Implementation

The Reserve Bank and the commercial banks have been preparing to implement Basel II, and it has been decided to allow banks some more time in adhering to new norms. As against the deadline of March 31, 2007 for compliance with Basel II, it was decided in October 2006 that foreign banks operating in India and Indian banks having presence outside India would migrate to the standardized approach for credit risk and the basic indicator approach for operational risk under Basel II with effect from March 31, 2008, while all other scheduled commercial banks are required to migrate to Basel II by March 31, 2009.

It is widely acknowledged that implementation of Basel II poses significant challenge to both banks and the regulators. Basel II implementation may also be seen as a compliance challenge. But at the same time, it offers two major opportunities to banks, *viz*., refinement of risk management systems: and improvement in capital efficiency. The transition from Basel I to Basel II essentially involves a move from capital adequacy to capital efficiency. This transition in how capital is used and how much capital is needed will become a significant factor in return-on-equity strategy for years to come.

The reliance on the market to assess the friskiness of banks would lead to increased focus on transparency and market disclosure, critical information describing the risk profile, capital structure and capital adequacy. Besides making banks more accountable and responsive to better-informed investors, these processes enable banks to strike the right balance between risk and rewards and to improve the access to markets. Improvements in market discipline also call for greater coordination between banks and regulators.

## Improving Risk Management Systems

Basel II has brought into focus the need for a more

comprehensive risk management framework to deal with various risks, including credit and market risk and their inter-linkages. Banks in India are also moving from the individual silo system to an enterprise-wide risk management system. While the first milestone would be risk integration across the entity, the next step would entail risk aggregation across the group both in the specific risk areas as also across the risks. Banks would, therefore, be required to allocate significant resources towards this endeavour. In India, the risk-based approach to supervision is also serving as a catalyst to banks' migration to the integrated risk management systems. However, taking into account the diversity in the Indian banking systems, stabilising the RBS as an effective supervisory mechanism is another challenge.

**Corporate Governance**

To a large extent, many risk management failures reflect a breakdown in corporate governance which arise due to poor management of conflict of interest, inadequate understanding of key banking risks, and poor Board oversight of the mechanisms for risk management and internal audit. Corporate governance is, therefore, the foundation for effective risk managements in banks and, thus, the foundation for a sound financial system. Therefore, the choices which banks make when they establish their risk management and corporate governance systems have important ramifications for financial stability. Banks may have to cultivate a good governance culture building in appropriate checks and balances in their operations. There are four important forms of oversight that should be included in the organisational structure of nay bank in order to ensure appropriate checks and balances; (i) oversight by the board of directors or supervisory board; (ii) oversight by individuals not involved in the day-to-day running of the various business areas; (iii) direct line supervision of different business area; and (iv) independent risk management, compliance and audit functions. In addition, it is important that key personnel are fit and proper for their jobs. Furthermore, the general principles of sound corporate governance should also be applied to all banks, irrespective of their unique ownership structures.

## Implementation of New Accounting Standards

Derivative activity in banks has been increasing at a brisk pace. While the risk management framework for derivative trading, which is a relatively new area for Indian banks (particularly in the more structured products) is an essential pre-requisite, the absence of clear accounting guidelines in this area is a matter of significant concern. The World Bank's ROSC on Accounting and Auditing in India has commented on the absence of an accounting standard which deals with recognition, measurement and disclosures pertaining to financial instruments. The Accounting Standards Board of the Institute of Chartered Accountants of India (ICAI) is considering issue of Accounting Standards in respect of financial instruments. These will be the Indian parallel to International Accounting Standards 32 and 39. The proposed Accounting Standards will be of considerable significance for financial entities and could, therefore, have implications for the financial sectors. The formal introduction of these Accounting Standards by the ICAI is likely to take some time in view of the processes involved. In the meanwhile, the Reserve Bank is considering the need for banks and financial entities adopting the broad underlying principles of IAS 39. Since this is likely to give rise to some regulatory/prudential issues, all relevant aspects are being comprehensively examined. The proposals in this regard would, as is normal, be discussed with the market participants before introduction. Adoption and implementation of these principles are likely to pose a great challenge to both the banks and the Reserve Bank.

## Supervision of Financial Conglomerates

The financial landscape is increasingly witnessing entry of some of the bigger banks into other financial segments like merchant banking, insurance etc. Emergence of several new players with diversified presence across major segments make it imperative for supervision to be spread across various segments of the financial sector. In this direction, an inter-regulatory Working Group was constituted with members from the Reserve Banks, SEBI and IRDA. The framework proposed by the Group is complementary to the existing regulatory structure wherein the individual entities are regulated by the respective regulators and the identified financial conglomerates are subjected to focused regulatory oversight through a mechanism of inter-regulatory exchange of information. As a first step in this direction. An inter-agency Working Group on Financial Conglomerates (FC) comprising the above three supervisory bodies identified 23 FCs and a pilot process for obtaining information from these conglomerates has been initiated. The complexities involved in the supervision of financial conglomerates are a challenge not only to the Reserve Bank of India but also to the other regulatory agencies, which need to have a close and continued coordination on an on-going basis.

In view of increased focus on empowering supervisors to undertake consolidated supervision of bank groups and since the Core Principles for Effective Banking Supervision issued by the Basel Committee on Banking Supervision have underscored consolidated supervision as an independent principle, the Reserve Bank had introduced, as an initial step, consolidated accounting and other quantitative methods to facilitate consolidated supervision. The components of consolidated supervision include, consolidated financial statements intended for public disclosure, consolidated prudential reports intended for supervisory assessment of risks and application of certain prudential regulations on group basis. In due course, consolidated supervision as introduced above would evolve to cover banks in mixed conglomerates, where the parent may be non-financial entities or parents may be financial entities coming under the jurisdiction of other regulators.

## Application of Advanced Technology

The role technology in banking in creating new business models and processes, in maintaining competitive advantage, in enhancing quality of risk management systems in banks, and in revolutionizing distribution channels, cannot be overemphasised. Recognising the benefits of modernising their technology infrastructure, banks are taking the right initiatives. While doing so, banks have four options to choose from: they can build a new system themselves, or buy best of the modules, or buy a comprehensive solution, or outsource. A further challenge which banks face in this regard is to ensure that they derive maximum advantage from their investments in technology and avoid wasteful expenditure which might arise on account of uncoordinated and piecemeal adoption of technology: adoption of inappropriate/inconsistent technology and adoption of obsolete technology. A case in point is the implementation of core banking solution by some banks without assessing its scalability or adaptability to meet Basel II requirements.

## Financial Inclusion

While banks are focusing on the methodologies of meeting the increasing demand placed on them, there are legitimate concerns with regard to the banking practices that tend to exclude rather than attract vast sections of population, in particular pensioners, self-employed and those employed in unorganized sector. While commercial considerations are not doubt important, banks have been bestowed with several privileges, especially of seeking public deposits on a highly leveraged basis, and consequently they should be obliged to provide banking services to all segments of the population, on equitable basis. Further, experience has shown that consumers' interests are at times not accorded full protection and their grievances are not properly attended to. Feedback received reveals recent trends of levying unreasonably high service/user charges and enhancement of user charges without proper and prior intimation. It is in this context that the Governor, Reserve Bank of India had mentioned in the Annual Policy Statement 2005-06 that the Reserve Bank will take initiatives to encourage greater degree of financial inclusion in the country: (1) setting up of a mechanism for ensuring fair treatment of consumers, and (2) effective redressal of customer grievances.

## Conclusion

With the increasing levels of globalisation of the Indian banking industry, evolution of universal banks and bundling of financial services, competition in the banking industry will intensify further. The banking industry has the potential and the ability to rise to the occasion as demonstrated by the rapid pace of automation which has already had a profound impact on raising the standard of banking services. The financial strength of individual banks, which are major participants in the financial system, is the first line of defence against financial risks. Strong capital positions and balance sheets place banks in a better position to deal with and absorb the economic shocks.

## Notes

1. The financial implementations of this strategy, along with reduction of inter-personal and inter-regional disparities, have constituted the basic goals of fiscal policy in post-colonial India. Apropos the literature on assignment of instruments to targets, it is important to task whether even in principle fiscal policy could simultaneously meet all these goals. (See, *Tinbergen, Jan, On the Theory of Economic Policy*, North Holland: Amsterdam, 1952) However, the present paper is confined to the record of actual performance.
2. For a detailed analysis of savings and investment behaviour of different institutional sectors, see Bagehi, Amaresh and Nayak, P., "Public Finance and the Planning Process: The Indian

Experience", paper presented at the International Seminar on Public Economics, New Delhi, January 1990.

3. See *Economic Survey, Ministry of Finance, Government of India*, 1991-92.
4. Buiter, W.H. and Patel, V. R. "Debt, Deficits and Inflation: An Application to the Public Finance of India", in the *Journal of Public Economics,* Volume 47 No. 2, 1990; Gengerg, H., *Fiscal Policy, Debt, Growth and Inflation in a Long Run Perspective: An analytical Framework with an Application to India*, World Bank, 1989; Rangarajan, C., Basu Anupam and Jadhav, Narendra, "Dynamics of Interaction Between Government Deficit and Domestic Debt in India", paper presented at the International Seminar on Public Economics, New Delhi, 1990.
5. This thesis was developed in greater detail in Mundle, Sudipto, "Food, Finance and Foreign Trade: The Limits of High Growth in India", where it was argued that the then prevailing high growth would not be sustainable.
6. Reddy, K.N., Growth of *Public Expenditure in India* 1872-1968, Delhi: Sterling publishers, 1972; Premehand, A, Control of Public Expenditure in India: A Historical and Analytical Account of the Administrative, Audit and Parliamentary Problem, Delhi: Allied Publishers, 1963; Toyer, J., Public Expenditure and Indian Development Policy 1960-1970 Cambridge University Press, 1981 among others. For the work done during the more recent period, see Sarma, Atul and Tulasidhar, V.B., *Economic Impact of Government Expenditure: An Analysis in Input Output Framework,* Delhi: Concept Pubilishing Co, 1984; Mundle, Sudipto, "Pattern of Public Expenditure in India: A Financial Perspective of the Development State", paper presented at a conference on 'The State and International Linkages', the Hague, 1988 and Rao, M. Govinda, and Tulasidhar, V.B., "Public Expenditure in India: Emerging Trends", NIPFP Working Paper No 5/1991, 1991.
7. See Mundle, Sudipto and Mukhopadhyay, Hiranya, "A Note on Central Government Expenditures", paper presented to the Finance Minister, New Delhi, November 1991. Excerpts of this paper were published in the *Economic Times*, 20 January 1992, See also the paper by Chelliah, Raja, J., "Growth of Indian Public Debt", in this volume.
8. "Distributional Coalitions" is taken to mean a narrow special

interest group having disproportionate organizational power for collective action. See, Olson, Mancur, Rise and Decline of the Nations New Haven: Yale University Press, 1982.

9. For a more detailed discussion of these issues and an earlier estimate of subsides in India See Mundle, Sudipto, and Rao, M. Govinda, "Volume and Composition of Government Subsidies in India, 1987-88", in the *Economic and Political Weekly*, 4 May, 1991. The earlier estimates have now been revised and are being reported here for the first times.
10. According to the Scheme, the Reserve Bank of India would not be obliged to honour the cheques of the states having overdrafts beyond seven continuous working days.
11. These Growth rates relate to the period upto 1987-88. Compensation is later years was a consequence of the salary revision subsequent to the Fourth Central Pay Commission Report. The revision is estimated to have increased the salary bill by 18 per cent.
12. The Central transfers to the states in 1991-92 increased by less than 7 per cent over the previous year in nominal terms and the estimated increased in 1992-93 is just over 8 per cent.

# 7 EXPORT VARIABLES AND ECONOMIC GROWTH

## Constant Market Share

Export promotion is a major objective of India's economic policy today. The fulfilment of this objective depends heavily on the international competitiveness of her exportable. While the concept of international competitiveness can be said to consist of different factors, ultimately the litmus test of the competitive position of a country *vis-à-vis* other countries is in the relative market share of its exportable in the world market.

There are many factors that can affect a country's international competitiveness. It is a painstaking but useful task to identify these constituents and examine their influences on competitiveness. Such an exercise would be of great value to a policy-maker. However, this is beyond the scope of the present study where the focus is only on the price factors. In particular, an analysis of the extent to which the price factors here important in the international competitiveness of India's exportable during the last two decade is made here.

Many authors have examined closely, and from various angles, the international competitiveness of a country's exportables.

In the literature subjecting this topic to scrutiny, the Constant Market Share (CMS) analysis has occupied a significant place. It is a simplified method for examining a country's export performance. The concept of market share is the basis for this type of analysis. The extensive application of the CMS norm belongs to two main categories. The simpler version statistically decomposes the source of export performance and distinguishes between changes in market penetration (market share) and changes in the size of these markets. Thus, here CMS analysis uses aggregate export data to measure the difference between the constant share norm and actual export performance. By this procedure, export performance is assumed to be invariant regarding commodity desegregation. We can find an application of this procedure in Hickman *et al.* (1979), and Mekesell and Farah (1981), to name just two studies.

The more comprehensive version of CMS analysis takes into account the commodity composition effect along with the market size effects, the world market effect the competitiveness effect. In this method, competitiveness is actually a residual term. First applied to export growth by Tyszynski (1951), this approach has since then been employed by many authors. It has also been used by a few authors to study India's export performance (see Biswas ,1982, Leela, 1985, Tiwari, 1986). These studies try to explain a country's export performance in terms of general competitiveness. Though the existence of price and non-price factors affecting competitiveness have been recognized, their specific influences were not properly investigated in these studies. While non-price factors and their changes are difficult to quantify, on the other hands, price competitiveness can be measured at least approximately through various relevant indicators. Price factors also include costs, profits and all such underlying influences. Of the studies dealing with price competitiveness, we may mention two, which have been conducted keeping the Indian context in, mind, namely, papers by Verghese (1979) and Narmbiar and Mehta (1989).

The remaining part of the section is divided into three sub-sections. Sub-sections 5.1 and 5.2 describe the methodology and also the results obtained from two separate but related studies that were conducted by use. Finally, sub-section 5.3 attempts an analysis of the economic rationale underlying the observed results and overall conclusions are offered.

## Methodology

We have concentrated on the general competitiveness as well as the price competitiveness of India's exportable during the two decades; the 1970s and the 1980s. To that ends, two related but separate studies have been undertaken by us. The first tries to throw light on India's export performance in the OECD countries by comparison with eight newly industrialized countries (NICs), and the other is related to India's export performance in manufactures, relative to thirteen major exporters of manufactures in the world market. In both cases, the influence of price factors on competitiveness has been examined.

For the first part of our study, our decision to take the OECD as the target groups of importers was not a very difficult one. The OECD, consisting of twenty-four developed, industrialized countries, clearly serves as the most crucial market for world trade. India's export performance and its competitive position in the OECD market are judged *vis-à-vis* eight NICs. These are Brazil, Mexico, Hong Kong, the Republic of Korea, Singapore, Malaysia, Thailand and Indonesia. The NICs are now emerging as prominent figures in the economic scenario of the world, and it would be worthwhile to see how far India, a developing Third World country, has been able to compete with them in a crucial international market during the last two decades.

The method of CMS analysis developed by Hickman *et al.* (1979) has been used here to study India's export performance with respect to its total exports (of all commodities) in the OECD region. It should be emphasized that the CMS analysis is merely a measurement technique for decomposing the growth of a variable, and should not be viewed as a behavioural relationship.

In our study we have divided the OECD into five groups: namely, the EEC; the EFTA and Turkey; USA and Canada; Australia and New Zealand; and Japan. The European Economic Community(EEC) consists of (1)

Belgium, (2) Luxembourg, (3) Denmark, (4) France, (5) Federal Republic of Germany, (6) Greece, (7) Ireland, (8) Italy, (9) Netherlands, (10) Portugal, (11) Spain and (12) the UK; The European Free Trade Area (EFTA) consists of (1) Austria, (2) Finland, (3) Iceland, (4) Norway, (5) Sweden and (6) Switzerland. Obvious geographical and economic considerations have led us to divide the OECD into the above-mentioned categories. Turkey has been grouped with the EFTA only because it does not merit a separate grouping.

For the algebraic representation of the CMS model we must introduce the following definitions.

$X_{ijt}$ - Export from country I to region j in year t.

$X_{it} = \Sigma^{n}_{j=1} X_{ijt}$ = Total exports of the country I to all regions (that is, to the OECD markets) in the year t.

$M_{it} = \Sigma^{n}_{j=1} X_{ijt}$ = Total imports of the $j^{th}$ region from all of the m exporters.

$W_t = \Sigma^{m}_{j=1} X_{it} = \Sigma^{n}_{j=1} M_{ijt}$ = Total export to the OECD market by all the m exporters or total imports by all the n region from all the m exporters in year t.

$\alpha_{ijt} = \frac{X_{ijt}}{M_{jt}}$ = The market share of the exporting country I in region j in year t.

$\beta_{ijt} = \frac{Mjt}{W_t}$ = The import share of region j of the total imports by all regions in year t.

$Y_{it} = \frac{X_{jt}}{W_t}$ = The market share of the country I in terms of total export to all regions.

j = 1 ... n = Where n = 5 regional markets in the OECD

j = 1 … n Where m = 9 exporting countries (India and eight NICS) to the OECD market.

0 The subscript used to denote the base year.

Applying these definitions and summing over all five regional markets, we can derive expression (1) that decomposes total export by country I in year t to the OECD market into four components.

$$X_{it} = \Sigma^5_{j=1} X_{ijt} = [\Sigma^5_{j=1} \alpha_{jo} \beta_{jo}]\, W_1 +$$
$$[\Sigma^5_{j=1} \beta_{jo} \Delta\alpha_{jo}]\, W_1 +$$
$$[\Sigma^5_{j=1} \alpha_{ijo} \Delta\beta_{jo}]\, W_1 +$$
$$[\Sigma^5_{j=1} \beta_{ijo} \Delta\alpha_{jit}]\, W_1 + \qquad (4.1)$$

**Constant Market Share (CMS)**

The first term gives the constant market share or the value of exports for country I in year t, assuming that the country's share of the OECD market has remained unchanged since the base period. To show this, we note that in the base period $\Delta\beta_{jt} = \Delta\alpha_{ijt} = 0$; so that (1) reduces to

$$Xjo = [\Sigma^5_{j=1} \alpha_{ijo} \beta_{jo}] W_o$$

where:

$$Yjo = [\Sigma 5j{=}1\, \alpha_{ijo} \beta_{jo}] \qquad (4.2)$$

**The Competitive Effect**

The second term summarizes the effect of changes in the I[th] country's market shares ($\Delta\alpha_{ijt}$) for all regions since the base period, holding constant the relative size ($\beta_{jo}$) of the various importing regions. This term isolates the influence of changes in the competitiveness of country I in specific OECD markets.

## The Market Size Effect

The third term measures the net effect of shift in the size of the various regional markets, holding constant the I$^{th}$ country's share in ach market. On account of this market size effect, the market share of country I in the total exports may increase without any change in its export competitiveness, provided that the markets that are to relatively greater importance to country I grow more rapidly than the rate of growth of total exports.

## The Interaction Effect

Finally, the last term measures the interaction between changes in market shares and market sizes. The interaction effect serves largely as a residual term, and takes into account changes that cannot be attributed exclusively to either the competitive effect or the market size effect.

The export share of country I in the total exports (by the nine exporters in our study) to the OECD Market may be obtained by dividing the expression (4.1) by $W_t$:

$$Yit = \frac{X_{it}}{W_t} = [\Sigma^5_{j=1}\, \alpha_{ijo}\beta_{jo}] + [\Sigma^5_{j=1}\, \beta_{jo}\Delta\alpha_{ijt}] + [\Sigma^5_{j=1}\, \alpha_{ijo}\Delta\beta_{jt}] + [\Sigma^5_{j=1}\, \Delta\alpha_{ijt}\Delta\beta_{jt}] \quad (4.3)$$

Since the first term on the right side is the base period market share, (4.3) may also be written as:

$$\Delta Y_{it} = Y_{it} - Y_{io} = [\Sigma^5_{j=1}\, \beta_{jo}\Delta\alpha_{ijt}] + [\Sigma^5_{j=1}\, \alpha_{ijo}\Delta\beta_{jt}] + [\Sigma^5_{j=1}\, \Delta\alpha_{ijt}\Delta\beta_{jt}] \quad (4.4)$$

Where (4.4) decomposes changes in the export share between the base period and year t into its three component effects.

It is convenient to express the change in the export share in the form of a ratio to the base period share by dividing expression (4.4) by $Y_{io}$:

$$\frac{\Delta Y_{it}}{Y_{io}} = \frac{[\Sigma^5_{j=1} \beta_{jo} \Delta\alpha_{ijt}]}{Y_{io}} + \frac{[\Sigma^5_{j=1} \alpha_{ijo} \Delta\beta_{jt}]}{Y_{io}} + \frac{[\Sigma^5_{j=1} \alpha_{ijt} \Delta\beta_{jt}]}{Y_{io}} + \quad (4.5)$$

Thus, the percentage change in the export share is decomposed into three parts. These are percentage changes in export share explained by (a) the competitiveness effect, (b) the market size effect, and (c) the interaction effect.

We have calculated the three components of expression (4.5) for India for the period 1971 to 1990 on an annual basis.

The next stage of our study involves regression analysis. The purpose of conducting this type of analysis is to examine the influence of price factors on the competitiveness effect. The percentage change in export share that is explained by the competitiveness effect is the dependent variable in our regression model. For the explanatory variable we have taken the percentage changes in India's relative wholesale price (WPI) with respect to the weighted average (weighted G.M) for wholesale prices of its competitions. The wholesale price for each country has been adjusted for exchange rates to express them in dollar terms.

The second part of the study concentrates on manufacturing exports from India to the world market. Manufacture is a growing sector of world trade. Hence, for the study of a country's international competitiveness its performance in the export of manufactures is very important. The ultimate purpose of this study is to determine the extent to which competitiveness in the manufacturing sector can be explained by price factors.

The market share of India in the manufacturing sector relative to its competitors, has been used as an index of competitiveness. Non-availability of adequate data has led us to work with the relative market share instead of directly with the competitiveness effect. Working with relative market shares would, however, in no way dilute the scope of the study. For, as we shall note later in this study (Table 7.2), the competitiveness effect is clearly the dominant factor in determining market share, in respect of all exportable. Therefore, the relative market share can act as a very good substitute for the competitiveness effect.

What exactly is meant by the term 'manufacture'? There are three variables relating to manufactures: exports, wage cost, and price. A problem of comparability arises here in order to link the data of the first with the latter two.

Export data on manufacture are available as per the SITC[3] classification, whereas data relating to unit wage cost in manufacture are available under ISIC classification.

To make the export figures compatible with the cost figures, we have made some approximation in the definition and scope of 'manufactures'. To be specific, the following items have been added to the SITC groups 5, 6, 7, and 8, which constitute the category 'manufactures' (figures in brackets indicate respective SITC codes):

(i) Food and live animal (0) less live animal for food (001) less feeding staff for animal (081).
(ii) Beverages and Tobacco (1).
(iii) Crude material excluding fuels (2) less oil seeds, Oleaginous fruit (22) less Textile fibres and waste (26) less Metalliferous ores scraps (28) less Crude animal vegetable material (29).
(iv) Petroleum product refined (334).

(v) Animal, vegetable oil fat (4).

After these adjustments, the two definitions of 'manufactures' almost coincide with ach other.

For computing the unit wage cost, we have undertaken the following procedure. First, data were collected on wage-rates (on a per hour, per day or per month basis), total annual employment (paid), and hours worked per person (on per week or per day basis) in the manufacturing sector for each of the countries in our sample. Second, all these figures were combined to arrive at the annual total wage cost figure in manufactures. These total cost figures were then divided by total output (in value terms) of manufactures to get the unit wage cost.

For this part of the analysis data were also collected on prices. For most of the countries in the sample, indices were taken for the industrial manufacturing sector to the extent that they were available. But non-availability of such data for Sweden. Hong Kong and the Republic of Korea determined the use of different price indices for these countries. In particular, the price index was used for exported goods for Sweden, the consumer price index for Hong King, and the wholesale price index for Korea. Such approximations were made on account of the fact that no data on other suitable price indices are apparently available for these countries.

The dependent variable in the regression model for this particular case is the relative market share of India with respect to thirteen major competitors. They are: (1) Australia, (2) Canada, (3) France, (4) Federal Republic of Germany, (5) Japan, (6) Sweden, (7) Netherlands, (8) USA, (9) UK, (10) Italy, (11) the Republic of Korea, (12) Hong Kong, and (13) Singapore. First, we wanted to include not only developed industrialized countries but a few newly industrialized ones as well. Second, the availability of appropriate data was also a decisive factor in selection. On this ground, a few countries had to be excluded which would otherwise have qualified as major exporters of manufactures.

Relative market shares have been calculated in accordance with the formula given below:

Suppose, $X_{it}$ = Export of manufacture by country I in year t, where i = 1.. 14; t= 1971 to 1988.

$$Y_t = \sum_{i=1}^{14} X_{it}$$ = Total export of manufacture by the fourteen exporters in year t.

$$S_{it} = \frac{X_{it}}{Y_t}$$ = Share of country i in the total export of manufacture by the fourteen exporters in year t.

$$MKit = \frac{Sit}{\left(\prod_{j=1, j\neq i}^{13} S_{jt}\right)^{1/13}}$$ = Relative market share of country i with respect to thirteen competitors in year t.

Out explanatory variables are India's relative unit wage-cost in manufacture and relative price index.

The relative unit wage-cost for country i in the year t is defined as

$$RC_{it} = \frac{LC_{it}}{\left(\prod_{j=1, j\neq i}^{13} LC_{jt}^{\,jt}\, \Sigma^{jt}\right)_j^{i} / s \quad s}$$

where LCit = unit wage-cost for country i in the year j.

the relative price index for country i is defined as:

$$WP_{it} = \frac{P_{it}}{\left(\prod_{j=1, j\neq i}^{13} P_{jt}^{\,jt}\, \Sigma^{jt}\right)_j^{i} / s \quad s}$$

Where, Pit = price index for country i in the year t.

Our study in this particular case covers the eighteen-year period 1971 to 1988. Actually, lack of up-to date statistics on prices and wage cost has led us to fix 1988 as the terminal year of our study, thus leaving out the last two year of the decade.

## Result and Interpretation

The results of the empirical exercise are presented here and an attempt made to analysis them. In the first part of this section well shall discuss the results obtained from the study related to India's export competitiveness in the OECD market. Thereafter, results related to India's export performance in the manufacturing sector are analysis.

**Table 7.1:** Annual Percentage Change in India's Export Performance in the OECD Market (1971-90)

| *Year* | *Percentage change in export share* | *Percentage change in export share explained by effèct* | *Percentage change in export share explained by market size effect* | *Percentage change in export share explained by interaction effect* |
|---|---|---|---|---|
| 1971-72 | -8.390 | -8.810 | 0.220 | 0.200 |
| 1972-73 | -20.470 | -21.590 | 2.120 | -1.000 |
| 1973-74 | -11.100 | -8.700 | -0.370 | -2.030 |
| 1974-75 | 3.610 | 2.810 | 1.300 | -0.500 |
| 1975-76 | 3.505 | 3.530 | 0.037 | 0.038 |
| 1976-77 | -5.828 | -5.570 | -0.250 | -0.008 |
| 1977-78 | -8.910 | -6.690 | -2.230 | 0.010 |
| 1978-79 | -9.110 | -10.370 | 1.400 | -0.140 |
| 1979-80 | -20.920 | 17.200 | -4.490 | 0.770 |
| 1980-81 | -12.520 | -13.570 | 1.630 | -0.580 |
| 1981-82 | -13.590 | -13.480 | -0.190 | 0.080 |
| 1982-83 | 26.430 | 28.960 | -2.940 | 0.410 |
| 1983-84 | -11.480 | -10.010 | -1.580 | -.110 |
| 1984-85 | 5.150 | 5.700 | -0.460 | -0.090 |
| 1985-86 | 24.350 | 22.570 | 1.130 | 0.470 |
| 1986-87 | -2.018 | -2.190 | 0.110 | 0.062 |
| 1987-88 | -5.800 | -7.030 | 1.560 | -0.330 |
| 1988-89 | -1.822 | -0.975 | -0.638 | -0.209 |
| 1989-90 | 1.886 | -1.010 | 2.950 | -0.054 |

*Source of Raw Data:* United Nations (various years), *International Trade Statistics* Year Book, Vol. 1.

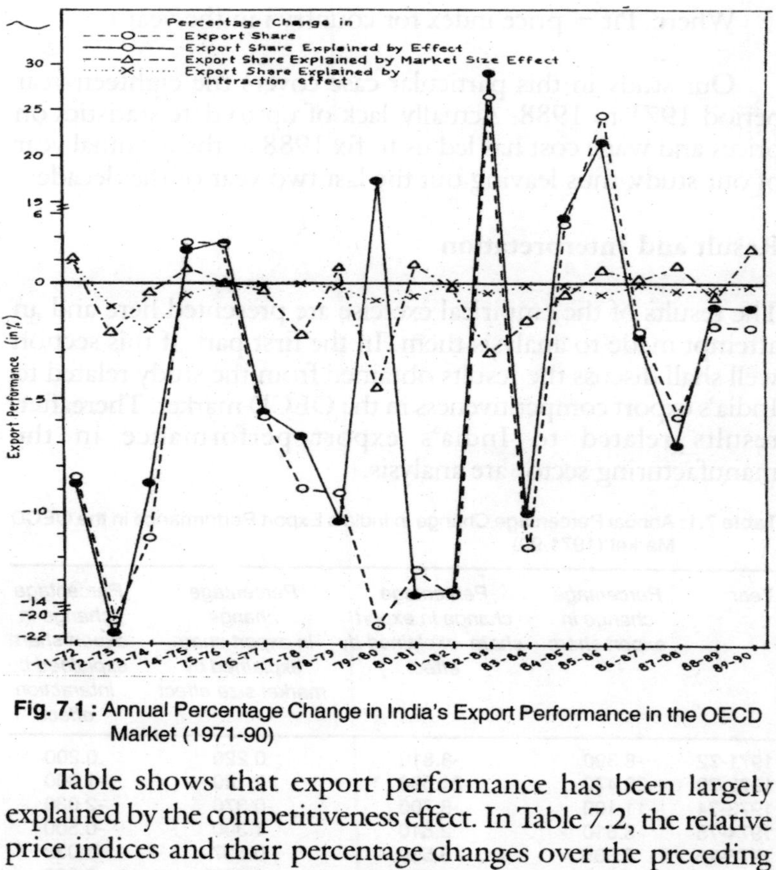


**Fig. 7.1 :** Annual Percentage Change in India's Export Performance in the OECD Market (1971-90)

Table shows that export performance has been largely explained by the competitiveness effect. In Table 7.2, the relative price indices and their percentage changes over the preceding year are shown for the period 1971-90. From this table it can be seen that there has been a downward movement of the relative wholesale price for India over time. This is an indication of an improvement in India's price competitiveness.

To examine the influence of price factors on competitiveness, we have conducted regression analysis with the following relationships:

$$C_t = a_1 + b_1 (DP_t)$$
$$C_t = a_2 + b_2 (DP_{t-1})$$
$$C_t = a_3 + b_3 (DP_t) + b_{32} (DP_{t-1})$$

**Table 7.2** : Relative Wholesale Price Indices for Indian and their Percentage Changes (1971-90)

| *Year* | *Relative wholesaler price indices for India (RWP)* | *% age change in relative wholesale price indices (current)* | | *% age change in relative wholesale price indices (lagged by one year)* |
|---|---|---|---|---|
| | | *Period* | $DP_t$ | |
| 1971 | 1.220 | 1970-71 | – | – |
| 1972 | 1.250 | 1971-72 | 2.46 | – |
| 1973 | 1.180 | 1972-73 | -5.60 | 2.46 |
| 1974 | 1.170 | 1973-74 | -0.85 | -5.60 |
| 1975 | 1.120 | 1974-75 | -4.27 | -0.85 |
| 1976 | 0.949 | 1975-76 | -15.27 | -4.27 |
| 1977 | 0.969 | 1976-77 | 2.11 | -15.27 |
| 1978 | 0.967 | 1977-78 | -0.21 | 2.11 |
| 1979 | 0.983 | 1978-79 | 1.65 | -0.21 |
| 1980 | 1.050 | 1979-80 | 6.81 | 1.65 |
| 1981 | 0.983 | 1980-81 | -6.38 | 6.81 |
| 1982 | 0.997 | 1981-82 | 1.42 | -6.38 |
| 1983 | 1.090 | 1982-83 | 9.33 | 1.42 |
| 1984 | 0.997 | 1983-84 | -8.53 | 9.33 |
| 1985 | 1.000 | 1984-85 | 0.30 | -8.53 |
| 1986 | 1.080 | 1985-86 | 8.00 | 0.30 |
| 1987 | 1.060 | 1986-87 | -1.85 | 8.00 |
| 1988 | 0.056 | 1987-88 | -9.81 | -1.85 |
| 1989 | 0.834 | 1988-89 | -12.76 | -9.81 |
| 1990 | 0.782 | 1989-90 | -6.32 | -12.76 |

*Note:* Base year for wholesale price indices is 1985.
*Source :* International Monetary Fund and Financial Statistics.

Where,

$C_t$ = Percentage change in export share explained by the competitiveness effect in year t.

$DP_t$ = Percentage change in relative wholesale price in year t with respect to year t-1.

$DP_{t-1}$ = Percentage change in relative wholesale price in year t-1 with respect to year t-2.

All these relationships have been estimated for three sets of data. We first considered the entire period or our survey 1972-90, and then performed the exercise for the sub-periods 1972-80 and 1981-90. The estimated result are presented in Table 7.3.

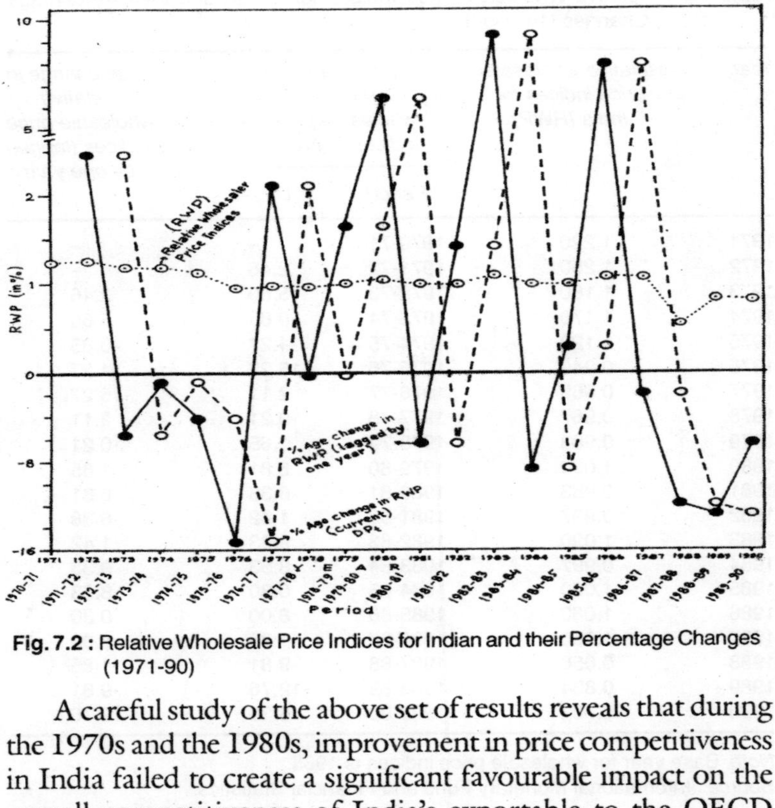


**Fig. 7.2 :** Relative Wholesale Price Indices for Indian and their Percentage Changes (1971-90)

A careful study of the above set of results reveals that during the 1970s and the 1980s, improvement in price competitiveness in India failed to create a significant favourable impact on the overall competitiveness of India's exportable to the OECD market. Let us now study the results in some detail.

Regression equations with $DP_t$ as the explanatory variable show that only for 1972-80 do we have a negative coefficient (for $DP_t$). The t-value is seen to be insignificant. However, the value of $R^2$ is quite small (about 0.30).

When we consider the entire time-span of our study, we find a positive and insignificant coefficient for $DP_t$ and a very low value of $R^2$ (about 0.09). On the other hand, the results for the last decade (1981-90) show a positive and highly significant relationship between changes in competitiveness and $DP_t$. The relationship is seen to be significant at the 5 per cent level, while

**Table 7.3 :** Regression Equations Analyzing the Effect of Percentage Change in Price of Percentage Change in Export Share Explained by Competitiveness Effect for India

| *Period* | *Dependent variable* | *Explanatory $DP_t$* | *Variables $DP_{t-1}$* | *Constant term* | *Sum of squares residual* | *$R^2$* | *D.W.* |
|---|---|---|---|---|---|---|---|
| 1972-90 | $C_t$ | 0.27080 (0.41518) t(17) = .65223 | – | -2.9888(2.8843) t(17) = -1.0362 | 2442.3 | 0.0244 | 1.6583 |
| 1972-80 | $C_t$ | 0.77839 (0.45068) t(7) = -1.7271 | – | -9.9921(2.8695) t(7) = -3.4822 | 492.3659 | 0.29881 | 1.9163 |
| 1981-90 | $C_t$ | 1.1578 (0.419320) t(8) = 2.7611* | – | 4.3454(3.1156) t(8) = 1.3947 | 674.6892 | 0.48795 | 2.2087 |
| 1973-90 | $C_t$ | – | – 0.19293(0.43264) t(16) = -0.44592 | -3.6683(3.0295) t(16) = -1.2109 | 2451.1 | 0.01228 | 1.7358 |
| 1973-80 | $C_t$ | – | – 0.56905(0.66562) t(6) = -2.6071 | -10.4951(4.0255) t(6) = 0.85492 | 625.3367 | 0.10859 | 1.2925 |
| 1981-90 | $C_t$ | – | – 0.15419(0.53278) t(8) = -0.28940 | 1.0359(4.0923) t(8) = .25314 | 1304.0 | 0.01036 | 2.4906 |
| 1973-90 | $C_t$ | -0.19549 (0.43984) t(15) = 0.69395 | 0.30649(0.44167) t(15) = -0.69395 | -2.9533(3.2476) t(15) = 0.90939 | 2374.9 | 0.0430 | 1.7058 |
| 1973-80 | $C_t$ | -0.62851 (-5.143) t(5) = -1.0999 | -0.8596(0.48290) t(5) = -1.7801 | -12.3051(3.05967) t(5) = -3.4212 | 382.7579 | 0.45438 | 1.4952 |
| 1981-90 | $C_t$ | -0.21121 (1.1701) t(7) = -0.52483 | 1.1701(0.44033) t(7) = 2.6573* | 4.1134(3.2969) t(7) = 1.2477 | 649.1459 | 0.50734 | 2.4260 |

* Significant at 10% and 5% levels of significance but insignificant at 1% level of significance.

*Note:-* 1. Figures in parentheses indicate standard errors of the respective coefficients.

2. t(n) value of 't' statistic for the coefficient with 'n' degrees of freedom.

$R^2$ is also fairly high (about 0.55). Clearly, there was an interdecade structural change in the relationship between Ct and $DP_t$ which assumes a value of 8.19 for our data as against the tabulated value of 6.36 for $F_{2.15}$ at the 1 per cent level.

From the above discussion, it may be concluded that in the Indian context, current price change have not shown any significant tendency to exert a favourable influence on the competitiveness of its exportable over the last two decades. Such results may be economically justified only if non-price factors exert considerable influence on export performance.

To carry out a more detailed study on the relevance of price factors, we have also tried to examine the influence of the percentage change in prices with a one-year lag ($DP_{t-1}$) on $C_t$. It is likely that buyers react to a change in price not instantaneously but after a certain time interval. Moreover, even if we assume that the buyers react favourably to a change in price competitiveness, a certain time may elapse before the actual transactions take place.

In view of the above considerations, we considered price-changes with a lag of one year. Hence, our decision to work with $DP_{t-1}$.

The results of the regression analysis performance with $DP_{t-1}$ as the explanatory variable are documented in table. It is quite clear that Ct and $DP_{t-1}$ are related in a more economically justifiable manner for this period, as all the three coefficients of $DP_{t-1}$ that is, 1973-90, for 1973-80 and for 1980-90 are seen to be negative. However, they are insignificant, and no structural change in observable.

The estimated results from our multiple regression model (with both $DP_t$ and $DP_{t-1}$) are presented in Table 7.3. It is seen that changes in current wholesale prices are positively related to $C_t$ for the periods 1973-90 and 1981-90, ad negatively related to $C_t$ for the period 1973-80. While the relationship is insignificant for the eighteen-year time-span 1973-90, it is highly significant (at the 5 per cent level) when only the last decade is considered. On the other hand, for the period 1973-80, the relationship between $C_t$ and $DP_t$ is insignificant. The results are therefore almost similar to those obtained from out two-variable model, with the lone exception that $DP_t$ is now seen to be significantly related to $C_t$ for entire period of our survey.

Again, when we examine relating $DP_{t-1}$, we see that it is negatively related to change in competitiveness for all the three periods considered by us. The relationship is seen to be insignificant in all the cases. Therefore, the relationship obtained from our multiple regression analysis in respect of $DP_{t-1}$ and $C_t$ exactly corresponds to the obtained from the two variable tests.

The joint explanatory power of $DP_t$ and $DP_{t-1}$ (as revealed by the values of $R^2$ and tested by the observed F-Statistics) reveal different characteristics for the three period under consideration. For the span 1973-90, the explanatory power is seen to be quite low ($R^2 = 0.043$), and the observed F is statistically insignificant higher with 1973-80, however, the explanatory power (as revealed by $R^2$) is considerably higher with $R^2 = 0.4544$, though $DP_t$ and $DP_{t-1}$ are seen to be jointly insignificant, as the observed F again fall short of the tabulated F-value. On the other hand, quite in keeping with our earlier findings, the joint explanatory power is quite high for the period 1981-90 ($R^2 = 0.5073$), and this is confirmed in the value of F, which is found to be statistically significant.

Thus, the evidence collected from our regression analysis suggests that neither the current change in the relative wholesale prices, nor the lagged changes in the same, show a consistently negative relationship with changes in competitiveness. Price competitiveness, therefore, has failed to translate itself into export competitiveness over the last two decades.

The figures for relative market shares, relative wage-costs and relative prices are given in Table 7.3. Relative unit wage-costs have been employed with a one-year lag in our linear regression model it is expected that costs affect prices and hence can affect market penetrations only after a certain time lag. It would not therefore be a very rewarding exercise to regress relative market share on current relative unit costs.

**Table 7.4 :** Relative Market Share in Manufacture, Relative Wage Cost and Relative Price Indices of Manufacture for India.

| *Year* | *Relative market share in manufacture (MK)* | *Relative unit wage cost (RC)* | *Relative price (SP)* |
|---|---|---|---|
| 1971 | 0.188 | 0.515 | – |
| 1972 | 0.186 | 0.498 | – |
| 1973 | 0.141 | 0.461 | – |
| 1974 | 0.163 | 0.358 | – |
| 1975 | 0.161 | 0.332 | – |
| 1976 | 0.173 | 0.517 | – |
| 1977 | 0.150 | 0.524 | – |
| 1978 | 0.155 | 0.513 | – |
| 1979 | 0.152 | 0.463 | – |
| 1980 | 0.132 | 0.403 | 1.000 |
| 1981 | 0.130 | 0.375 | 1.010 |
| 1982 | 0.128 | 0.355 | 0.957 |
| 1983 | 0.145 | 0.348 | 0.968 |
| 1984 | 0.142 | 0.353 | 0.967 |
| 1985 | 0.125 | 0.294 | 0.977 |
| 1986 | 0.130 | – | 0.874 |
| 1987 | 0.143 | – | 0.802 |
| 1988 | 0.145 | – | 0.736 |

*Note:* The base year for the price indices in 1980.
*Source of Raw Data :*

1. IMF, International Finance Statistics (various years).
2. UN, National Accounts Statistics (various years).
3. UN, Statistics Yearbook (various years).
4. UN, Year book of Asia and Pacific (various years).
5. ILO, Year book of Labour Statistics (various years).

Our model consist of the following equations:

$$MK_t = a_1 + b_1 PC$$
$$MK_t = a_2 + b_2 WP_t$$
$$MK_t = a_3 + b_3 WP_{t-1}$$

Where,

MKt = India's relative market share in manufacture in year t.

PC = RCt-1 = India's relative unit wage-cost in manufacture in year t-1.

WPt = India's relative price in year t.

WPt-1 = India's relative price in year t-1.

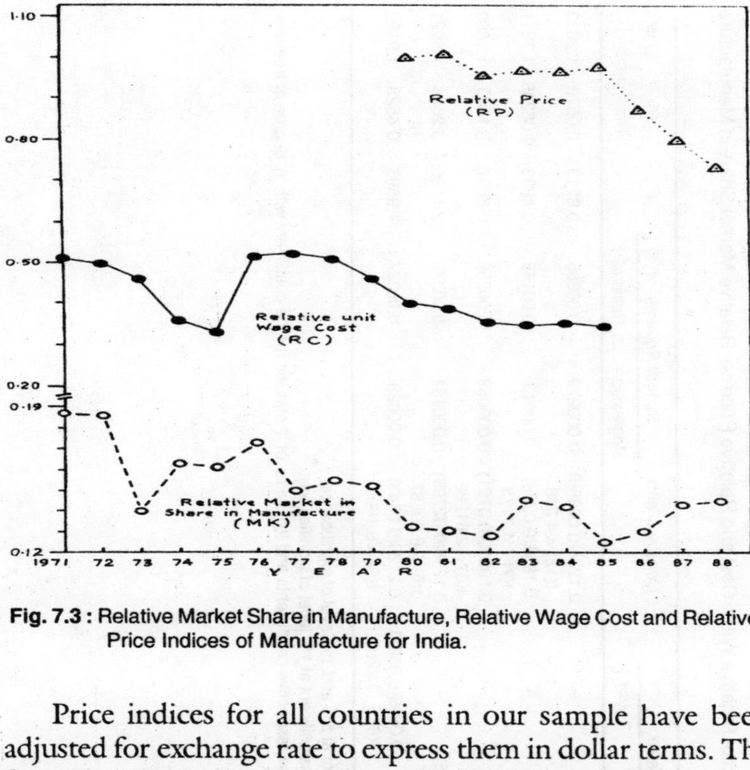


**Fig. 7.3 :** Relative Market Share in Manufacture, Relative Wage Cost and Relative Price Indices of Manufacture for India.

Price indices for all countries in our sample have been adjusted for exchange rate to express them in dollar terms. The first relationship has been estimated for three sets of data.

We have considered the period 1972-83 (for wage cost is available to us up to 1985) and the two sub-periods 1971-80 and 1981-85. The last relationships in our model have been estimated only for the sub-period 1981-85 (this has been guided by the availability of data). The results obtained are presented in Table 7.5.

We have considered the period 1972-85 (the data for wage cost is available to us up to 1985) and the two sub-periods 1971-80. The last two relationships in our model have been estimated only for the sub-period 1981-85 (this has been guided by the availability of data). The results obtained are presented in Table 7.5.

**Table 7.5 :** Regression Equation Analyzing the Effect of Relative Wage Cost and Relative Price on Relative Market Share in Manufacture for India.

| *Period* | *Dependent Variable* | *Explanatory Variable* | | | *ConstantTerm* | *Sum of Squares* | | *F* | $R^2$ | *D.W.* |
|---|---|---|---|---|---|---|---|---|---|---|
| | | *PC* | *WPt* | *WPt-1* | | *Regression* | *Residual* | | | |
| 1972-83 | MK | 0.0614(0.0658) t(12) = 0.9334 | – | – | 0.1224(0.02868) t(12) = 4.268 | 0.000279 | 0.00385 | 0.8713 | 0.0676 | 1.2633 |
| 1972-80 | MK | -0.0565(0.0827) t(7) = -0.6829 | – | – | 0.1832(0.0388) t(7) = 4.7173 | 0.00013 | 0.00198 | 0.4663 | 0.06246 | 1.7211 |
| 1981-85 | MK | -0.1698(0.2045) t(3) = -0.8304 | – | – | 0.19630(0.0751) t(3) = 2.61288 | 0.000059 | 0.00258 | 0.6897 | 0.1869 | 1.9689 |
| 1981-88 | MK | – | -0.0444(0.0305) t(6) = -1.4535* | – | 0.1768(0.02799) t(6) = 6.30537 | 0.000131 | 0.00373 | 2.1126 | 0.2604 | 1.8921 |
| 1981-88 | MK | – | – | -0.0808(0.0363) t(6) = -2.2269 | 0.2123(0.0343) t(6) = 6.1800 | 0.00023 | 0.00027 | 4.9593 | 0.4525 | 1.9190 |

* Significant at 10% level of significance but insignificant at 5% and 1% level of significance.

** Significant at 10% and 5% level of significance but insignificant at 1% level of significance.

*Note:* 1. Figures in parentheses indicate standard errors of the respective coefficients and t(n) value of 't' statistic for the coefficient with 'n' degree of freedom.

The estimated value for the coefficient of PC are insignificant in all the three time-period considered by us. For 1972-85 the relationship between PC and MK is positive, but the t value for the coefficient of MK is seen to be insignificant.

The value of $R^2$ is also very small ($R^2 = 0.0676$). For the two sub-periods 1972-80 and 1981-85, the coefficients for PC are negative but insignificant. The explanatory power of PC is also very low as indicated by the value of $R^2$ ($R^2 = 0.06246$ for 1972 to 1980 and $R^2 = 0.1869$ for 1981 to 1985).

From the Table 7.5 we van seen once again that the relative market share is negatively related with relative price (both current and lagged). The t value for the coefficient of $WP_t$ is statistically significant at the 10 per cent level. The coefficient of $WP_{t-1}$ significant at the 5 per cent level.

The values of $R^2$ in the two cases indicate that 276 per cent of the variation in the relative market share is explained by current relative price and the explanatory power of the lagged price is 45 per cent.

We can infer from the above results that at the aggregated level at least, the cost factors as represented by relative unit wage cost do not affect relative share significantly. This is not to suggest, of course, that this absence of a significant relationship will persist at the micro level also. On the other hand, even at the aggregated level, prices (particularly lagged prices) can better explain relative export shares. However, as the explanatory power of neither of the is very high, our earlier conclusion that non-price factors are more important in explaining competitiveness still holds good. While the first part of our study postulated an insignificant and positive relationship between relative prices and competitiveness, we now have a more economically defensible position.

## Conclusions

Our analysis of the results in sub-sections 7.1 and 7.2 quite unambiguously point to the fact that price factors do not explain changes in aggregate competitiveness in a significant way. These conclusions have to be modified slightly when we consider only India's manufacturing exports, though the explanatory powers relative prices are still not very high. On the other hand, costs are seen not to affect the competitiveness of the manufacturing at all.

One possible explanation of an absence of a significant relationship between prices (and costs) and overall competitiveness is as follows: relating aggregate measures of price and costs to aggregate measures of export competitiveness in not the same as relating prices and costs to exports at the micro individual commodity level. Demand and supply function for individual commodities cannot be aggregated to yield a demand and supply function for all commodities. Each commodity has its own demand and supply functions in each of the trading countries. Therefore, the true picture at the micro level may not be reflected fully in our study.

There are various other factors which can influence competitiveness, and hence dilute its relationships with costs and prices. On the one hand, there are several non-price factors which include quality (in marketing and after-sale services as well), while on the other, there are government policies (both domestic and foreign), various multilateral and bilateral trade relationships with trade partners, and many other influencing factors. It needs a careful and extensive study (which is beyond scope of this section) to find out the individual impact of each of these factors on export competitiveness.

In conclusion, it asserted that government policies must be sufficiently tuned to influence the non-price factors. The importance of achieving 'price-competitiveness' is perhaps overemphasized in policy-prescriptions.

## Issues Related to Exchange Rates, Co-integration and Export

India's export performance in the last two decades (1970-90) may be seen at two levels-one is the aggregative performance and the other is a disaggregated study. The aggregative study tries to address the question. Did depreciation of the Indian rupee lead to better export performance? On the other hand, the focus of the disaggregated study is, in a nutshell, on issues such as the bilateral export performance of India *vis-à-vis* its major trade partners. This may be carried out through a time-series analysis of India's exports may be analysed is through an analysis of India's market share, commodity-wise along with a comparison of India's performance with its major competitors for those commodities in the international market. Since the commodity-wise relative export performance of India is discussed in other sections of this chapter, this section will exclusively focus on the export performance of Indian in an aggregated fashion.

**India's Aggregated Export Performance, 1970-90**

India's economic performance certainly provides a lot of thought-provoking material for theorists and empirical economists dealing with international trade. The country went through a record massive devaluation in the year-1966, when the rupee was devalued by 57.5 per cent. From 1991 onwards, India has moved into the flexible exchange rate regime, wherein the current account transactions now allow full convertibility of currency. However, as has already been pointed out in a earlier chapter, this also led to a huge depreciation of the Indian currency. The question which obviously looms large in the minds of all economists is the efficacy of the devaluation/depreciation of a currency in overcoming the short-run balance of payment difficulties. There are a number of theories that deal with these questions, and their exist a number of empirical studies which have tried to test the famous Marshall-Lerner condition of the effects of devaluation on exports, imports and balance of payments for different countries (Balassa, 1987). India forms the subject matter of a fair amount of such work. However,

Indian studies took a significantly new twist with the induction of co-integration analysis into the picture, mainly by Sarkar (1994, 1995) and Hag and Upadhyay (1994). We have devoted a special section to the discussion of co-integration in the context of export growth analysis in India, as this king of analysis makes little sense in the discussion of the time-series properties of export growth *vis-a-vis* the exchange rate movement in India.

In the context of India, there is a heated debated regarding the following two fundamental issues:

(1) Does the devaluation contribute to inflation sufficiently to offset the initial relative price advantage within a short time?
(2) are the elasticities of demand for Indian exports and imports such that the devaluation leads to a decline in the terms of trade (or rise in the real exchange rate) of such a magnitude that will offset the gain from quantity increase?

As expected, no definite consensus has been reached in this debate. If one tries to proceed chronologically, Marwah (1970) used an econometric model to compare two sets of solutions-one with devaluation and the other without. The results show that real consumption is reduced in 1966-67 and the total output lagged by a year (1967-68). In addition, substantial improvements could be expected in the balance of trade.

Bhagwati and Srinivasan (1975), as already quoted, argued that the coincidence of the drought situation with devaluation led to the rapid rise in prices along with reduced government expenditure. Due to the existence of various export and import duties, the real net devaluation was much lower than the nominal devaluation in 1966. In the absence of abnormal monsoon conditions, and with a substantial reduction in the duties, the effects of devaluation would have been substantial.

Sen (1986) found that the devaluation of 1966 had a fairly sizeable positive effect on India's balance of trade. Although the export volume had actually declined during the two years, this was primarily due to drought. Correcting for this factor, exports (particularly of non-traditional terms) were found to have improved. Despite the fact that the elasticity of substitution between imports and domestic factors is probably quite low, the volume of imports could be expected to fall at a given level. The continuing inflationary trend in that period is caused by the drought. It is shown that in the absence of exogenous factors, the effects of devaluation would persist for a longer period. But in the long run, the devaluation may seem to have had a marked contradictory effect on the Indian economy.

# 8 SUMMARY, CONCLUSION AND LIMITATION

The seventies was the period of instability and uncertainty in the western countries. It was affected by high and varying rates of inflation and fluctuations in output. Fixed exchanges rates system which earlier stability to domestic price levels broke down and the problem of inflation became rather more acute. Even the controls on interest rates and credit could not nay longer cope the problem of inflation. So, it was realized that targeting of the growth of money supply should be made which should emphasize the movement of monetary policy away from credit policy based on controls over interest rates and volume of credit to the monetary policy based on money supply and growth.

Keeping in view the above, major industrial countries of the world adopted monetary targeting as the basis for money supply and growth. West Germany, Japan and Australia adopted monetary targeting in 1974; Switzerland, Canada and United States of America in 1975; and United Kingdom, France and Italy in 1976. In India too, a Committee under the Chairmanship of Sukhamoy Chakravarty was set up in December 1982 to provide a comprehensive review of the monetary system and suggest measures for improving the effectiveness of monetary policy. This Committee submitted its report to the Reserve Bank of India in April 1985. It recommended adoption monetary targeting (preferable $M_3$) with feedback in the form of a range rather than a specific magnitude as a part of the comprehensive scheme for restructuring the monetary policy.

The then Finance Minister V.P. Singh accepted the Chakravarty Committee's proposal of monetary targeting in the 1986-87 budget. The Reserve Bank, however, had adopted the policy of monetary targeting in 1985-86 when it for the first time prescribed a ceiling for monetary expansion ($M_3$). In each year since 1985-86, it has been prescribed by the RBI that the expansion in $M_3$ should not exceed (or should be less than) the average of the previous three years. Following the framework suggested for monetary targeting by the Chakravarty Committee, Mody made an attempt to predict the rate of expansion of money supply during the Seventh Plan period (1985-86 to 1989-90) (Mody, 1986) of the basis of certain calculations he observed that the amount of deficit financing as envisaged in the Seventh Plan was consistent with the approach suggested by the Chakravarty Committee.

The Chakravarty Committee pointed out that the successful operation of monetary targeting hinges on the following two critical assumptions.

(1) The demand for money is fairly predictable over the relevant time frame with reasonable accuracy having regard to the relationship between money, output and prices. In other works, the demand for money is fairly stable over time.
(2) The money multiplier is reasonably stable and predictable. In addition to the above two pre-requisites, the other pre-requisites for the success and setting of monetary targets are Sheila, Page, 1992.
(3) Third, the income velocity of money remains stable;
(4) Fourth, the acceptable rise in prices is based on the proposition that it is the money supply which causes prices to change and not *vice versa*; and
(5) Fifth, the monetary base or the reserve money is subject to control by the monetary authorities. In other works, money supply is exogenously determined i.e. it is a policy controlled variable.

Thus, the success of monetary targeting requires stability of the demand for money function and of money multiplier and the income velocity of money. It also requires that the causal relation runs from money supply to prices and finally that the money supply is an exogenously determined or a policy controlled variable.

In the present study, an attempt has been made to examine whether our economy ripe for monetary targeting as an instrument of monetary policy. Specifically, the study aims at achieving the following objectives.

(i) Reviewing the literature on money and monetary policy in India with special reference to the issues involved in monetary targeting;
(ii) Examining the working of monetary policy in India since 1970;
(iii) Examining if the pre-requisites for money targeting are satisfied in India; and
(iv) If so, whether the rates of growth of money supply is targeted in terms of $M_1$ or $M_3$.

The study pertains to the period from 1971-90. The selection of this period has been dictated by the fact that the comparable data on different measures of money supply $M_1$ and $M_3$ (new series) with a revised methodology are available from 1970 onwards. For analysis, however, simple statistical tools like ratios, averages and growth rates have been used. In addition, the ordinary least squares method was used for estimation of the regression equations. Cochrane-Orcutt interactive method was used wherever it was required to correct data for serial auto-correlation. The data have been taken from various issues of *Reserve Bank of India Bulletin,* Report on Currency and Finance, Economic Survey of Indian National Accounts Statistics, Statistical Tables relating to Banks in India, etc. In some cases, quarterly data have also been used in this study for analysis.

The main findings of the study are briefly outlined below:

(1) The decade-wise estimation of the demand for money function revealed that all estimated regression equations had negative intercept. But when converted into antilog, these intercepts turn out to be positive indicating that the demand from money is positive at all level of income. This seems plausible because the transactions and precautionary demand for money is always positive at all level of income. Further, the income elasticity of demand for money was found positive and significant in the previous decade (1971-80). But, in the later decade (1981-90), it declined to around 0.5. The interest rate (short-term as well as long-term) elasticity of demand for money was found insignificant in both the periods. It implies that interest rate has not been an important determinant of demand for money function in India. But the interest rate elasticity of real balances was found to be around 0.5 in the first decade (1971-80) which was found significant at one per cent level. In the later decade, the elasticity of demand for money with respect to real balances remained positive, rose to around one and was found significant at one per cent level. All the equations, however, explained about 99 per cent of the variations in demand for money and were found free from the problem of serial auto-correlation. In addition, the Chow's F-test revealed that the demand for money function with $M_1$ as the dependent variable did not undergo any structural change while that with $M_3$ as the dependent variable underwent a structural changes in the later period at five per cent level of significance. Thus, the broad conclusion that emerges from our study is that the demand for money function with $M_1$ as the dependent variable has remained stable while that with $M_3$ as the dependent variable depicted instability over the period under consideration.

(2) The study reveals that $M_1$ has grown at a rate slower than the rate of growth of $M_3$ in both the sub-periods

1971-80 and 1981-90 as well as taking the period 1971-90 as a whole. The main reason from rapid growth of $M_3$ is the faster growth of time deposits over these periods. Further, the narrow money multiplier, $M_1$ declined from an average of 1.59 during 1971-80 to 1.15 during 1981-90 and the broad money multiplier, $M_3$ rose from 2.73 to 3.08 over the same period. This was confirmed when money multipliers $M_1$ and $M_3$ were regressed on time. But the fall in $M_1$ and rise in $M_3$ over the period under consideration was not smooth. Both the money multipliers depicted a fluctuating trend which can be explained in terms of the variations in the various ratios such as the cash-demand deposits ratio, time-demand deposits ratio, excess reserves-demand deposits ratio, the required reserves and the statutory liquidity ratios. Decade-wise estimated regression results revealed that while the narrow money multiplier ($M_1$) remained statistically constant, the broad money multiplier ($M_3$) rose significantly during 1971-80. But, in the later decade (1981-90) these trends reversed now, while $M_1$ declined significantly, $M_3$ tended to stationeries. Further, the co-efficient of variation of $M_1$ and $M_3$ declined in the later decade in both the cases, though this decline in case of $M_3$ was more than in case of $M_1$. However, in both decades, the coefficient of variation in the case of $M_1$ was less than that in case of $M_3$. In short, it may be broadly concluded that both $M_1$ and $M_3$ are stable over short period in India. Further, because of smaller coefficient of variation, $M_1$ depicts relatively more stability.

(3) Given that the money multiplier is stable in India, it lends credence the belief that money supply is exogenously determined in India. It was also found that most of the variations in money supply were explained by reserve money. Further, Reserve Bank of India credit to government turned out to be the main contributory

factor towards the expansion of reserve money. It alone explained almost 90 per cent of the variations in reserve money. The study also revealed that it is not only the current but also the lagged variations in reserve money, which determine the movements in money supply in the economy. Further, the current and the lagged variations in reserve money explained relatively more variations in $M_3$ than in $M_1$.

Regression analysis reviews the New View on the determinant of money supply. According to this view the amount of deposits are determined by the demand for loans by the public (money demand). Hence, the monetary policy that uses interest rate as an intermediated target to change money supply of the economy has an element of endogeneity in its policy making. Indian monetary policy making is clearly the one that takes interest rate as its intermediate target when money supply change is intended. Our results shown that there is, in fact, evidence that about 40 per cent of the money supply changes is made as a result of initial increase in demand for money.

(4) The application of Sims' test to examine the issue of causality between money supply and prices revealed that the estimated co-efficients of the lagged, current as well as future values of $M_3$ as a group as well as those of its reverse were insignificant. The regressions were run with 6 past, current and 4 future lags; 8 past, current and 4 future lags; and 10 past, current and 4 future lags. These regressions were run on 4 future lags also. However, the predictive power of the equation was highest when P was regressed on $M_1$ with 8 past, current and 4 future lags. Hence it was concluded that there exists a unidirectional causality from $M_1$ to P and not from $M_3$ to P.

(5) The main objective of monetary targeting is to control inflation. Hence, the success of monetary targeting can

be judged from the ability of the model of price determination used predict the prices. For this purpose, the robustness of the model was judged by comparing the predicted with actual price level by estimating the inequality co-efficient proposed by Theil. We took the quarterly data from 1986 onwards, i.e., the year when monetary targeting was adopted. The inequality co-efficient between actual and estimated prices was found nearer to zero (0.0002 for the period 1986 (1) to 1988 (IV) with $M_1$ as the explanatory variable. But this co-efficient moved away from zero (0.14 for the period 1986 (I) to 1988 (IV) when $M_3$ was used as the regressant. From this, it was concluded that the rate of growth of money be targeted in terms of $M_1$ rather than $M_3$.

(6) The study revealed that the income velocity of money (narrow) declined from 4.97 to 4.26 while that of broad money declined from 3.32 to 1.51 over the period from 1970-71 to 1989-90. Thus, the income velocity of money (both narrow as well as broad) declined over the period under consideration. This was due to the fact that the national income grew at rate slower than the rate of growth of money supply. But the decline was found statistically insignificant. Hence income velocity of money may be taken to have remained more or less stable over the period under consideration. With a view to determining the factors influencing income velocity of money, it was regressed on two sets of variables: one consisting of rate of growth of national income and of money supply, and the other consisting of rate of interest, ratio, of currency to demand deposits and the ratio, of household financial assets to national income. The income velocity of money was also regressed on all the variables taken together. The results obtained are:

(i) the explanatory power ($R^2$) of the equation with rate of growth of national income and of money supply (both $M_1$ and $M_3$) as the explanatory variables declined in the later period 1981-90;

(ii) the explanatory power of the equation, on the other hand, with rate of interests, ratio of currency to demand deposits and the ratio of household financial assets to income as the regressants representing financial depending increased in the later period in the case of income velocity of money both narrow as well as broad;

(iii) when all the factors were taken together, in the case of both narrow as well as broad income velocity of money, the regression co-efficient of national income turned out to be insignificant while that of HFA/Y was significant during both the sub-periods 1971-80 and 1981-90. But money supply and C/DD in case of income velocity of money (narrow) and rate of interest in case of income velocity of money (broad) turned out to be the significant factors influencing velocity during 1971-80. But during 1981-90, in addition to HFA/Y, it was the rate of interest which influenced significantly narrow and it was the C/DD which influenced significantly income velocity of broad money.

Thus is was only the ratio of HFA/Y representing financial deepening which turned out to be an important factor, which influenced significantly income velocity of money (both narrow and broad) in both periods. However, in both period its regression co-efficient was negative, which may be explained by the fact that over time as the people continued spending relatively a large proportion of their income of financial assets such as shares and debentures, bank deposits, national saving schemes etc., a larger proportion of their purchasing power got immobilized. This might have resulted into a negative relation between HFA/Y and income velocity of money.

(7) The prime object of monetary policy since the early seventies has been to contain the inflationary pressures, which continued building up throughout the seventies and the eighties in the economy. During this period, the Reserve Bank made use of restrictive credit and monetary policies. The Reserve Bank made these policies more rigorous when there was financial stringency of relaxed when the monetary situation eased. In other words, the Reserve Bank adopted what it called a 'flexible' or 'cautious' credit policy during the period under consideration. The CRR, both in average and incremental forms, the SLR, and the refinance facilities from the Reserve Bank constituted the prime instruments of credit policy. This period also witnessed the re-emergence of interest rate as the instrument of credit policy. This Reserve Bank also made use of policy of moral suasion, besides the selective credit controls. Another feature of credit policy in this period was the adoption of the policy of quantitative ceilings on credit expansion since 1973-74 busy seasons till 1982-83. During this period, the Reserve Bank prescribed ceilings in terms of the expansion of non-food bank credit and incremental credit-deposit ratio. The study revealed that the actual expansion in non-food bank credit was higher than the prescribed ceiling during all the period under consideration excepting 1974-75 and 1981-82 (April-March) busy season. During these latter periods, the expansion in non-food bank credit was slightly less than the prescribed ceiling. Indeed, the monetary and credit policies till mid-eighties operated primarily on only one element of monetary expansion viz. credit to commercial sector to moderate overall monetary expansion. However, it was recognized that the major factor

responsible for the expansion in money supply in India was the net bank credit to the government sector. This had effect of increasing the reserve or the primary money in the economy, which caused secondary expansion in money supply. With a view to restrict directly the expansion in money supply, the Reserve Bank from 1984-85 onwards started using money supply as an intermediate target for the operation of monetary policy and started prescribing quantitative ceilings on the expansion in $M_3$. The study revealed that the rate of inflation was comparatively lower when money supply used as the intermediate target variable. However, since the adoption of the technique of monetary targeting too, the expansion in $M_3$ continued to be larger than the prescribed quantitative limits.

(8) Finally, it be mentioned that if monetary targets are to be meaningful operationally, then the rules of the game required that there should be close co-ordination between fiscal policies and monetary policies. The consideration of monetary targets as an instrument of monetary policy cannot be divorced from the manner in which the extent to which the public expenditure in being regulated. This would appear to be an organic link between conceptualization of monetary target and strict adherence to the need for improving efficiency in the utilization of resources. The success of this technique would hinge very much on the political will of the government to contain the growth of non-productive expenditure and its readiness to play the game according to the rules. The observance of this requirement implies greater maneuverability for the reserve bank to conduct the monetary policy.

Thus, the broad conclusion that emerges from our study is that the conditions in the monetary sector and Fiscal actions in India are ripe for the adoption of monetary targeting as a technique for the operation of monetary policy in India. This is supported by the relative stability of demand for money, of money multiplier, and of income velocity of money in the case of only narrow money supply ($M_1$) to price level in India. Finally, narrow money supply ($M_1$) was found exogenously determined. Therefore, it is concluded that money be targeted in terms of $M_1$ rather than $M_3$ in India.

The present study has tried to use a different empirical evidence for finding the crowding out effect because it has been defined here in a broader terms. When there is an increase in government budget deficit it has been observed that there are three simultaneous effects as expected. First, the traditional positive effect on the interest rate seconds the positive effect on the prices and third, a positive effect on the value of domestic exchange rate. Application of these hypotheses to the data that there is no evidence of increased interest rates due to higher budget deficit, nor is there evidence of higher prices due to budget deficit. This is not completely unexpected as in a vast section of the economy process are controlled by the government (like the railway fare, airline fares, petrol prices, etc.) and the interest rates are completely controlled by the Reserve Bank of India. Our analysis further shows that even if the exchange rates have responded to the budget deficit as the theoretical principles would expect, the low value of t-statistic shows that the results are not very conclusive. At the end, one can take this exercise as an attempt to question the empirical evidence of crowding out hypothesis in the same spirit as the other studies of developed economies.

# BIBLIOGRAPHY


Akeriof, G.A. and Milbourne, R.M. 'The Short-Run Demand for Money', *Economic Journal*, December 1980, pp. 885-900.

Akerlof, G. A. 'The Short-Run Demand for Money: A New Look at an Old Problem', *American Economic Review*, May 1982, pp. 35-40.

Allan, H. Meltzer, 'The Demand for Money: The Evidence from the Time Series. *Journal of Political Economy*. Vol. 71, June 1963, pp. 219-46.

Almon, S. 'The Distributed Lag between Capital Appopriations and Expenditures', *Econometrica,* Vol. 33, January 1965, pp. 174-81

Almon, S., 'The Distributed Lag between Capital Appropriations and Expenditures', *Econometrica*, Vol. 33, January 1965, pp. 147-81.

Arora, H. K. 'Crowding Out in the Context of a Developed Country', *Indian Journal of Quantitative Economics*, Vol. 4, No. 1, 1988, pp. 1-20.

Bagchi, Amaresh and Nayak, P.B., "Public Finance and the Planning Process: The Indian Experience', Paper presented at the International Seminar on Public Economics, New Delhi, January 1990.

Bailey, M. (1956), 'The Welfare Cost of Inflationary Finance". *Journal of Political Economy*, 64.

Bardhan, P., *"A Political-Economy Perspective on Development"*, this volume, 1992.

Barnanke, B. and M. Gertler (1995), "Inside the Black Box: the Credit Channel of Monetary Policy Transmission", *Journal of Economic Perspectives*, 9(4).

Barro, Robert J. 'Inflation, the Payment Period, and the Demand for Money', *Journal of Political Economy,* Vol. 78. November 1970, pp. 545-56.

Baumol, W. J. & J. Tobin, 'The Transactions Demand for Cash: An Inventory Theoretic Approach', *Quarterly Journal of Economics*, Vol. 66, November 1952, pp. 545-56.

Belied, H. and K.S. Lyon, 'Government Expenditure and the Ex-Ante Crowding-Out Effect: An Examination', *Applied Economics*, Vol. 21, No. 10, October 1989, pp. 1411-20.

Benjamin, Friedman, 'Crowding Out or Crowding In? Economic Consequences of Financing Government Deficit', *Brookings Papers on Economic Activity*, Vol. 3, 1978, pp. 593-654.

Bronfenbrenner, M. and Thomas, M. 'Liquidity Functions in the American Economy', *Econometrics*, Vol. 28 October 1960, pp. 810-34.

Bruner, Karl and Meltzer, Allan H. 'Predicting Velocity: Implications for Theory and Policy', *Journal of Finance*, Vol. 18, May 1963, pp. 319-54.

Buter, W.H. and Paterl, U.R., 'Det, Deficits and Inflation: An Application to the Public Finance of India, in the *Journal of Public Economics,* Vol. 47. No. 2, 1992.

Cagan, P. (1956), 'The Monetary Dynamics of Hyperinflation', in M. *Friedman (ed), Studies in the Quantity Theory of Money*, University of Chicago Press, Chicago.

Chan, A. and E. Gustafson, 'An Empirical Examination of Government Expenditure and the Ex-Ante Crowding-Out Effect for the British Economy'. *Applied Economics*, Vol. 23, No. 2, February 1991, p. 305.

Chatak, S. (1981), *Monetary Economics in Developing Countries*, Macmillan, London.

Chelliah, Raja J., *'Growth of Indian Public Debt'*. This Volume, 1992.

Clower, R. W. and P.W. Howitt, 'The Transactions Theory of Demand for Money: A Reconsideration', *Journal of Political Economy*, June 1978, pp. 449-66.

Coen, Tuelings and Marc Koopmanschap, 'An Econometric Model of Crowding Out of Lower Education Levels'.

*European Economic Review*, Vol. 33, No. 8, Octover 1989, p. 1653.

CSO (2007a), Quick Estimates of National Income, Consumption Expenditure, Saving and Capital Formation, 2005-06, Press Release dated January 31, 2007.

CSO (2007b), Advance Estimates of Nation Income, 2006-07, Press Release dated February 7, 2007.

Das Gupta, A. *Personal Taxation and Private Financial Savings in India,* Delhi: National Institute of Public Finance and Policy, 1989.

David, Bowles, Holley Ulbrich and Myles Wallace, 'Default Risk, Interest Differentials and Fiscal Policy: A New Look at Crowding Out', *Eastern Economic Journal*, Vol. 15, No. 3, July 1989, p. 203.

David, Laidler and J. Michael Parak, The Demand for Money in the United Kingdom, 1956-67. *Preliminary Estimates, Manchester School*, Vol. 18, September 1970, pp. 714-809.

Deadman, D. and Ghatak, S.I. 'On the Stability of Demand for Money in India', *The Indian Economic Journal* Vol. 29, No. 1, July-September 1981, pp. 41-45.

Deaver, J. (1970), 'The Chilean Inflation and the Demand for Money', in D. Meiselman (ed). *Varieties of Monetary Experience. University of Chicago Press,* Chicago.

Dennis, Placone, Holley Ulbrich and Myles Wallace. 'The Crowding Out Debate. It's Over When It's Over and It Isn't Over Yet', *Journal of Post-Keynesian Economics*. Vol. 8, Fall 1985, pp. 91-96.

Dornbusch, R. (1992), 'Lessons from Experience with High Inflation' *World Bank Economic Review*, 6 (1).

Fisher, I., (1930), *The Theory of Interest*, Macmillan, New York.

Genberg, H., Fiscal Policy, Det, Growth and Inflation in a Long-Run Perspective. An Analytical Framework with an Application to India, World Bank, October 1989.

Ghatak, R. '*Rural Money Markets in India*'. Macmillan Publishers, New York, 1976.

Gillis, M., (ed.), *Tax Reform in Developing Countries*, London: Duke University Press, 1989.

Goldman, Sachs (2007), India's Rising Growth Potential, *Global Economic Paper No.* 152.

Greenspan, A. (2005), Testimony before the Committee on Banking, Housing and Urban Affairs, US Senate, February 16.

Gupta, S.B. (1983), *Monetary Economics: Institutions*, Theory and Policy S. Chand and Co., New Delhi.

Havrilesky, T. M. and J. T. Boorman, *Monetary Macroeconomics*, AHM Publishing Company, Illinois, 1978.

Hinrichs, H. H., "*A General Theory of Tax Structure Change During Economic Development*", Harvard Law School International Tax Programme, Cambridge, Mass.

In terms of these guideline (i) the increase in non-food credit in the first half of 1981-82 was not to be in excess of the increase in the first half of 1980-81, (ii) non-food credit expansion in 1981 slack season was to be marginally lower than the expansion in 1980 slack season.

Interim Report of the Tax Reforms Committee, (Chairman: Raja J. Chelliah), Government of India, New Delhi, 1991.

International Monetary Fund and International Financial Statistics.

International Standard Industrial Classification for all Economic Activities.

Ishac, Diwan, 'Foreign Debt. Crowding Out and Capital Flight', *Journal of International Money and Finance*, Vol. 8, No. 1, March 1989, p. 121.

James, Tobin, 'The Interest Elasticity and Transactions Demand for Cash' *Review of Economics and Statistics*. Vol. 38, August 1956, pp. 241-47.

John, M. Keynes, *The General Theory of Employment, Interest and Money*, Harcourt, Brace and Co. London, 1936.

John, Tatam, 'Two Views of the Effects of Government Budget Deficits in the 1980s' *Federal Reserve Bank of St. Louis Review*. Vol. 67, October 1985, pp. 5-16.

Johnson, J. '*Econometric Methods*', McGraw Hills, New York, 1963, Chapter, 9.

Kaldor, Nicholas *'The General Theory of Employment, Interest and Money'*, Harcourt, Brace and Co. London, 1936.

Karl, Brunner and Allan H. Meltzer, 'Predicting Velocity: Implications for Theory and Policy', *Journal of Finance*, Vol. 18, May 1963, pp. 319-54.

Keith, Hartley and John Singleton, 'Defense R & D and Crowding Out', *Science and Public Policy*, Vol. 17, No. 3, June 1990, p. 152.

Keith, M. Carlson and Roger W. Spenser, 'Crowding Out and its Critics', *Federal Reserve Bank of St. Louis Review*, Vol. 57, No. 12, December 1975, pp. 2-17.

Keynes, J. M. (1936), *The General Theory of Employment, Interest and Money Harcourt*, Brace and World Inc., New York.

Kiguel, M.A. and N. Liviatan (1992), 'When Do Heterodox Stabilization Programms Work? Lessons from Experience', *World Bank Research Observer*, 7(1).

Kulkarni, Kishore *'First Principles of Monetary Theory'*, Kenda/ Hunt Publishing Company, Dubuque, Lowa, 3rd edition 1996.

Kulkarni, Kishore, 'Further Empirical Evidence on Stability of Demand for Money in India'. *Journal of Economics*, Special Number, April 1986, pp. 18-34.

Laidler, David *'The Demand for Money'*.

Laidler, David and Parak, J. Michael *'The Demand for Money in the United Kingdom,* 1956-67', Preliminary Estimates, Manchester School, Vol. 18, September 1980, pp. 714-809.

Maria, S. Gochoco, 'Financing Decisions and the "Crowding Out" Effect: The Case of Philippines', *Economic Letters*, Vol. 32, No. 4, April 1990, p. 331.

Mark, E. Wohar, 'How Effective is Fiscal Policy? The US Experience', *Review of World Economics*, Vol. 124, No. 3, Summer 1988.

McCallum, B.T. (1989), Monetary Economics, Macmillan, New York. – and J.G. HOEHN (1983), 'Instrument Choice for Money for Money Stock Control with Contemporaneous and Lagged Requirements', *Journal of Money, Credit, and Banking,* 15.

Mckinnon, Ronald I. 'Money and Capital in Economic Development', The Bookings Institution, Washington, D.C., 1973.

Michael, Haliassos, 'Sustainability of Macroeconomic Policies. Inflation Targeting and Crowding Out', *Southern Economic Journal*, Vol. 57, No. 4, April 1991, p. 1010

Michael, J. Bodkin, 'Taxation, Saving, and the Rate of Interest', *Journal of Political Economy*, Part II, 86, S3-S27, April 1978.

Michael, M. Hutchinson and David H. Pyle, 'The Real Interest Rate/Budget Deficit Link: International Evidence, 1973-82', *Federal Reserve Bank, San Francisco, Economic Review*, No. 4, Fall 1984, pp. 26-35.

Miller, S. M. and F.S. Russek, 'Are the Twin Deficits Really Related?, *Contemporary Policy Issues*, Vol. 7, No. 4, October 1989, pp. 91-115.

Milton, Friedman, 'The Demand for Money-Some Theoretical and Empirical Results' *Journal of Political Economy*, Vol. 67, June 1959, pp. 327-51.

Milton, Friedman, "A *Theory of the Consumption Function*, Princeton University Press. NJ, 1957.

Milton, Friedman. 'The Quantity Theory of Money— A Restatement', In *Studies in the Quantity Theory of Money* Milton Friedman (ed). University of Chicago Press, 1956.

Minhas, B.S., Jain, L. R. and Tendulkar, S.D., "Declining Incidence of Poverty in the 1980s: Evidence Versus Artefacts", in *the Economic and Political Weekly,* July 1991.

Mohan, Rakesh (2004), "Orderly Global Economic Recovery: Are Exchange Rate Adjustments Effective Any More?" *Reserve Bank of India Bulletin*, April.

Mohan, Rakesh (2005), "Communications in Central Bank: A Perspective", *Reserve Bank of India Bulletin*, October.

Mohan, Rakesh (2005): Some Apparent Puzzles for Contemporary Monetary Policy, Speech Delivered at the Conference on China's and India's Changing Economic

Structures: Domestic and Regional Implications at Beijing during October 27-28.

Mohan, Rakesh (2006): New Economic Geography and Monetary Policy in a Flattening world, observation as an Overview Panelist at a Symposium sponsored by the Federal Reserve Bank of Kansas City at Jackson Hole, Wyoming, August 24-26.

Mohan, Rakesh (2006a), "Coping with Liquidity Management in India: Practitioner's View", *Reserve Bank of India Bulletin*, April.

Mohan, Rakesh (2006b), "Evolution of Central Banking in India", *Reserve Bank of India Bulletin*, June,

Mohan, Rakesh (2006c), "Monetary Policy and Exchange Rate frameworks: The Indian Experience", *Reserve Bank of India Bulletin*, June.

Mohanty, M.S., Gert Schnabel and Pablo Garcia-Luna (2006): Banks and Aggregate Credit: What is New? BIS Papers No. 28, August.

Moore, Basil 'The Endogenous Money Supply', *Journal of Post-Keynesian Economics*, Vol. X, No. 3, Spring 1988, pp. 372-86.

Mundle, Sudipto and Mukhopadhyay, Hiranya, "A Note on Central Government Expenditures", paper presented to the Finance Minister, November 1991, New Delhi, (excerpts published in the *Economic Times*, 20 January 1992).

Mundle, Sudipto and Rao, M. Govinda, "Volume and Composition of Government Subsidies in India, 1987-88", in the *Economic and Political Weekly*, 4 May, 1991.

Mundle, Sudipto, "Food, Finance and Foreign Trade: The Limits of High Growth in India", Department of Economics, Cambridge University, mimeo, 1990.

Mundle, Sudipto, "Pattern of Public Expenditure in India: A Financial Perspective of the Development State", paper presented at a conference on "The State and International Linkages. The Hague, October 1988.

Musgrave, R. A., "Tax Reform in Developing countries" in Newbery, D., and Stern, N., eds, *The Theory of Taxation for Developing Countries*: World Bank, 1987.

Nag, A. and A. Das (2002), "Credit Growth and Response to Capital Requirements: Evidence from Indian Public Sector Banks", *Economic and Political Weekly*, August 10.

Nicholas, Kaldor, 'How Monetarism Failed', *Challenge*, May-June 1985, pp. 4-13.

Nitsuhiro, Fukao and Takashi Okubo, 'International Linkage of Interest Rates: The Case of Japan and the United States', *International Economic Review*, Vol. 25, No. 1, February 1984, pp. 193-207.

Olson, Mancur, *Rise and Decline of Nations*, New Haven: Yale University Press, 1982.

One aspect to this reform has been to bring short-term interest rate in better alignment with other interest rates in the system.

Pandit, B.L., A. Mittal, M. Roy ands. Ghosh (2006), "Transmission of Monetary Policy and the Bank lending Channel: Analysis and Evidence for India", Development Research Group Study No. 25, Reserve Bank of India.

Pathak, D.S. 'Demand for Money in Developing Kenya— An Econometric Study (1969-78)', *The Indian Economic Journal,* Vol. 29, No. 1, July-September 1981, pp. 1-10.

Paul, Evans, 'Do Large Deficits Produce High Interest Rates?', *American Economic Review*, Vol. 75, No. 1, March 1985, pp. 68-87.

Pierce, J. L. and T.D. Thomson (1972), 'Some Issues in Controlling the Stock of Money', in Controlling Monetary Aggregates II: *The Implementation, Federal Reserve Bank of Boston Conference Series*, 9.

Polle, W. (1970), 'Optimal Choice of Monetary Policy Instruments in a Simple Stochastic Macro Model', *Quarterly Journal of Economics*, 84.

Poole, W. (1970), "Optimal Choice of Monetary Policy Instrument in a Simple Stochastic Macro Model", *Quarterly Journal of Economics*, 84 (2), May, 197-216.

Poole, W. (2004a), *Report of the Advisory Committee to Advise on the Administered Interest Rates and Rationalisation of Saving Instruments* (Chairman: Dr. Rakesh Mohan), RBI, July.

Poole, W. (2004b), *Report on Currency and Finance, 2003-04*, December.

Poole, W. (2006), *Annual Policy Statement for 2006-07*, April.

Poole, W.(2002), *Report on Currency and Finance 2000-01*, January, Mumbai.

Poole, William 'Whither Money Demand/Brookings Papers on *Economic Activity,* Vol. 3, 1970, pp. 485-500.

Premchand, A., *Control of Public Expenditure in India: A Historical and ana Alytical Account of the Administrative, Audit and Parliamentary Process*, Delhi: Allied Publishers, 1963

Rangarajan, C., Basu, Anupam and Jadhav, Narendra, "Dynamics of Interaction Between Government Deficit and Domestic Debt in India", Paper presented at the International Seminar of Public Economics, New Delhi, January 1990.

Rao, C.H.H., *"Agriculture: Policy and Performance"*, this volume, 1992.

Rao, M. Govinda and Aggarwal, V., "Central Transfers to Offset Fiscal Disadvantages of the States", in the *Indian Economic Review*, Volume 26, No. 1, 1991.

Rao, M. Govinda and Mundle, Sudipto, "An Analysis of Changes in State Government Subsidies: 1977-87" Paper presented at the World Bank-NIPFP Seminar on State Finances, 19-20 April 1991.

Rao, M. Govinda and Tulasidhar, V. B., "Public Expenditure in India: Emerging Trends", NIPFP Working Paper No. 5/ 1991, 1991.

Rao, M. Govinda, "Proposals for State Level Budgetary Reforms", in the *Economic and Political Weekly*, February 1992.

RBI (2006): Handbook of Statistics on the Indian Economy 2005-06, Reserve Bank of India.

RBI (2007a): Macroeconomic and Monetary Developments: *Third Quarter Review*, 2006-07, Reserve Bank of India.

RBI (2007b): Third Quarter Review of Annual Statement on Monetary Policy for the Year, 2006-07, Reserve Bank of India.

Reddy, K. N., *Growth of Public Expenditure in India*, 1972-1968, Delhi: Sterling Publishers, 1972.

Reddy, Y.V. (2001), "Communications Policy of the Reserve Bank of India", *Reserve Bank of India Bulletin*, September,

Reddy, Y.V. (2006), "Central Bank Communication: Some Random Thoughts", *Reserve Bank of India Bulletin*, January.

Report on Currency and Finance, 1970-71, p. 37.

Report on Currency and Finance, 1971-72, p. 79.

Report on Currency and Finance, 1971-72, p. 79.

Report on Currency and Finance, 1974-75, p. 75.

Report on Currency and Finance, 1980-81, pp. 101-102

Report on Currency and Finance, 1980-81, pp. 101-102.

Report on Currency and Finance, 1984-85, p. 151.

Report on Currency and Finance, 1986-87, p. 135.

Report on Currency and Finance, 1986-87, p. 135.

Report on Currency and Finance, 1989-90, pp. 136-37.

Richard, Arnott and Joseph E. Stiglitz, 'Moral Hazard and Non-Market Institutions: Dysfunctional Crowding Out or Peer Monitoring?' The *American Economic Review*, Vol. 81, No. 1, March 1991, p. 179.

Richard, Cebula, 'New Evidence on Financial Crowding Out'. *Public Choice*, Vol. 46, 1985, pp. 305-309.

Robert, A. Black and Claire G. Gilmore, 'Crowding Out During Britain's Industrial Revolution', The *Journal of Economic History*, Vol. 50, No. 1, March 1990, p. 109.

Robert, J. Barro, 'Inflation, the Payment Period, and the Demand for Money'. *Journal of Political Economy*, Vol. 78, November/December 1970, pp. 1228-63.

Roger, C. Kormendi, 'Government Debt, Government Spending and Private Sector Behaviour', *American Economic Review*, Vol. 73, December 1983, pp. 994.

Ronald, I. Mackinnon, *Money and Capital in Economic Development*, The Bookings Institution, Washington, D.C., 1973.

Ronald, Teigen, 'Demand and Supply Functions for Money in the United States. Some Structural Estimates', *Econometrica*, Vol. 32, October 1964, pp. 477-509.

Sampath, R. K. and Zakir Hussain, 'Demand for Money in India', *The Indian Economic Journal*, Vol. 29, No. 1, July-September 1981, pp. 17-36.

Samuelson, P. A., "Diagrammatic Exposition of a Theory of Public Expenditures", in the *Review of Economics and Statistics*, November, 1955.

Samuelson, P. A., "Pure Theory of Public Expenditure", in the *Review of Economics and Statistics*, November 1954.

Sarma, Atul and Tulasidhar, V.B., *Economic Impact of Government Expenditure: An Analysis in Input Output Framework*, Delhi: Concept Publishing Co., 1984.

Singh, Tarlok 'Determinants of Demand for Money in India', *The Indian Journal of Economics,* Annual Number, Vol. LXV, No. 256, July 1984, pp. 83-97.

Singh, Tarlok 'Modeling the Demand for Money in India', *International Journal of Development Banking,* Vol. 8, No. 2, July 1990, pp. 33-42.

Solocha, A. and T.P. Bundt. 'International Crowding-Out: The US Debt and Foreign Interest Rates'. *Quarterly Journal of Business and Economics*. Vol. 29, No. 1, Winter 1990, pp. 28-45.

Standard International Trade Classifications.

Sun-Yong Kim and Raymond E. Lombra, 'Why the Empirical Relationship Between Deficits and Interest Rates Appears to Fragile', *Journal of Economics and Business*, Vol. 41, No. 3, August 1989, pp. 241-51.

Teigen, Ronald 'Demand and Supply Functions for Money in the United States, Some Structural Estimates', *Econometrical,* Vol. 32, October 1964, pp. 477-509.

The Bank stipulated a ceiling in respect of individual bank's total borrowings from the Reserve Bank as follow: of the banks, total demand and time liabilities as on September 28, 1973, (i) 1.5 per cent for the period between December 8, 1973 and January 11, 1974; (ii) 2 per cent for the period between January 12, 1974 and April 5, 1974; and (iii) one per cent thereafter till May 31, 1974.

The banks were advised on December 11, 1971 to grant Defence packing-cum-supply credit limits on merit against confirmed Defence orders or acceptance of tenders as also to sub-contractors providing materials etc. to primary suppliers fulfilling Defence orders.

This was done following the recommendation of the Committee to Review the Working of the Monetary System (Chakravarty Committee) develop the treasury bills as a monetary instrument with flexible rates. This was also made an approved instrument for SLR purpose for details, see Report on Currency and Finance, 1986-87, pp. 145-46.

This was expected to enable banks to better equitable cost of raising the funds and the return on those funds.

Thomas, J. Courchene and A.K. Kelly, 'Money Supply and Money Demand: An Econometric analysis for Canada', *Journal of Money Credit and Banking*, Vol. 3, May 1971, pp. 368-71.

Tinbergen, Jan, On the *Theory of Economic Policy*, North Holland: Amsterdam, 1952.

Tobin, J. "Money and Income: Post Hoc Ergo Propter Hoc?" *Why, Journal of Economics*, Vol. 84, No.1, 1970, pp. 301-17.

Tobin, J., 'Monetary Policy: Rules, Targets & Shocks', *Journal of Money, Banking and Credit*, Vol. 15, No. 4, Nov. 1983, pp. 508-17.

Tobin, James 'The Interest Elasticity and Transactions Demand for Cash' *Review of Economics and Statistics*, Vol. 38, August 1956, pp. 241-47.

Toye, J., *Public Expenditure and Indian Development Policy* 1960-1970. Cabridge University Press, 1981.

Traditionally, SLR is considered as an instrument of reallocation of credit between public and private sectors. In a situation where the control a banks credit to government is large, it can minimize the expansionary impact of fiscal operations and the growth of reserve money.

Van, Heerden, J.H.P. 'Income and Interest Rate Elasticities of the Demand for Money in South Africa, 1970-1979', The *Indian Economic Journal*, Vol. 29, No. 1, July-September 1981, pp. 89-79.

Vasudeva, A. 'Demand for Money in India— A Survey of Literature'. *Reserve Bank of India Staff Papers*. Vol. 2, No. 1, June 1977, pp. 58-83.

William, H. Buiter, 'Crowding-Out and Effectiveness of Fiscal Policy', *Journal of Public Economics*, Vol. 7, pp. 302-28.

# INDEX